THE
SPIRITUAL ENGINEERING
OF SACRED ECSTASY

The Keeneys

CONTENTS

PART ONE

INTRODUCTION TO
SPIRITUAL ENGINEERING

Sacred Ecstatics aims for soul igniting communion and union with the divine source and force of creation, sometimes called the Creator, Lord, Jehovah, Allah, Brahman, God, Goddess, Holy Father, Holy Mother, the Big Holy, or what the Quakers called The Light.[a] A full blown ecstatic experience with divinity has a somatic outcome: a mysterious force takes up residence inside your body as a sacred vibration that is unlike anything known before. It forever empowers your ecstatic relationship with the divine and transforms you into a well-tuned spiritual instrument. Sacred Ecstatics guides those seeking this highest spiritual experience, teaching what is required for the initial reception of the sacred vibration as well as how to later access

---

[a] Though there are a plentitude of names to indicate the most hallowed sacred name, we will interchangeably use "God," "the divine," and a few other metaphors that are personally and emotionally potent to us. Our use of several names is meant to acknowledge that the utmost originator of life and all its mystery is beyond conceptual understanding and linguistic indication. We avoid any debate about the advantages or disadvantages of one name over another because it distracts and distances you from an experience of divinity. For us, "God" is the simplest spelling of the utmost mystery, holiness, numinosity, luminosity, and creativity whose loving grace, unconditional forgiveness, vast wisdom, and incredible power to change and uplift are infinite.

and nurture it. We invite you to step into a whole new numinous reality in which your personal relationship with a higher power brings transformative creative change and extraordinary ecstatic joy.

Spiritual engineering addresses the actual phenomena inherent in the emergence, sustenance, enhancement, and advancement of sacred ecstatic experience, especially reception of the sacred vibration. It enables us to make explicit the specific actions involved in each step of the three-part recipe of Sacred Ecstatics:[1] (1) building sacred ground, (2) spiritual cooking, and (3) a transformed return to the everyday. Successful execution of each step requires applying the basic skills of spiritual engineering, the practical know-how behind setting your soul on fire, and living an ecstatic spiritual life.

The initial preparatory skills involve gathering the required "ingredients" that are always present in the production of heightened ecstatic experience. Once the ingredients are gathered, the subsequent skill set addresses how to blend them and form what we call a "mystical prayer wheel." Next, the wheel is turned with ecstatic prayer, the dynamic that builds sacred ground and generates spiritual heat. It turns with increasing momentum until a big room[b] emerges and an ecstatic fire is ignited for spiritual cooking to spontaneously begin. This is when God powerfully operates and radically changes you through higher attunement, realignment, reconstruction, re-education, renewal, healing, transformation, and other ecstatic ways that are beyond human understanding. Finally, when a round of spiritual cooking is done, special action is prescribed that helps you sustain the changes brought on by the former ecstatic experience, carrying it within you throughout the everyday.

The three main forms of Sacred Ecstatics are its group *intensives* where people come together to spiritually cook, one-to-one *sessions* with a client seeking healing or spiritual growth,

---

[b] Sacred Ecstatics uses the term, "big room," to indicate the vast space required to host sacred experience. You must make enough room for God in order to have a personal experience with divinity.

and daily home *workouts* that either focus on a particular skill practice, a pre-arranged sequence of practices, or a whole "ecstatic travel track" that can be done alone or with others. An ecstatic travel track is a specially designed audio or video recording that takes you through all the steps of the Sacred Ecstatics recipe. Here you may venture to the ecstatic ways of the Caribbean, Africa, Japan, or anywhere in the spiritual world the track leads.

The home cooking workouts in particular bring a new contribution to the practice of ecstatic spirituality. Like a musician you can practice your instrument — which in this case is your own body — at home. All the performing arts rest on well-developed skills or techniques that are used to masterfully express a whole performance. Similarly, spiritual engineering builds your ecstatic chops to help you better conduct the sacred art of spiritual cooking.

Sacred ecstasy is a universal human experience that is not bound by any particular tradition, culture, or geographic locale. And yet it has often been suppressed, misunderstood, or forgotten entirely. After all, ecstasy frees the body, unbinds the mind, expands the heart, and sets the soul on fire. It arrives to challenge the hegemonic rule of concrete belief, stilled practice, and distilled spirituality. Practically every spiritual tradition has made it taboo and done its best to ensure that ecstasy is no longer truly ecstatic and that spirituality has very little spirit. Fortunately, sacred ecstasy can never be totally suppressed — the pinnacle spiritual experience can happen anywhere to anyone if the conditions are right.

Whereas long-standing ecstatic lineages tacitly passed on their knowledge from one generation to another, we aim to make explicit what was formerly unspoken so that the pragmatics of spiritual cooking can be learned today by any sincere seekers, regardless of their religious tradition. Spiritual engineering takes you past debating belief and interpretation and straight to the practical art and technique of spiritual cooking and sacred ecstasy. This section, Part One, sets forth a general introduction to spiritual engineering, followed by Part

Two, which discusses the basic skill practices required for effectively executing the three-step recipe of Sacred Ecstatics. Part Three offers specific tips for how to better bring spiritual engineering knowledge to intensives, sessions, and workouts. Finally, in Part Four we introduce some of the visionary dreams that inspired the development of this pragmatic orientation to ecstatic spirituality. An appendix provides a glossary of the basic terms of spiritual engineering and Sacred Ecstatics in general.

SACRED ECSTASY
AND THE SACRED VIBRATION

Sacred ecstasy is the extreme emotion that comes from feeling direct contact with divinity. It begins with communion, the sharing of intimate spiritual feelings and thoughts with God. Here you hold nothing back in your communication as all forms of expression are drawn upon, from words to groans, shouts, songs, and even the movements of dance. Prayer is communion with God, and when it is most expressive and effective, it draws you nearer and nearer to God until there is mystical union — no distance remains between the Creator and the created. This is when sacred emotion reaches its maximal threshold and becomes unadulterated ecstasy. When you are one with the divine, something more than an emotional explosion of joy takes place that few people have ever heard about. A sacred vibration is installed inside you — the divine literally places the power of holiness into your flesh. Your life can never be the same for now you are a vessel that holds the sacred vibration, something that can be awakened and further empowered by particular rhythms, melodic tones, hallowed words, sacred songs, and physical movement.

It is challenging to choose a name for this mysterious, sacred vibration because it is more than a pulse, energy, power, or force. It contains similarities to but is also qualitatively different from "qi," "reiki," "kundalini," and the "universal life force."

4

Namely, its strength is non-subtle and it involves a specially blended mix of intense sacred emotion, somatic vibration, and the widest range of joyful celebratory expression. Most importantly, the sacred vibration can only be received inside the experience of sacred ecstasy, the heightened emotion that bursts through when you commune and unite with the divine. When its vibratory pulse is in operation, sacred emotion with all its motion and commotion are reactivated. As a carrier of the sacred vibration, you must learn how to keep it in play so that every breath and everything expressed offers praise to God, the Big Holy, the *mysterium tremendum et fascinans*.

While contemporary spiritual seekers have largely lost touch with this kind of vibratory ecstatic experience that somatically and emotionally embraces the divine, it is known and revered among the custodians of the oldest living spiritual and healing tradition in the world, that of the Kalahari Bushmen. The mysterious vibrational power associated with sacred ecstasy is called *n/om* in the Kalahari and it is regarded as the most important gift a human being can receive. Without it, singing, dancing, healing, or visioning cannot fully come to life. N/om is simultaneously the match, fuel, and fire required for sacred work to commence. We regard n/om as equivalent to the sacred vibration—it is the same complex mix of vibrational energy, sacred emotion, body movement, and the voiced tones and rhythms of the songs that awakens and amplifies its circulation in the body.

We use the double name, "sacred vibration" because it helps highlight the primary experiential components that are present: a *vibration* in the body and the accompanying emotion and expressive commotion that are inspired by the *sacred*. The sacred vibration is also equivalent to the holy spirit as it is known among ecstatic Christians who describe it as a fire in the bones or an electrical current that fills the body. As Bishop John, a Shaker from St. Vincent articulates: "The power of God is an electric force that comes into your body. It's like lightning . . . I vibrate from my head right down through my body. I feel jolts of electricity."[2] We join the Bushmen, the Caribbean Shakers, and other ecstatic lineages in regarding the reception of the sacred vibration as what brings true spiritual empowerment and the highest bliss of ecstasy, the marks of being touched by God. You were born to be an instrument of this sacred vibration rather than a psychological state of consciousness, but likely have never been plugged into its mighty power source and had your life ecstatically switched on.

You are a different person once you receive this initiatory experience of the old school mystics, shamans, healers, preachers, and spiritual teachers. In addition to filling you with non-subtle energy, the sacred vibration's unique heightened emotion goes past all former delight, joy, and love. You immediately realize why words like "rapture," "bliss," and "ecstasy" were originally meant to indicate this extraordinarily *felt* mystical experience. Sacred emotion is a divinely lit, heartfelt fire that far surpasses even the most striking flashes of cognitive realization. Under its intoxicating influence, you cannot help but become a spirited celebrant making a joyful noise while trembling in a shaking dance.

Dare we say that no life-altering form of spirituality, healing, creative pursuit, or world-changing action can arise without the sacred vibration? Mirra Alfassa, partner of Sri Aurobindo, proposed an answer to this question: "One must have the supreme Vibration in order to participate in that Movement [the divine changing of the world], which I am beginning to feel in the cells of the body." [3] Sacred ecstasy combines the most extreme joy with the highest degree of somatic excitation, bringing a frenzied rapture that William James characterized as "deliciousness . . . beyond anything known in ordinary consciousness."[4] Sufis describe this as a "total absorption with God" while contemporary mystic Evelyn Underhill characterizes it as an "inebriation of the Infinite" and "the perfect consummation of the Love of God."[5]

Over all else, spiritual seekers throughout the world should be hunting for this extraordinary experience that converts one into an ecstatic instrument that blasts a joyful noise and shines the brightest light. The sacred vibration is the motor of a spiritual life. Without it, you can't spiritually go anywhere. It is both the sacred means and the achievement of the highest outcome you seek. Celebrating the experience of holiness, divinity, and all its mystery and joy is the ultimate beginning and end, the alpha and omega of Sacred Ecstatics. Above all else, you must seek God, and when the two of you meet, your soul will truly heat. Spiritual cooking is not a one-time occurrence, but a whole new way of life that constantly returns you to the fire of ecstatic renewal and never-ending creation.

REVERSE ENGINEERING THE PINNACLE
SPIRITUAL EXPERIENCE

The main mission of Sacred Ecstatics is to make the ultimate spiritual experience more available to others. We have reverse-engineered what takes place in the Kalahari and other ecstatic lineages so that the sacred vibration can be more readily installed and its ecstasy felt. We hope to help usher in a new spiritual movement in modern times that takes us back to the original human spiritual passion and orientation — hunting, receiving, and sharing the sacred vibration.

The inspiration to more analytically examine Sacred Ecstatics from a practical engineering perspective arose from a series of visionary dreams[c] about Charles Henry (1859–1926), a sensory physiologist and multidisciplinary scholar at Sorbonne University in Paris. Our goal became the identification, articulation, and prescription of the key ingredients and processes that underlie what the Bushmen call "getting cooked by God" or what we more generally call "getting spiritually cooked." Spiritual cooking refers to the radically transformative experiential process that instills the sacred vibration whenever you are ecstatically excited and set on fire by the divine. The laboratory work of Charles Henry suggests that the highest mystical experience can be evoked when the body is approached

---

[c] We include reports on these visions in Part Four of this book.

as a musical-like instrument that is appropriately tuned to conduct and transform vibration. This orientation helps render you capable of catching and amplifying sacred emotion in a way not otherwise possible. To begin your personal hunt for the sacred vibration, you essentially need to be spiritually reengineered and remade into a well-tuned instrument that can resonate with it.

Beyond the basic practices that arrange a favorable climate for experiencing sacred ecstasy and installation of the sacred vibration, a focus on spiritual engineering invites a radically different perspective for relating to all practices from any religious orientation. Rather than accentuate, compare, and contrast beliefs, we primarily search for the presence of the sacred vibration and discern whether a tradition contributes any practical know-how for its transmission, amplification, and reactivation.

Sacred Ecstatics is a special syncretic blend of time-proven techniques, strategies, and heuristics used by the Kalahari Bushmen of southern Africa, the Shakers of the Caribbean, the early parishioners of sanctified black churches in the United States, and the seiki jutsu practitioners of old Japan. These traditions are the main pragmatic roots of Sacred Ecstatics, though other contributions to the holy pyrotechnics (spiritual fire setting), autokinetics (spontaneous body movements), and ecstatic performing arts (sacred dance and music) of spiritual ecstasy (mystically excited bliss) continue to influence and contribute to our spiritual engineering knowledge.

From the start, we study and experience what an ecstatic lineage says they are doing to get spiritually cooked, and this includes using their key metaphors and phrases for describing this experience and the means of accomplishing it. Our spiritual engineering research further unpacks and discerns the ecstatic phenomena actually taking place with the body—its specific actions, the patterns that organize a sequence of action, and the coupling of all this to interactions with other people. We highlight anything that is relevant to authentically achieving ecstatic experience— from a certain body movement or vocal expression to an internal emotion — and delineate how this unfolds and comes together in real time.

We take seriously what ecstatic traditions teach about installing the sacred vibration. In particular, most ecstatic lineages find that the sacred vibration is best packaged and delivered in a *song* that contains the needed sacred emotion. Receiving such a song links you to the heartfelt pulse of higher spiritual power. From the perspective of spiritual engineering, singing or instrumentally performing a sacred song generates an acoustic vibration that is specially empowered with the emotion that originally inspired its composition. Music also inspires physical movement of the body, and this transduction from auditory to mechanical vibration further helps convey music's emotion. In short, when a moving body, sacred emotion, and song are blended together, it creates the optimal conditions for transmitting the sacred vibration.

Ecstatic lineages offer different kinds of practical expertise concerning the expression of song and its relationship to movement, both of which are required to awaken the heightened emotion that brings forth sacred vibration. Some traditions offer more knowledge about body movement while others bring more skills in cooking with music's rhythms and tones. Embracing syncretism in the spiritual engineering of Sacred Ecstatics enables greater access to any and all available know-how concerning the art of spiritual cooking.

THE ROPE TO GOD: MORE FIRE AND EMOTION, LESS TALK AND ABSTRACTION

Sacred Ecstatics follows the practical wisdom of the Kalahari Bushmen and pays the most respect and attention to what they call a "rope to God." When the sacred vibration becomes sufficiently empowered, you experience being more in touch with the rope, conduit, pipeline, or link to its divine source. Remember that the sacred vibration arrives when you are brought close to divinity through wholehearted communion and ecstatic union—this is how it is initially received, and later, when the vibration is reawakened, you are brought back in touch with the divine. The "rope" is both a metaphor for your relationship with God and a reference to the actual tugging, pulling, and tapping of your body that may be felt during heightened spiritual cooking. The more the sacred vibration is activated, the stronger your rope to God becomes.

Your rope to God holds your personal, emotional relationship to the creator, and when it is strong, you more naturally trust and interfere less with whatever comes forth in your spiritual life. Always remember to give the utmost respect and attention to this rope, that which mystically resides above your head. While it may now be a thin and fragile thread, know that more experience with spiritual cooking and its activation of the sacred vibration helps this rope become empowered. Once you truly feel a strong rope to God you will no longer exaggerate the importance of discussing, naming, debating, or even wondering about the definition, conceptual meaning, or ontological existence of divinity. You will give more importance to feeling God as a living presence whose spiritual force and wonder-working power circulate within as a supreme ecstatic vibration, emotion, and motion nurtured by the songs that make you leap and dance with joy! Release all hindering thought and unnecessary contemplation that reside below your rope. Stop overpondering the meaning of life and instead start moving to its heartbeat. Move from trying to know it all to feeling it all. Focus on taking care of your connection to the divine so its life-giving power can take care of the rest of you.

You are not ready to resourcefully talk about any important aspect of spirituality until you are in direct emotional contact with the divine. Resisting, distancing, or disqualifying the experience of sacred emotion is only an indication that you are not feeling it in your life. Be careful about any spiritual teaching that exorcizes the divine and devalues sacred emotion. Bring more spiritual street smarts to your search—make sure it is understood that the closer you get to divine mystery, the more that the higher emotion, motion, and commotion of sacred ecstasy will be embraced. There is no way to come close to divine mystery without feeling its presence and being moved by its life-changing power. Emotional distance hardens your heart and makes you resent or disqualify those who are ecstatically happy. Nothing but strong emotion can bring on the spiritual heat that melts and converts ice to liquid and steam. Once the divine, God, the Light, or the Big Holy touches your heart, everything about you changes. You forever seek a more personal relationship with divinity that is beyond conceptual understanding, something felt within that energizes a newborn spiritual life. This is what it means to seek spiritual cooking rather than only alter the conceptual lenses for spiritual looking.

PRINCIPLES OF SPIRITUAL ENGINEERING

We now present some important principles that specify how to approach ecstatic cooking so that the mystical rope can do its job with the least interference, the clearest reception, and the greatest strength. Keep in mind that these are orienting perspectives that help you perform the spiritual engineering practices we introduce in Part Two. Spiritual engineering facilitates and enhances your capacity to emotionally, sonically, and physically resonate with the divine. Follow its practical orientation and instructions to learn how to play your body instrument in a way that enables you to commune with and be subsumed by God.

Emphasizing the Importance of Sacred Emotion

The sacred vibration is an ecstatic mix of sacred emotion, sacred song (with both its rhythms and tones), and sacred movement that collectively resides within the body. While all these ingredients are necessary, sacred emotion is the most important. After all, ultimate bliss is itself an emotion, so the end result of receiving the sacred vibration is technically an extreme amplification of a particular kind of joyful feeling that has to be present from the start. Sacred emotion is more than whatever common joy you have known before—it is both the longing for and the fulfillment of extreme joy, love, wonder, and awe felt when you are near the Creator. Heightened sacred emotion can overcome and transform all other kinds of emotion. Even if you begin full of heartache and sadness, God's ecstatic firestorm will turn it into the utmost joy.

Sacred emotion drives the whole ecstatic process. Without the presence of this emotion at the onset, the pinnacle spiritual experience cannot be reached. From the perspective of spiritual engineering, you are going to have to access and feel some emotion early on, however small, and then build it up so it reaches its full-blown ecstatic peak. Because music helps awaken emotion, its practical value to ecstatic experience is obvious. Sacred music in particular is more likely to activate sacred emotion and was created for that purpose, so pay particular attention to this genre of music.

Once the sacred vibration is installed, the body spontaneously trembles, vibrates, and shakes whenever sacred emotion is felt. This is not just any kind of body shake; it is the ultimate shake that is inspired and triggered by sacred emotion. The activation of a muscle clonus (involuntary muscle spasm) or any willfully forced movement and choreography will not lead you to the sacred vibration. The mysterious pulse you seek starts with a special alignment of body movement, rhythm, tone, and emotion that amplifies all these ingredients until the divinely activated vibrational force comes forth.

Deeply felt emotional connection to divinity is the vital ingredient almost always absent in contemporary methods and technological devices that try to induce mystical, shamanic, or spiritual experience. There is no getting around it: full sensory immersion into mystical light, divine love, and spiritual power requires a heartfelt relationship to their sacred source. Anyone can verbally claim to be full of heart and soul, and even declare familiarity with the heated ecstasy of spiritual cooking. But spiritual engineering sweeps away all such declarations and replaces them with a request to perform a song and dance. If you feel sacred ecstasy and carry the sacred vibration in your body, it will come through in your expression, from the sound of your voice to the way you move. The spiritual engineering of Sacred Ecstatics helps you ignite, feel, and express rather than recite, name, and interpret the sacred vibration and everything associated with its activation, enhancement, ongoing development, and daily use.

The Body Instrument

The spiritual engineering of Sacred Ecstatics invites you to regard the human body—your own and that of others—as a musical-like instrument that uses mechanical movement to produce sound, whether it is pulsing vocal chords, blowing air, clapping hands, stomping feet, or applying finger pressure on another instrument's strings or keys. The body is a unique kind of instrument, however, because it not only generates sound and movement; it is also influenced by externally produced acoustic and mechanical vibration. Amidst a field of mechanical and acoustic vibration—internally and externally produced—spiritual cooking, sacred ecstasy, and the sacred vibration are born.

In addition to transmitting and receiving mechanical and acoustic vibration, the body connects and amplifies them. The sound of a musical instrument is amplified with the help of a resonator that enables acoustic vibration to be better heard and felt. The body of the instrument, whether it is that of a violin, guitar, piano, clarinet, or horn, is such a resonator. The same is true of your body—it is a system of resonators that especially includes the bones that are ideal for conducting vibration. To build up the sacred vibration, the acoustic vibration of sacred music is resonated through your somatic instrument while aligned with your body's mechanical movement. You increase the emotion you feel from a song when it excites more spontaneous movement of your body. At the same time, such an elevation of physical movement brings a rise in music's subsequently expressed emotion. When sacred emotion, acoustic vibration from music, and mechanical vibration from physical movement are all coordinated and amplified to reach their peak intensity, the sacred vibration starts to form.

The body instrument can also shift its experienced instrumental form, especially as you get nearer the big room where everything is changing.[d] Specifically, your body may act like a vocal instrument for singing, or a percussion instrument for making rhythm, or it can simulate any other instrument you can imagine from a guitar to a horn, saxophone, or flute. Like the instruments found in an orchestra, however, the one supreme instrument that can play like a whole ensemble — simultaneously making rhythm, accompanying with harmonic chords, and producing melodic lines — is the piano. This instrument can do it all. As jazz pianist Oscar Peterson is reputed to have said, "I believe in using the entire piano as a single instrument capable of expressing every possible musical idea."[6] Your body as an instrument also can be played as a grand body piano enabling the fullest range of musical experience.

In 1924 Charles Henry proposed a remarkable future treatment orientation where the whole human body would be conceptualized, physically played, and neurologically excited as a body keyboard[7] that activates what he called the "biopsychic resonator." Henry hypothesized that when played in the right way, the body keyboard creates the optimal resonance and maximal excitation required for mystical illumination and bliss. He approached the induction of mystical experience as both an engineer and an aesthetician, discerning the underlying processes and specifying the performance action required to masterfully produce it.

When the body is approached as a keyboard or piano-like instrument, it can be regarded as having the equivalent parts. A piano's resonators include the strings, soundboard, and wooden

---

[d] Sacred Ecstatics proposes that the bigger the existential room hosting experience, the more everything within it is changing and transforming, having less attachment to classification, static definition, and any presumed stability or solidity of form. Communion and union with the divine are only possible in the big room.

case in which acoustic vibration takes place. Your sinew, solid structures, spatial cavities, and whole encasement are analogous to these parts of the piano. The human body is a natural resonator whose tissue, organs, bones, and fluids all generate and respond to vibration. The other components of the piano, the hammers and keys in particular, create the mechanical vibrations that activate sound. Your limbs provide the means for equivalent action as they enable feet, hands, and fingers to apply pressure and induce mechanical vibration.

Like any musical instrument, a piano must be tuned, regulated, and made ready to play. The human body also is need of constant tuning and regulation, something best accomplished by a spiritually cooked tuner. In addition, it is valuable to have your instrument played by someone who already knows the songs and has the chops to play them in a way that induces ecstatic experience. This is why you benefit from contact with spiritually cooked people — to experience how it feels when your body instrument is both well tuned and masterfully played. Later when you are sufficiently cooked, you will be able to tune and play your own keyboard and other body keyboards as well.

While the spine is a particularly good conductor of vibration whose vertebrae have been likened to a diatonic musical scale,[8] we follow Charles Henry and regard the whole body, with the spine included, as a resonating keyboard instrument. Somatic vibration arises with the body's production of acoustic sound, including a voice that whispers, shouts, tones, and sings, and with the body's mechanical movement of hands and feet that clap, slap, pound, and stomp. Again, the body's acoustic and mechanical vibrations may be further influenced by externally produced sound and the touch of someone else whose tactile pressure, duration, and mechanical vibration can constantly vary. The spiritual engineering of Sacred Ecstatics especially focuses on how the body keyboard produces, receives, aligns, and amplifies the acoustic and mechanical vibrations associated with sacred music. When the latter's held emotion reaches the highest ecstasy, the sacred vibration bursts forth, pierces the body, and is immediately installed within.

A Sacred Ecstatics session, intensive, or workout begins with you imagining that you are like a piano sitting on stage waiting to be played. As things progress you become spiritually heated by moving with the rhythms and melodic tones that strike up the band and stir the soul. Getting spiritually cooked, ascending the spiritual thermometer,[e] climbing the rope to God, playing the sacred musical scale, entering the big room of mystery, feeling a fire in the bones, and setting your soul on fire are all descriptive ways of pointing to the experience of your body instrument being played with divine inspiration and ecstatic virtuosity.

The basic practices of spiritual engineering help you become more familiar with your tunable, adjustable, and playable somatic instrument and work with its ability to activate diverse vibrations across the whole experiential spectrum. To find your body keyboard, you may have to first handle other body instruments, that is, experience your body shape shift through different instrumental forms until you finally arrive at the grand body piano. In other words, you will most likely have to drum, sing, and perhaps blow Gabriel's horn before meeting the entire range of tones, melodic lines, harmonies, and rhythms that can be played on the mystical keyboard Charles Henry envisioned long ago.

The Ecstatic Amplifier: Sound and Movement as a "Call and Response"

The sacred vibration is an ecstatic mix of song (both its tones and rhythms), physical body movement, and divinely inspired emotion. The spiritual cooking of all ecstatic spiritual traditions brings forth the sacred vibration through linking sound and movement in a mutually enhancing way. Here, sound (especially the musical tones and rhythms of vocal or instrumental expression) evokes physical movement (especially

---

[e] We devote an entire chapter to the spiritual thermometer in *Sacred Ecstatics: The Recipe for Setting Your Soul on Fire.*

celebrative trembling, shaking, quaking, and dancing) as the latter calls forth more sound. This back and forth interplay is a "call and response" interaction that is inspired, triggered, and fueled by sacred emotion. The emotion stirred by the sound of sacred music can be depicted as a call for the body to respond with praiseworthy movement. Likewise, the excitement of experiencing the body move can be regarded as a call for a vocal or instrumental response that expresses appreciation and praise.

Infusing emotion into both sound and movement is required for each to amplify the other in a back and forth exchange. When this oscillating dynamic of sound (inspired acoustic vibration) and body movement (inspired mechanical vibration) is closely intertwined and well timed, the emotion held in each is amplified in kind. This is how emotion is elevated until it peaks as fully blown sacred ecstasy. The Bushmen describe the arrival of heightened sacred emotion, usually brought on by singing a special song, as "waking up" and "raising the heart," which immediately triggers spontaneous body trembling and shaking and, in turn, triggers more emotion and sound making. The "call and response" of sound and movement is what amplifies the emotionality of ecstatic spirituality. The circular amplification of emotion through this pairing of sound and movement moves you toward the mountaintop transformative experience: installation of the sacred vibration within your body. Once you receive the sacred vibration, it is conducted and spread throughout your flesh and bones as both an electrical-like current and an ecstatic fire that spiritually cooks you.

Don't forget that the emotion of which we speak is not like any typical emotion. It is inspired by a personally felt relationship with divine mystery. This feeling may begin with a sense of wonder and awe that brings goose bumps to your skin or it may become a deep and tearful feeling of appreciation and gratitude that something vast and great watches over and cares for you. In its more elevated ecstatic forms, sacred emotion feels like a direct contact experience with God where you are physically struck by divine lightning, lit by sacred fire, or zapped by holy electricity. Its ecstasy is the initiatory moment when you fully realize that you are becoming a newborn spiritual being—the conversion, rebirth, and reconstruction required for all forms of spiritual anointment from healing to mysticism, shamanism, ministry, and true membership in spiritual community.

The kind of movement and sound that result from the highest surge of sacred emotion is the special kind of expression that conveys ecstasy. It is a spontaneous and enthusiastic response of celebration for something mysteriously wonderful and overwhelmingly blissful. When sacred emotion hits the highest bar, you immediately want to praise what you feel with a mighty leap of delight and a wild, joyful noise. Based on this discussion of spiritual engineering, you can now better appreciate the following description of ecstatic experience previously quoted in *Sacred Ecstatics:*

> I used to wonder what made people shout, but now I don't. There is a joy on the inside, and it wells up so strong that we can't keep still. It is fire in the bones. Any time that fire touches a man, he will jump.[f]

This statement contains a description of all components of the sacred vibration: sound ("shout"), sacred emotion ("joy"), movement ("jump"), as well as the process of amplification required to blend them ("it wells up so strong that we can't keep still"). Being emotionally touched and moved by divine mystery may call you to take a stand, wave your arms, clap your hands, or shake the whole of your body as you shout with elation. When the call and response reaches a high enough energetic threshold, it crosses over into the fire of spiritual cooking. This is when the sacred vibration awakens to powerfully attune and resonate your body instrument with the divine—something

---

[f] This is taken from the religious testimony of an African American preacher who was born into slavery before the Civil War in the United States. Clifton Johnson, *God Struck Me Dead: Religious Conversion Experiences and Autobiographies of Ex-Slaves* (Philadelphia, PA: Pilgrim Press, 1969), 74.

only felt in the ecstatic heat of a big room rather than conceptually understood in the cold small container of spoken words. The sacred vibration can only emerge when you are emotionally (inspirationally), acoustically (musically), and mechanically (kinesthetically) amplified and in synch enough to converge all its ingredients.

Get Soulfully Tuned: Be a Little Off to Sound More On

A piano tuning is complex and involves more than setting the pitch. Most piano keys have several strings associated with them to produce a single musical note. Only one string is perfectly tuned while the other strings are adjusted to slightly deviate from this pitch. This "tempering" makes the tone have an oscillating "beat." Creating this tiny amount of deviation or "offness" of the strings rather than having them perfectly matched gives every note and musical scale a more aesthetically pleasing sound. The variation can neither be too much nor too little; it must be just right, and this is part of what constitutes a great tuning and contributes to the soul of a piano's sound.

Good spiritual engineering also brings this kind of variation to your sound and rhythm, providing the "offness" and swinging oscillation required for soulful expression. The introduction of syncopation, complex rhythm, polyrhythm, tonal dissonance, blue notes, embellished melodies, and the like brings different kinds of deviations, oscillating swings, and variations including off beats, torn rags in the time, an improvised melodic surprise, or a dissonant trip from an unexpected riff. This is what creates a soulful temperament. From the perspective of ecstatic spiritual engineering, the popular new age shaman's concept of "soul loss" more accurately refers to loss of both the beat and offbeat required for you to soulfully swing. The absence of soul is found in those who lose relationship to spontaneity and ongoing change, relying on memorization rather than improvisation. The cure is syncopation, not more entrainment to the monotony of dead beats and uninspiring tones. To truly recover your soul, you need more ecstatic jazz in your life.

For the sacred vibration to be soulfully in play, the strings and resonator of your body instrument must be able to catch its vibe. Capturing soulful resonance happens automatically if your habits of thought and action don't interfere and your instrument is skillfully tuned and tempered. All ecstatic traditions acknowledge that there is usually a preliminary period of preparation required in which people are tuned and made more receptive to the sacred vibration. The various formats and offerings of Sacred Ecstatics help prepare you for a soul tune-up—making you ready to catch and be caught by the sacred vibration through experiencing the soulful emotion, sounds, rhythms, and movement that come with it.

Developing Good Habits

Spiritual engineering sometimes uses the paradoxical strategy of prescribing the opposite of what you may think you should do in order to better assure that you achieve the desired goal. For instance, you may be asked to *not move* in order to be moved in a radically different kind of way. We call this "going against the grain of your ineffective habits." Unless you grew up as a Kalahari Bushman in southern Africa or in some other ecstatic culture, you were most likely raised and educated (and this includes your somatic, kinesthetic, emotional, musical, and rhythmic education) in an ecstatically cold culture that lacks experience with receiving and transmitting the sacred vibration, amplifying intense sacred emotion, expressing spontaneous ecstatic movement, and performing soulful rhythm and improvised, embellished music. Not to worry, because cooling habits can be unlearned and undone, and you can learn to lay down new hot tracks and sizzling grooves. This is what the practices of spiritual engineering help accomplish—they introduce you to the cooking habits, skills, and tracks that have been laid by ecstatics who came before you.

To assure that interfering habits are disabled, go ahead and try out beginner's "I really don't know how to act" mind. Avoid reintroducing any habit that cools and calms rather than heats and excites your body instrument's performance, and this includes any and all wild movements or sounds that are imagined to be ecstatic and spiritually hot, but actually are not. Remember, "ecstatic" in this context refers to the presence of the sacred vibration, something not recognized, known, or embodied in what today's spiritually "cool" culture refers to as ecstatic dance, energy movement, therapeutic shaking, or sound healing.

Putting your body in charge of its expression rather than directed, controlled, and choreographed by your overly conscious mind provides a good start. However, there is more to the spiritual engineering of Sacred Ecstatics than a shift from movement directed by the body rather than the mind. You are ultimately aiming to be under the influence of an ineffable divine mystery that is beyond your mind and body. It's best to not indulge in wondering too much about what this means or whether it's happening yet or not. Value involuntary, body directed movement over consciously directed movement, and then go further by surrendering everything to a higher mysterious power. Aim to ultimately be emotionally and physically moved by divine resonance. In the beginning, keep it simple. Follow the spiritual engineering directions provided, including our suggestions for improvisation and experimentation.

Catching the Feeling

Remember that sacred emotion is the most important ingredient in spiritual cooking. When you first begin experimenting with Sacred Ecstatics, don't be in a rush to make something happen—first aim to catch the feeling held inside the rhythms, music, movement, and expression you witness in others who are cooked. It takes time to learn how to ecstatically prepare, tune, regulate, and play your body instrument. When you imitate another's cooked expression without feeling it deeply resonate within, you learn how to posture rather than authentically catch, hook up to, and finally embody what is being expressed. You may have been taught that it's good to "fake it until you make it." Unfortunately in this context, that advice only encourages habitual faking rather than spiritual baking. Instead, your inner emotion must strengthen and amplify until it is felt 110 percent. As one preacher said, "Before God can use a man, that man must be hooked in the heart."[9] Once you are hooked, caught, or lassoed by your love and longing for the divine, your ecstatic expression pours forth spontaneously with enough heat to set everyone around you on fire.

The Inner Body

Charles Henry proposed that in order for you to feel the original emotion that inspired any art or performance, your "internal machinery"[10] or "inner body" must recreate the rhythmic movements of whatever it confronts, whether it is music, dance, art, or mystical ecstasy. Speaking of art, Henry argued that we are not able to

> consciously comprehend emotion that an artist tries to express, but we can be made to feel it; artists set down those outer manifestations of their emotion that our body will mechanically imitate, however lightly, so as to place us in the indefinable psychological state that caused them.[11]

Based on Henry's insight, we offer a practical learning strategy for catching the feeling of what you hear and/or see in an intensive, session, or video of ecstatic cooking: get in synch with the rhythms of the aural and movement expression of someone who is truly cooking, doing so with your inner body before you try expressing it externally. The rhythmic activity of a spiritually cooked person should be mirrored and mimed by your inner ecstatic spiritual body before external performance is ready to commence. Gather and blend the ingredients internally to catch the feeling, vibe, and ecstatic pulse of how others are cooking. It is easier to master ecstatic expression on the inside because any limiting or impoverished external body habits are held back. Get it right on the inside and then allow the emotion of sound and movement to become strong enough to inspire the launch of external expression.

It is important to recognize that your internal performance brings actual sensory-motor activity and neuronal excitation to the external physical body. One of the great physicians of our time, Dr. Robert Fulford, used to imagine doing physical exercises while lying in bed each morning. He learned to activate his nervous system, muscles, and whole body with the micromovements associated with an imagined performance, and this helped keep him fit.

Do the most on the inside and the least on the outside, allowing the latter to gradually build up. When you first clap or sing with others who are cooked, make sure you are inaudible when you do it externally. It's better to accentuate your inner emotion and hear others while you whisper the song and are physically unable to hear your voice, rather than sonically drown out what needs to be held within and heard without. Imagine that you are making the sound you hear others make. This allows both your emotion and voice to get in synch with what you are aiming to embody. Don't immediately make your sound too audible or your movement too visually noticeable. Wait for God to turn up the volume and intensity. Never hold back your inner emotion and devotion to divine influence, but always hold back anything that appears, sounds, and smells like you are externally doing your own thing that is out of synch and voluntarily imposed.

This same process occurs when you find yourself absorbed into music that you passionately enjoy and are swept away with. For instance, while attending a concert you may get caught by its emotional excitement and feel like you are one of the musicians, even feeling your hands move as if they are playing the guitar or holding a microphone. You are so connected to the music that there is no need to separate who is the performer and who is the audience. Musicians also sometimes feel a reversal when the music really gets a hold on their body. Pianists, for example, may experience the piano keys moving their fingers rather than the other way around. When you merge with the whole of music, the striking of a piano's hammer becomes indistinguishable from what is struck in your soul and the strings of your heart are the same as those on the soundboard. The keys, piano, and music then feel like they are playing you.

A perfect inner body enactment of spiritually cooked expression helps build the right kind of habits for your body instrument—encouraging ecstatic emotion to be caught and amplified until it launches spontaneous absorption, fusion, and fully integrated expression. It is useful to imagine that you were born with a whole, perfect inner ecstatic spiritual body that has been waiting to lead the rest of you. Over the years, your external physical form has become dissociated from this perfect inner form and gone astray, acquiring habits that throw you out of tune and leave you in the cold. You will have to reawaken your inner body so it can relearn how to ecstatically walk, run, dance, shake, sing, drum, and play its instruments all over again. You need to earn back the trust of your inner body, allowing it to be more ecstatically engaged. With the ongoing attunement and development of your inner body, it will take the lead and your outer body will eventually catch on without your having to teach it a thing.

As you ecstatically work out your inner body, remember that the call and response of sound and movement, fueled by amplified emotion, must always be involved. The spiritual engineering practices of Sacred Ecstatics encourage you to pursue inner ecstasy rather than inner peace, inner movement rather than inner stillness, and inner heightened emotion rather than detached feelings. It teaches you to move with spiritual fervor on the inside that causes a fire to spread to the outside, waking up the mysteries of emotion, perception, and action that go past trance and help you enter the singing dance of spiritual cooking and sacred ecstasy.

Ongoing Change and Entrainment Busting

The heightened ecstatic experience of a fully tuned and cooked body instrument requires constant change, something that cannot be accomplished by recycling the same incantation, prayer, rhythm, song, or movement pattern, over and over again. Any spiritual practice, whether it is meditation, ecstatic dance, shamanic journeying, energy healing, ceremony, or church, must not get stuck in one gear or it won't go anywhere. Your emotion, movement, rhythm, tone, expression, spiritual temperature, vibration, instrumental form, and all the rest of it must constantly change. This requires being inside the big room of Sacred Ecstatics, an experiential place the Kalahari Bushmen call "First Creation." This is where you will find *the changing*, the vital force of change that raises the temperature and gets you spiritually cooked, as well as makes you tuned and instrumentally performed. Spiritual heat and sacred ground's expansion bring divine improvisation, not obedience to any frozen form, distillation of process, or the quietude of ecstatic ineptitude.

Therefore, avoid excessive periods of entrainment and the non-vibrant trance states caused by synchronizing yourself with a redundant, monotonous rhythm like a metronome, steady tom-tom beat, or the sleepy drone tone of hypnotic talk. Becoming too locked into a repetitive movement or rhythm is a sign that you are far from the big room and its infusion of change. You are also distant from God and more locked inside trickster mockery, fable, and confabulation rather than amidst the heat of spiritual cooking.

When you find yourself experientially wrapped and bound inside a humdrum hypnotic trance, you are in need of what we call an "entrainment buster"—sudden movements and spontaneous shouts that help wake up your ecstatic, mystical senses and startle your body to wiggle and shake itself free. As spiritual engineering knowledge and practice of its skills bring you ecstatic habits and your experience with Sacred Ecstatics grows, these interrupts of a lost and meandering mind will happen spontaneously. The more well-tuned and regulated your body instrument, the more it is able to trigger the wake up calls, gearshifts, and ecstatic boosters that enable you to stay on the spiritual mainline rather than float away on trickster driftwood.

In ecstatic gatherings conductors initiate the necessary interrupts and changes. They also stand ready to vary a rhythm, tone, movement, or song at any time. For instance, after a fast and furious song, Caribbean Shakers may switch to a slow song that, rather than cool things down, will paradoxically feel like a call for stronger shouting and more jolting movements. *Changes* in any direction of any kind are what continuously amplify, magnify, and heat up the sacred vibration. To keep things spiritually heated and creatively charged, everything must change—the ecstatic gears must constantly shift. Follow as best you can and then expect to be interrupted by another change for you to follow differently.

Becoming an Ecstatic Spiritual Engineer

Remember that no beginning student of Sacred Ecstatics is able to immediately embody all the basic practices of spiritual engineering. It takes time to master an art and this includes the transformative ecstatic art of tuning, regulating, and playing your body instrument so it spiritually cooks. Before you earn your Sacred Ecstatics "driver's license" for traveling on the rope, "hunting license" for tracking the sacred vibration, "musician's union card" for getting a gig as a big room instrumentalist, and "chef's diploma" from a higher culinary institute, you must initially learn how to enact the recipe by successfully gathering and blending the ingredients and turning the mystical wheel.

It can't be said enough that sacred ecstasy is not primarily a matter of belief, but of action that effectively elevates sacred emotion until it bursts into supreme ecstasy. It's often difficult for people to understand how little their running trickster commentary matters when it comes to turning up the heat and getting cooked. Once you receive the sacred vibration, however, you will know without a doubt that it cannot be reawakened by thought alone. The ignition of ecstasy is not an intention. Regardless of your physical or mental state when you begin an intensive, session, or workout, the action you need to take is the same: gather and blend the ingredients and board the mystical wheel that transports you to the big room fire. Follow the practical wisdom passed down through numerous generations and it will lead you in the right direction. Welcome to the life that spiritually engineers endless voyages to sacred ecstasy. Here you exalt dance over ideological stance, song over story, fascinating rhythm over monotonous beat, spiritual heat over frozen belief, experimentalism over fundamentalism, excitation over relaxation, vibration over contemplation, spiritual cooking over mindful meditation, and divine mystery over personal mastery.

OVERVIEW OF THE SPIRITUAL ENGINEERING BASIC PRACTICES

The basic practices of spiritual engineering will be presented in depth in Part Two. These practices develop the skills required for optimal spiritual cooking, enabling more effective enactment of all the steps of the Sacred Ecstatics recipe. As always, the purpose of good spiritual engineering is to prepare you for reception of the sacred vibration, tune you as an instrument for divine performance, and empower your rope to God.

The first set of spiritual engineering practices focus on gathering and embodying the four ingredients needed for spiritual cooking. The first three ingredients prepare your body (1) to be more responsive to a changing rhythm (the ingredient of a fascinating rhythm); (2) freeing it to move more spontaneously (the ingredient of seiki movement); (3) and making it more somatically responsive to changes of tone (the ingredient of tonal alignment). Sacred music then brings the fourth ingredient — sacred emotion — that further inspires and intensifies all the others. After the four basic ingredients are gathered, you advance to the next level of skill that involves ecstatically blending them together. This is accomplished through establishing a basic call and response that gets each ingredient calling and responding to all the others. This results in the formation of the mystical prayer wheel whose initial turning builds sacred ground. The wheel's turning is the ecstatic dynamic that expands and heats the room, eventually lighting the ecstatic fire of spiritual cooking itself.

The more the wheel turns, the more the function of the wheel changes—moving from expanding to heating and cooking, and even to becoming a wheel of transportation for spiritual traveling, something that takes place when spiritual cooking is in full force. This kind of spiritual traveling is not passive and visually imagined, but entails the wholehearted and whole-bodied enactment of the movements, rhythms, tones, and songs associated with a particular ecstatic locale. Every experiential destination is housed in the big room where all is changing, which means you never can predict where you'll ecstatically travel or what might happen. Finally, you will learn how to effectively return to the everyday and pour the heat, mystery, and experienced changes of the big room back into the world, sharing what you received in order to further sustain and nurture it.

In a Sacred Ecstatics intensive or a session, the gathering of ingredients and their blending into a turning mystical wheel are led and guided by someone anointed as a conductor. This provides an opportunity for you to cook with others under the supervision of someone who brings expertise in spiritual cooking. We also teach you how to privately make a quick gathering and blending of these ingredients into a wheel that may be interspersed throughout the activities of your day—what we call *the ecstatic prelude*. In addition, time can be set aside for working on the specific practices for gathering and blending as well as following along to the ecstatic travel tracks that enable you to spiritually cook at home.

Note that receiving the sacred vibration is not something that can take place at the snap of your fingers. Furthermore, it is extremely rare to receive the sacred vibration and develop a strong rope to God without some guidance and physical contact with a spiritually cooked conductor. You must repeatedly be brought inside the spiritual heat of the big room in order to develop your ability to move through the steps of the recipe, become better prepared to receive the sacred vibration, and strengthen your rope. Keep in mind that the same spiritual engineering know-how applies both to beginning and seasoned participants; no matter how cooked you get, you will always need to gather and blend the ingredients and turn the mystical wheel in order to climb the thermometer to the big room.

What is most important is that you learn to make rhythms, tones, movement, and sacred emotion more important than the chatter of inner and outer commentary, narration, and interpretive analysis. Making the highest pragmatic and paradigmatic shift from the reign of cogitation to the primacy of ecstatic excitation is the first crossroads you face. You, like most people in modern times, are likely deeply habituated to approaching healing and spirituality through mostly cognitive means. You seek the right thought, belief, spiritual law, or theoretical understanding, assuming that it will help bring the desired change. However, there is another less known road that takes you straight to the spiritual heat. This is the path of Sacred Ecstatics. On this road you learn to take ecstatically engineered action no matter what you think you understand or don't understand about your life, whether it concerns the past, present, or future. Whatever your state of being, it's time to gather the ingredients, blend them into a mystical wheel, and turn your life around by enacting the recipe for setting your soul on fire.

PART TWO

THE BASIC PRACTICES

The following spiritual engineering practices are divided into three sections: (1) preparation for spiritual cooking, which involves gathering the four ingredients; (2) the actual cooking itself, which begins with expanding and heating the room by blending the ingredients to form a mystical prayer wheel; and (3) reentering your everyday. In the beginning, you are asked to gather the following ingredients: a fascinating soulful rhythm, spontaneous movement, tonal alignment with somatic vibration, and sacred emotion infused by sacred music. It is the blending of these four ingredients that matters—you need all of them present and in relationship with one another to build sacred ground, light an ecstatic fire, and keep it burning. Each cooking ingredient depends on the other ingredients to maximize its contribution and effectiveness. Spend time working with each ingredient while also making sure that you arrange to work with all of them together so they are never isolated for too long.

Always start a round of Sacred Ecstatics—whether you are conducting a home workout, participating in a group intensive, or having a private session—remembering what it is you are trying to achieve. Sacred Ecstatics invites you to seek the highest outcome of setting your soul on fire and being spiritually cooked by God. This naturally happens when you are brought nearer the source and force of creation. Do not be bashful about aiming for the ultimate human experience whether it's called a saint's rapture, a shaman's shaking ecstasy, a Kalahari Bushman's n/om cooking, a seiki practitioner's seiki installation, a sanctified parishioner's baptism in fire, or a mystic's divine union. Begin by clearly and enthusiastically stating that you desire to enter infinity and be cooked by divinity. Take the vow that you will sincerely do your part to help this take place. Don't conduct Sacred Ecstatics in a half-baked manner; aim to be wholly baked by the Big Holy. Make the effort to go all the way and do your best not to drift from the divine target.

Although it's true that all spiritual outcomes are ultimately in higher hands, you must take action to get things started right. In the beginning, gathering and blending the four ingredients requires conscious will and disciplined effort. The same is true for learning any art. You may long to beautifully play a cello or masterfully dance the tango, but you will have to work hard to learn the basic skills required to perform either. Some people want the final accomplishment, but do not want to make the effort required to achieve it. Trickster stands ready to turn the wisdom of "thy will be done" or "it's in God's hands" into an excuse for being lazy, implying that work on your part might interfere with higher will and action. You must meet God at least halfway; there is no excuse for you to not practice, follow an anointed teacher's guidance, and learn how to become a more skilled divine instrument. Deciding to be a learner and an ecstatic burner requires giving up "know-it-all" mind and all the excuses it makes to not do everything required. Come to school with beginner's mind and be prepared to practice and train.

Mastering the art of spiritual cooking is not that different from learning music. You must learn the equivalent of how to play the notes and make a rhythm before producing a whole tune. At the same time, you must learn how to always sound like you are performing music even when you are practicing. Otherwise you will learn to play in a cold, stale, and aesthetically dead manner. The key to mastering music and spiritual cooking is found by maintaining the attitude that beginning practice and final performance are never too far away from one another.

Learn how to gather and blend each ingredient wholeheartedly rather than only going through the motions without sincere emotion and devotion. Your practice should always be expressed as your final performance.

Vincent van Gogh advised those who truly desired to paint: "If you hear a voice within you saying, 'You are not a painter,' *then by all means paint*, boy, and that voice will be silenced, but only by working."[12] Likewise when your heart sincerely longs to be near the divine, you may hear trickster's voice telling you that it is not possible. By all means in that very moment do all you can to head to the big room. There the music will silence all doubt and put to rest any trickster protest. Remember Thomas Edison who kept trying one experiment after another until he reached the outcome he sought. He proposed that "our greatest weakness lies in giving up." All the practices of Sacred Ecstatics must be performed in a spiritual laboratory where each session is an experimental trial that must be done again and again until the light eventually goes on. Be bold and tinker with infinity, experiment with divinity, and fire yourself up until you catch fire! If trial and error worked for the shamans, saints, and inventors who sought the light, there is no reason for you to remain in the dark. You are only one trial, one experiment, one note, one rhythm, one song, one step, one filament, and one match away from being spiritually set on fire.

STEP 1. GATHERING THE INGREDIENTS FOR SPIRITUAL COOKING

Ingredient 1: Fascinating Rhythm

Each of the four ingredients helps free you to be more kinesthetically sensitive, kinetically responsive, and somatically tuned to divine influence. As will be explained, certain *entrainment rhythms* are in part what maintain habits that block spontaneous movement and expression. Before spiritual cooking, you benefit from clearing away or shaking free the locked-in body rhythms that leave you somatically rigid and ecstatically frigid. Gathering the first ingredient—a fascinating rhythm—involves two parts: (1) busting the entrainment rhythms that recycle interfering habits and (2) recalibrating the way you respond to rhythm, this time paying more attention to rhythmic changes rather than just keeping time with a steady beat. Most spiritual ceremony begins by preparing the space for sacred work, like the ancient practice of smudging. You can think of working with the first ingredient as a form of preparatory ritual—a "budge smudge" or "rhythm detox." You need the smudge that uncouples you from toxic, lifeless rhythms and the budge that gets you moving with an uplifting, life-renewing rhythm. Rather than shoo away bad spirits, shake away deadbeat monotony. Make yourself available for God's soul time and the divine heartbeat that brings the spiritual heat.

Your Body Is a Vibrational Field and Polyrhythmic Mix

Are you aware that you are 99.99 percent empty space and that, if you were physically compressed, you'd be the size of a cube whose width measures around 1/500th of a centimeter? If there is really not that much to you, then why do you appear to take up so much space? The reason has to do with the fact that the atoms that make you a physical form never touch one another— they are separated by an electromagnetic force field. Said differently, you are primarily a complex arrangement of multiple vibrations, a polyrhythmic mix, wherein the amount of matter is what matters the least. What does matter is the vibrational field that organizes the space, placement, and relationship of your atoms. The various pulses of your rhythmic mix, found in your whole ecology of vibration, hold every level of recognizable pattern that is associated with your identity— from how you physically look to how you sound and move, as well as how you sense, think, and emote.

It's not any isolated thought or action (or atom, molecule, chemical, neuron, or brain part) that is responsible for your experience, but the rhythms binding them as a whole.

Fortunately, the basic biological rhythms for maintaining life, such as heartbeat and blood flow, are not easily removed. We are speaking of clearing the rhythms that bind impoverished mind-body habits, especially those that distance you from a felt relationship with the sacred. Untie the rhythmic thread that weaves a particular sequence of parts together and the presumed solid reality of each part magically vanishes. It's true that no man or woman is an island, and neither are the parts of your body or any aspect of human experience. The creation, maintenance, growth, and renewal of life require rhythms that connect the parts into a vibrant rather than lackluster whole. If your life is too boring and lifeless, or if you are stuck in the same cycle of impoverished patterns, then you are more in need of new fascinating rhythms than a psychological makeover.

Working with the "wholeness" of a human being is elusive if you don't recognize that rhythm is what connects the dots and glues the parts together. Perhaps holistic medicine's frustration with adequately capturing wholeness contributed to later favoring the names "integrative" and "complementary" rather than continue with an emphasis on "holistic." Similarly, once upon a time psychotherapy, especially early family therapy, toyed with the idea of treating a system rather than an individual, but quickly regressed to what is much easier to grasp — an individual's narratives and conversations rather than patterns of actually performed interaction that occupy a social situation. As a participant in this historical period of family therapy, Brad remembers how few leaders or teachers of the field could adequately define, illustrate, or demonstrate a so-called system. Looking back at the failed attempts of both holistic medicine and systemic-oriented therapies to escape being stranded on island-like thinking, what was missing was a clear way of conceptualizing the thread, string, or rope that weaves parts into a whole. What was neither seen nor heard was rhythm, pulse, and vibration — the force that holds, binds, sequences, circulates, and orchestrates parts to become a whole.

The Secret to Change: Clear the Stuck Rhythm

Duke Ellington had it right when his orchestra played, "It Don't Mean a Thing If It Ain't Got that Swing." Consider that the notes of a melody in a song are tied together and brought to life by rhythm. Remove the rhythm and the tones no longer produce a recognizable song; you are only left with a pile of disorganized, random sounds. Similarly regard all aspects of your experience as analogous to musical notes. It's rhythm that connects a whole sequence, pattern, or melody of ongoing experiences. Extinguish the rhythm and all its held content disassembles and falls apart. With this perspective we see that a common error in psychotherapy and medicine is the focus on isolating particular notes (such as problems, solutions, symptoms, cures, or other parts of experience) rather than the whole rhythmic pattern that connects, which includes your interactions with others. Treating the parts of human experience is no different than suggesting that a client needs less flats or more sharps, or additional C notes rather than B notes, not realizing that the notes alone are not as critically important as the rhythm holding them all together. If you clear away a monotonous, lifeless, or impoverishing rhythm and replace it with one that is more interesting and full of life, the same notes suddenly make beautiful music. Furthermore, a rhythm that is soulfully alive can inspire new notes and more exciting, improvisational arrangements. Change the rhythm that connects and other changes within will follow.

In engineering, entrainment refers to the *entrapment* of one substance by another substance, like aeration where gas is captured by a liquid. In human experience, entrainment generally refers to how your behavior (whether brain activity, body movement, or social conduct) becomes synchronized to a rhythm or frequency of vibration. A sequence of behavior becomes a habit when it is so synchronized that it seems entrapped or habituated inside a rhythmic loop that constantly recycles. Here we see that an isolated behavior that is deemed "impoverished," "problematic," or "pathological" persists or feels locked in due to rhythmic entrapment. While understand-

36

ing either the rhythmic origin of the behavior or its synchronization with a rhythm may be intellectually fascinating, practically speaking it rarely contributes to change and risks being iatrogenic. It's wiser to immediately intervene to bust the rhythm so the behavior is no longer stuck. The people-helping professions need less interpretation and more rhythm interruption. If the rhythm doesn't change, any conversation about it will simply be incorporated into the same rhythmic sequence, making the pattern even more resistant to change.

Anthropologist Edward Hall was also aware of the importance of rhythm in organizing human experience and in 1983 proposed: "Rhythm will, I believe, soon be proved to be the ultimate building block in not only personality, but also communication and health . . . the rhythm of a people may yet prove to be the most binding of all forces that hold human beings together."[13] He added that rhythm is a "hidden force, that, like gravity, holds groups together."[14] Rhythm actually holds all levels of phenomena together from atoms to personal habits and the choreographed interaction of social groups and whole cultures. The helping professions, from medicine to psychotherapy, are themselves in need of new rhythms that will alter the way they work with the rhythms of human experience.

Move from a Dead Beat to a Fascinating Rhythm

The use of rhythm in healing has been largely limited to synchronizing brainwaves with particular valued frequencies, especially those that are associated with relaxation. Biofeedback, also called brainwave synchronization, was founded on this principle — encouraging the brain to synchronize or entrain with chosen periodic rhythms of external stimuli that are auditory, visual, or tactile. Rhythmic-oriented healing, from biofeedback technology to music therapy, is generally biased toward Plato's early definition of rhythm as serving the "ordering of movement" or *kineseos taxis*.[15] Healing with rhythm has largely ignored or devalued any rhythm that does not have a predictable steady beat.

37

The smooth and steady coordination of body activity (including the brain) to even-keeled, unsurprising beats that supposedly induce mellow moods is promoted while ecstatic rhythms that evoke excitement and hyperarousal are ignored. This is arguably a cultural preference that promotes non-ecstatic rhythms while discriminating against those that are ecstatic, changing, and polyrhythmic. For example, Roberto Assagioli, founder of the humanistic psychology method called psychosynthesis, proposed that too much dissonance and irregular rhythms in music is psychologically damaging. He regarded music as an "aural drug"[16] and warned that music could cause a whole nation to become neurotic.

For Assaglioli, classical music was therapeutic, while jazz and rock and roll were pathological and injurious. His view echoed the naïve reaction of provincial parents who feared that adolescents would be under the devil's influence if they listened to the music of big bands, Elvis, or the Beatles. The same attitude is implicit in massage room and new age music whose rhythms are monotonous and absent of soulful syncopation. The so-called core shamanism of Michael Harner similarly exalts the importance of monotonous rhythm.[g] In summary, the healing and transformative arts of contemporary times have long

---

[g] The claim that the sonic driving of drum rhythms induces trance is typically an exaggerated generalization that lacks nuance and qualification. That idea was proposed in 1955 by Charles Pidoux, a physician who conducted ethnopsychiatric research among possession cults in Mali. See Jonathan Berger and Gabe Turrow, *Music, Science, and the Rhythmic Brain* (New York: Routledge, 2012). Entrainment to monotonous rhythm became Harner's core technique of inducing a trance presumed to be shamanic in nature. However, ethnographic studies and lab experiments have since demonstrated that drum rhythms are not a sufficient criterion to induce trance, nor is it necessary for producing trance (Ibid.). It is just as likely that monotonous rhythm is neither a primary nor necessary factor of shamanic experience. More importantly, the systemic complexity of the sacred nature of shamanism is trivialized and mocked when it is reduced to a simple causative factor. Perhaps the advocacy of steady monotonous rhythms by teachers of European descent is another example of colonization that imposes a preferred bleached rhythm over those beats that hold more diversity and complexity, and require more skill to produce.

advanced a bias toward rhythms that relax the body and entrance the mind. Sacred Ecstatics joins the ecstatic spiritual lineages that go in the opposite rhythmic direction. It calls on the drums that wake you up rather than provide an aural tranquilizer.

With this perspective, it is no surprise that African healers do not primarily direct their clients to go home and rest. They go for the energetic response rather than the relaxation response. The drums are called to play wildly as the community gathers for an ecstatic dance. Healing is found in the dance rather than the sick bed of rest. Rhythm is the medicine for an out of tune, out of synch, and out of whack human being. As Babatunde Olantunj describes this orientation, "Where I come from we say that rhythm is the soul of life, because the whole universe revolves around rhythm, and when we get out of rhythm, that's when we get into trouble."[17] Disease is associated with lacking the rhythms that have the vibrant swing of well-being. The key word here is "swing" because not any rhythm will do. You need a rhythm infused with the swing that rings the wake up call to come to life—a transformative rhythm that inspires change. When the rhythm changes, so does your experience, and this is the key to having a vital life: you need surprise, change, embellishment, and improvisation.[h]

The hierarchical exaltation of European calm over African excitement is no better exemplified than in Carl Jung's trip to an African village in the Sudan. He described his experience of the villagers' rhythms and movement in the autobiographical interviews that comprise the book, *Memories, Dreams, Reflections*.[18] The night began with children and adults of the community gathering for "savage singing, drumming, and trumpeting."[19] Jung was apprehensive from the start: "I did not know whether I ought to feel pleased or anxious about this mass

---

[h] Obviously, you also need your rest. The point is that human beings are in need of the whole cycle of relaxation and excitement. We have been led astray when only half the healing cycle—the quiet and still relaxed body—is regarded as the primary means of well-being, healing, or spirituality at the expense of heightened arousal.

display." Later when things started to spiritually heat up, he grew even more concerned that as "the rhythm of the dance and the drumming accelerated . . . the natives easily fall into a virtual state of possession . . . their excitement began to get out of bounds. . . . The dancers were being transformed into a wild horde, and I became worried about how it would end."[20]

Jung explained away his personal fear of ecstatic experience and demeaned the African as "primitive" with a "primal darkness" that only the light of psychological consciousness could alleviate. Rather than imply that Africans are in need of Western psychology, Jung could have explored whether a Western psychologist might benefit from an African rhythm that invites a process of personal transformation outside the boundaries of his conceptual understanding. Instead, he favored a European flavored universe, one that exalts sitting at rest at a desk construing psychological interpretation that lacks ecstatic reverberation. To his credit, Jung later confessed that he was as much examining himself as experiencing Africa:

> I had undertaken my African adventure with the
> secret purpose of escaping from Europe and its
> complex problems. . . . The trip revealed itself as
> less an investigation of primitive psychology . . .
> than a probing into the rather embarrassing
> question: What is going to happen to Jung the
> psychologist in the wilds of Africa?[21]

Unfortunately, Jung was so afraid of ecstatic experience that he left unchanged and more committed to perpetuating that which protected his cultural way and himself from rhythmic awakening.

Brad also found the same fear among popular contemporary teachers of shamanism. He was once invited to give a keynote address to a group of faculty who taught a neoshamanism method. After he ecstatically played a drum to a delighted audience, the founders of the organization were found recoiled with anxious concern. Brad was told by one of the most famous leaders of neoshamanism, "That kind of drumming is dangerous. It can induce psychotic episodes. A calm rhythm is much safer." At that moment, Brad knew that a cold and upside down form of non-ecstatic shamanism was being taught at most weekend shamanism workshops. The taboo against ecstatic rhythm and spontaneous shaking continues today among many of those who call themselves "shamanic practitioners."

Sacred Ecstatics begins by emphasizing rhythms and movements that are ecstatically evocative rather than calming or relaxing. In order to raise the spiritual temperature and cross over into non-ordinary states of heightened spiritual experience, you are in need of immediately being shaken and cleared of everyday habitual rhythms and instilled with ecstatic rhythms that awaken transformative vitality. Specifically, you must clear or at least loosen the grip of those rhythms that hold learned habits that stand in the way of your getting to the big room. Here, a toxic rhythm refers to the tick-tock clock kind of steady beat that, while easy to mount, does not inspire you to be improvisational or kinetically responsive to change, which is necessary for reaching ecstatic heights. With monotonous rhythm you become too easily entrained and trapped in clock time rather than freed by ecstatic time.

Lin-Manuel Miranda suggests: "When you're dealing with a constant rhythm, no matter how great your lyrics are, if you don't switch it up, people's heads are going to start bobbing. And they're going to stop listening to what you're saying, so consistently keep the ear fresh and keep the audience surprised." [22] Always highlight rhythmic changes over non-changing grooves. This is why authentic ecstatic drumming (and true shamanic drumming as well) is filled with off beats, altering beats, multiple beats, and interspersed arrhythmic chaos. It is meant to surprise you and trip you into waking up spontaneous body movement. Get off the well-beaten track and head your body toward the shake shack.

In summary, your experiential reality exists and persists through rhythmic entrainment. Be more excited than anxious to learn that you are more a rhythmic field than a psychological condition. As Miles Davis said, "My ego only needs a good rhythm section."[23] Interrupt, break, and clear away the rusty chains of entrainment and your experiential slate is instantly cleared and cleaned. This is the mind-blowing secret to escaping any stuck experience or limited reality: forget analyzing or interpreting the cause or nature of the presumed fixed state and bust the rhythm that maintains its existence. To advance forward and enter the big room of Sacred Ecstatics, you must untie or cut the cord of whatever rhythm prevents you from the ecstatic movement required to get there.

You cannot see or hear the rhythms that comprise your life — they are often invisible to the eye and inaudible to the ear just as all the rhythms, beats, pulses, and vibrations that hold your atoms together are beyond perception. There is no need to identify, diagnose, or understand your current rhythmic habits in order to clear and replace them with more vibrant rhythms. Apply skillful spiritual engineering from the get-go and bust entrainment rhythms that habitually lock you in an ecstatically chilled body. But keep in mind that if you don't immediately afterward catch a different kind of rhythm, one that is more ecstatically uplifting, you will soon fall back into the old rhythms that stand nearby. Board an ecstatic rhythm so you don't miss the soul train.

The Ecstatic Method of Catching a Fascinating Rhythm

Good spiritual engineering involves clearing and resetting the present rhythmic field, readying your body for an invigorating rhythmic ride. Before moving on to more creative and complex rhythms that frequently change, bust up any rhythmic entrainment by performing random action, unfamiliar movement, and surprising motion that include wiggling, flopping, and shaking the body. Remember that what you are clearing are interference patterns that block your chance to enter the big room where changing rhythms rule.

We offer a two-part method for learning to catch a fascinating rhythm. It begins with giving yourself a budge smudge/rhythm detox, followed by a unique way of moving to rhythms that fascinate rather than sedate. It can be done almost anywhere, either alone or with others. You can practice this method by itself or do it as part of a larger routine that includes working with the other ingredients. Although spiritual cooking requires blending all four ingredients together, keep in mind that working with each ingredient separately helps you hone the skills required to gather, activate, and embody each, making you better prepared for the later blend.

The Budge Smudge/Rhythm Detox: Taking the Walk of Evolution

When you walk into the room where you will ecstatically practice and perform, know that your immediate mission is to make a transition from the daily habits you walk in with to the vastly different reality of sacred ecstatic experience. To facilitate this transition we invite your body to physically enact what we call "the walk of evolution." You are going to perform a brief ecstatic reenactment of the emergence of life on earth, like an improvisational theatre exercise. What could be a more dramatic metaphor for making the transitional shift to Sacred Ecstatics than the whole history of life's evolution?

Proceed as follows: The moment you step into the room, imagine you are the first fish that came out of the primordial sea. What does a fish do when it is thrown out of the water? It flops. Go ahead and fantasize that you are the fish that has been thrown out of its familiar surroundings—flop spontaneously either on the floor or do so in a standing position if it is more comfortable to be a vertically inclined aquatic creature. Don't exaggerate or overexert this movement so you risk throwing your body even further out of alignment. Make a natural and effortless movement that is inspired by fish flopping, however small or large it is. You can even recruit one of your hands to serve as the whole fish.

After this reenacted moment in the evolution of life, take a few steps forward and now imagine you have further evolved. It is millions of years later than the appearance of the first fish and you are now the first dog getting out of a pond following a swim. What does a dog do after getting out of water? It performs one of the best shakes known to the animal kingdom — it shakes from head to tail.[i] Do the same and again make sure you don't overstrain your body by being too purposefully vigorous. Then proceed to sit down and assume you have arrived in the Africa, the cradle of humanity where syncopated drumming began.

Get Tripped by Rhythmic Surprise: The Key to Catching and Being Caught by a Fascinating Rhythm

At this time you are invited to play a recording of a percussion performance filled with polyrhythms and syncopation (we provide custom-made tracks for our mentorship students). Rather than move your body in time with a steady beat, however, pay more attention to instances when the rhythm changes and move your body in response to those changes in kind. A changing rhythm combined with a spontaneous somatic response to those changes is what soulfully charges the body and ecstatically wakes you up. If you are used to dancing to ecstatic rhythms, you may have to work harder to avoid falling into the habit of moving as you normally do. For this reason we strongly suggest that you perform this practice while seated. We ask you to do the opposite of what dance typically calls for: rather than strictly follow the beat, have your body respond more to the changes precipitated by spiritual heat.

You may find that your body both follows a beat with a steady motion *and* ecstatically responds with surprising movements that are triggered by sudden changes in the rhythm. This is fine as long as the latter remains the highlighted primary experience. In certain dance traditions, including the Kalahari Bushman healing dance, mastery requires both skillfully following a beat while at the same time being remarkably responsive to the interspersed rhythms and movements that not

---

[i] Qigong as well as the Chinese martial arts have long used animal mimicry as an exercise form. We have chosen two creatures that masterfully exemplify shaking action.

only surprise and delight but also bring heightened emotion and energy. As flamenco dancers say, the dancer aims for *duende,* another metaphor for n/om that is delivered by the surprise of an unexpected surge of movement that spreads life force throughout the performance room. In Bali, dancers are aware of two kinds of energies and their associated rhythms and movements. One of the energies, called *cesta kara,* is harnessed by many years of disciplined training. It fosters the perfection of form usually acquired by imitating a master dancer's performance. The other energy, called *taksu,* comes from the gods and it is unpredictable. The latter divine inspiration brings the improvised and spontaneous surprises that touch people's hearts and souls.[24]

Nikola Tesla was one of the first researchers to find that administering a mechanical vibration can "profoundly affect human life,"[25] helping improve major organ function as well as to promote a general state of well-being. He reported that "intense mechanical vibrations produce remarkable physiological effects" and mentioned that his friend Mark Twain "came to the laboratory in the worst shape, suffering from a variety of distressing and dangerous ailments, but in less than two months he regained his old vigor and ability of enjoying life to the fullest extent."[26]

Tesla's contraption demonstrated what a fish and dog already implicitly know: intense shaking, especially when it involves rapid oscillations (as Tesla discovered), is a natural adaptive response whether you are stepping outside your familiar surroundings or you are reentering them anew. What Tesla missed, however, is that once you clear away an impoverishing entrainment rhythm through a powerful dose of shaking motion, it needs to be immediately replaced by the kind of changing beat that inspires optimal vitality. Mount an ecstatic rhythm where entrainment, detrainment, and subsequently altered entrainment keep shifting to vary the groove, going both on and off a beat. You need just the right amount of "offness" to be ecstatically switched on. Then you will be naturally moved by both the predictable rhythms of earth and the unpredictable rhythms of heaven.

The walk of evolution, with its fish flopping and puppy dog shaking, brings you a Tesla-like shake-up, helping you be more moved by the subsequent unexpected rhythmic changes. When you hear and feel such a change, allow your body to freely move in response to it. Again, your body should be moved by the surprising changes of rhythm rather than only steadily moved by a repeating and ecstatically dampening beat. After a few minutes of clearing away lifeless monotony and catching a fascinating rhythm, you are ready to gather the next ingredient—seiki movement. In fact, you should find that you have already naturally transitioned into the unpredictable, spontaneous movement that seiki calls for.

Also know that fascinating rhythm alone can change your whole life if you infuse it throughout your everyday. Again, rather than consider yourself a psychological state of affairs, consider that what you are is primarily due to rhythmic phenomena. You are not a psychological complex; you are a polyrhythmic mix. Do you doubt this is true? Of course your mind would rather you exalt psychological, philosophical, scientific, and theological belief over the ecstatic ignition of your whole condition. Never mind that protest and move ahead of your head: eliminate the monotonous rhythm that keeps you in a holding pattern. We invite you to be an experimentalist rather than a spiritual, religious, or secularist fundamentalist. At least give it a test drive. Introduce a rhythmic shake-up to any habit, action sequence, interaction pattern, repeating thoughts, recycled ruts, ineffective patter, mindless or mindful chatter, and so forth. Go ahead and jazz 'er up, give your mood funks a funky rhythm, and give soul time a chance to work on you, clear you, endear you, and cheer you. Make the beat that brings the heat. Welcome to the overthrow of symbols by clashing cymbals as you sing George and Ira Gershwins' song, "Fascinating Rhythm":

Fascinating rhythm,
You've got me on the go.

Fascinating rhythm,
I'm all a quiver.
What a mess you're making,
The neighbors want to know,
Why I'm always shaking . . .[27]

You must shift the rhythms of your life to assure that your experience always changes. In this changing, life's vitality pulses through you, and this is what underlies transformation. For Sacred Ecstatics to start right, you must be loose enough to move in and out of one rhythmic pattern to another, and this especially includes the kind of syncopation that induces ecstatic palpitation. Clear the monotony whose existential boredom is always the deep problem underneath all surface problems, and steer toward the polyphony that brings creative invigoration.

Ingredient 2: Seiki Movement

Gathering the next ingredient involves sitting on a sturdy bench or chair and spending a few minutes with the traditional Japanese practice of *seiki jutsu*. Here a unique kind of spontaneous body movement is presumed to be activated by the invisible and mysterious force of *seiki*. In the Japanese tradition this particular sit-down practice is called *seiki taisou*. We simply refer to it as seiki movement. This practice provides an opportunity to learn how to free your body to move more spontaneously and involuntarily, something that is both a requirement for raising the spiritual temperature and a natural outcome of heightened spiritual cooking. When you call for seiki, you are inspired to let something beyond your mind's willpower and understanding move your body—the unimpeded flow of life itself, the changing of First Creation called seiki by an old school of Japanese energy practitioners.

The seiki practice teaches your body to be kinesthetically responsive to the constantly changing energy surges of seiki that constitute a fascinating rhythm. The changing flow, tides, current, and rhythmic pulse of seiki trigger your body to move in kind. Seiki is as capable of inducing a steady beat as it is of evoking a non-steady one. Here you find that a fascinating rhythm (ingredient 1) and spontaneous seiki movement (ingredient 2) are two sides of the same coin. The more responsive you are to changing rhythms, the better your seiki movement. Similarly, with good seiki movement, the better you catch, hold, and ride a fascinating rhythm.

Start this practice by saying one word out loud: "seiki." Speak the word "seiki" as if you are calling a person to come and visit you. Also make it the singular one-word answer to whatever question might arise for you concerning what takes place or what you think should take place on the bench. What are you doing? Seiki. What are you trying to achieve? Seiki. What does this mean? Seiki. What is the purpose and goal of this practice? Seiki. Would you further explain this? Seiki. What is seiki? Seiki. This is your time to focus on experiencing the spontaneous body movement that seiki brings and not be disturbed or distracted by any other questions, answers, thoughts, or pursuits.

Assume you have no idea what seiki actually is, even though you may be tempted to think that you understand it. Make no other comparison with qi, kundalini, reiki, or even the word "energy." Keep seiki a mystery, knowing only that it is non-subtle and unpredictable. Do not impose any elaborate thoughts that might interfere. Call whole-heartedly for seiki and assume it is on its way. If you sincerely call on seiki, it will show up and continuously move your body. In due time you will realize that knowing anything about seiki is irrelevant. Welcome and anticipate seiki's involuntary movements and pure, spontaneous expression.

The Seiki Call and Response

The ingredient of seiki movement provides the first opportunity to work with the *call and response* pattern that runs throughout all the practices, dynamics, and formats of Sacred Ecstatics. Without a calling, nothing can begin. Without a subsequent acknowledgment that something has arrived, you cannot achieve interactional traction. Call on the mysterious vital force of life itself and then respond whenever you suspect it has arrived. Verbally acknowledge whenever you notice that anything different takes place in the movement or sensation of your body. Most importantly, keep the call and response going. Don't do it once and stop. Keep calling and keep responding when something happens in return.

Again, say the word "seiki" aloud or some other simple call such as, "Seiki, I invite you to come." Keep calling until you feel your body unexpectedly move. The moment you experience any movement of the truly spontaneous kind, even if it is small, immediately respond by acknowledging its presence with an enthusiasm that is appropriate for the degree of seiki you feel. Perhaps you will feel your shoulder move a bit or a small head movement will transpire. Whatever takes place, immediately respond with simple words like, "Thank you" or "Come closer, seiki." Then wait for the next body movement. Your movement may be more of the same or something different may arise. Whatever the movement, respond again with appreciative recognition, voicing just the right amount of sincere emotion that matches the degree of movement that took place.

After calling for seiki, wait long enough for seiki to have a chance to respond, but if you feel that it might not have heard your request, then call again, this time doing it differently with a more sincere and persuasive tone to your voice. The call and response aims for this sequence, which will continue repeating as a circular pattern:

> verbal call for seiki → seiki body movement response → verbal acknowledgment of seiki's arrival (which is inherently another call for seiki to keep moving your body) → seiki body movement → verbal praise → and so on

In the beginning you only create a circular call and response between vocal expression and body movement. If a thought pops into your head, disregard it and do not give it any importance. The mysterious force of seiki is more interested in your body's spontaneity than the productions of your linguistic, journalistic, and diagnostic mind. If you are not sure whether your body moved after the call, but think it might have slightly moved or had a micromovement, readily assume it was seiki that moved you and acknowledge it in kind.

Learn how to regulate your call and response so it continues smoothly and isn't interrupted. While you don't want to exaggerate the emotion in your voice, you do need to call for seiki with enough feeling to inspire seiki to move you. In the beginning, use a tone that is sincere and congruent with how you are feeling at the moment. If you feel out of whack with little to no energy or enthusiasm, this means that you feel that seiki is far away. You may want to use your phone and pretend to dial s-e-i-k-i, making an imaginary long-distance call to Japan. Ask seiki to fly over and make a house call because you need it. Or if you feel excited and full of life, then start with the same amount of enthusiastic emotion when you call seiki: "Seiki, I'm ready for you!"

When you are feeling upset, cranky, irritable, or angry, recognize that even these moods provide a natural resource — there is a lot of energy inside them. Utilize this raw energy and ask seiki to come, knowing that is a good time for seiki to tap into the already built up tension within. "Seiki, I've got a lot of energy inside. Please come and convert this for your use." Don't call seiki with anger, but with a sincere request for it to take your body on a ride. After some practice, you will find how to smoothly time, sincerely voice, and spontaneously embody your seiki call and response in a way that takes your body on an energetic ride.

The emotion in your words is meant to express enthusiastic desire for seiki to come into your body. The words themselves are less important; it is the emotion conveyed that matters most. If your call is sincere, seiki will come. Make seiki feel at home and even encourage or court a close friendship with it. As emotion increases with your excitement for seiki's continued movement of your body, you may shift from speaking words to expressing energetic sounds that better convey your emotion. Allow this shift to take place naturally and don't force it.

The beginning call for seiki is usually vocally expressed and the initial response typically arrives as a body movement. As you stay engaged in this process, however, you find that your movement becomes both a call and response, just as your vocal expression becomes a call and a response. In other words, there are two directions for the call and response: (1) voice calls, body responds; and (2) body calls, voice responds. In each case, an effective response energetically matches the degree of what was felt during the call, but at the same time, it has enough extra emotion to inspire another response. Once the call and response turns in a circular pattern, it no longer matters whether the moving body or the speaking voice is calling or responding, as each becomes the mutual cause and effect of the other.

In terms of spiritual engineering, the call and response leads to a cybernetic positive feedback loop that acts like an ecstatic amplifier. You should aim to have this dynamic in play during all the spiritual engineering practices. While working with ingredient 2, the ongoing call and response of vocalized emotion and automatic movement amplifies the intensity of each. The close-knit dance of this duo is what enables seiki to awaken and circulate. More specifically, co-amplification of the voice's acoustic vibrations and the body's mechanical vibrations move you toward an experience where each vibrational form is experienced as inseparable from the other. This unity of vibration feels attuned with the rhythmic pulse of life itself—here called seiki.

Jump-starting an Effective Call for Seiki Movement

In Japan, numerous leading artists and scientists declared that seiki was responsible for their creativity and the inspiration for invention. Imagine if you also learned to tap into the remarkable force of seiki. The quality of your life would be suddenly transformed with creativity, novel invention, and overflowing inspiration. Japanese practitioners of seiki jutsu also believed that seiki was the fountain of youth and a natural means of healing. Imagine that all of this is available to you from seiki, doing so to jump-start your desire to call on its presence in your life.

We sometimes ask our students and clients to learn about the greatest practitioner of seiki jutsu in our time, Ikuko Osumi Sensei from Japan.[28] She was one of Brad's mentors and he wrote a book about her life and practice. Sensei became one of the greatest healers ever known and she could send concentrated seiki to arrive anywhere in the world. She was even described as a powerful shaman in an academic book on the religion of Shintoism. A meeting with her was usually life changing. Whatever outcome was achieved, she attributed it to seiki. Now imagine that after she passed on, she was taken to a meeting with the gods of the great religions. They praised the way she had lived her life, one that was never far away from seiki. As a reward they gave her the choice to select whatever form she wished to be reincarnated into and return to Earth. Without hesitation she said she would return as pure seiki. At that moment she became a puff of wind that, when sincerely called, could enter any room and fill it with seiki, and this includes the room where you practice your seiki movement.

You are welcome to call her to be with you during your seiki session. "Osumi Sensei, please visit me." Remember that she is now pure seiki so when she enters the room you will only know she is there when your body moves. When Osumi Sensei arrives, she may gently blow against your shoulder, or your arms, or any other part of your body. She can even concentrate her seiki wind to form a pointing finger that aims itself toward your body and commands for seiki movement to commence. When you are moved, make sure you say, "Hello, Osumi Sensei. Thank you from coming." Experiment with making your relationship with seiki more personal and mysterious, doing so to bring more enthusiastic emotion when you call for her to come and stay.

After verbally calling seiki, you can try jump-starting the seiki movement process by introducing any kind of "experimental" movement. It is fine to gently initiate a rock, a wiggle, a light bounce, a bob, or a sway and then quickly get out of the way. Wait for a sudden change of movement to arrive — consider it the arrival of seiki and vocally respond with an appropriate measure of gratitude. Make sure that you don't go into the kind of kinetic trance that occurs when you lock into the same steady beat movement for too long, whether it is rocking back and forth or bobbing up and down. To change your movement, you need a rhythmic disruption that enables you to jump from one movement to another. Learn to appreciate how a changing rhythm and changing movement are both evoked by seiki.

It is seiki's *spontaneity* that brings the energetic rush, brush, and shove of surprise. Seiki's next move is, by definition, always unknown, unpredictable, and unanticipated. Experiment with randomly changing your movements and their rhythms for no reason as you simultaneously call for seiki to move you. Calling on and responding to seiki is equivalent to jumping into the Wu Wei stream where the Tao takes you on a float trip. Move with all the changes, whether they are found in still or rapid currents, or in passing through a wading pool or taken down a whirlpool. Tinker and experiment with this ingredient. In other words, approach seiki with the seriousness of childlike play.

Do you think it is impossible to purposefully (or non-spontaneously) move in order to experience spontaneous movement? Surprise yourself by trying it anyway. Launch a movement and then another until you accidentally trip and fall into a spontaneous ecstatic groove. The more you hunt for perpetual changing motion and acknowledge when it is found, the more you develop the skill of turning the wheel of call and response that transports you to the big room. As you continue this daily practice, your body will eventually discover how to activate its own movement spontaneity. We call this your personal "seiki switch." It's like a button that starts the always unpredictable and completely improvised seiki performance of your body instrument.

No Drifting

Make sure you remain sitting during the seiki practice. Don't stand unless this movement happens on its own (traditionally seiki movement is done while seated). Focus entirely on pure spontaneity rather than accentuating the achievement of any particular form. It is better to have a spontaneous tiny wiggle than a forced big display of wild movement. Do not scream or make weird gross motor movements that would freak out your grandparents. At the same time, know that seiki may later visit you with a very big movement. If this happens, assign it no more value than any teensy weensy micromovement. Authentic spontaneity matters more than size, volume, and extremity.

Again, give no importance to any thoughts that arise, including random images that pop into your mind. Gathering the seiki movement ingredient provides a time for your body to be active and in charge while thoughts are rendered less important. Your mind is kept in check when you call for and respond to the movement of your body. When seiki movement arrives, your mind retreats and simply takes a ride in the backseat.

At the early stage of learning this practice, it may help to imagine that your spine is a special kind of seiki broomstick. The base of your spine holds the broom's brush. The top of the broomstick goes straight out of the top of your head and merges with the rope to God. Assume that "higher hands" are holding the broomstick and moving it in a simple back and forth sweeping motion. Consider this a sweeping of your existential floor. "Seiki, please sweep me clean." "Seiki, sweep me off my feet!" Seiki can clear away all the clutter of your mind and any non-ecstatic body habit. This broom also sweeps away previous assumptions about either stillness or movement and helps you avoid overthinking the meaning of entrainment or detrainment. It clears the ground and empties you of all that interferes with higher hands moving your body. First sweep and sway. When the floor is clean, there will be less resistance to other kinds of free and natural motion.

Moving with Spiritual Mystery

If you have a religious belief system or spiritual faith of any kind, you can use it to enhance your seiki movement practice. Although we encourage you to first experiment using only the word "seiki," you can also call on the holy spirit or some other name that inspires you. For example, you might start seiki movement by saying out loud, "Holy spirit, please come to me" or "Holy spirit, breathe on me." Then wait for the spirit to move you. As before, you will focus on how your body responds with an unexpected spontaneous movement. When you feel the spirit moving your body, vocally express acknowledgment and praise. The more the spirit moves you, the more you offer praise.

A well-timed call and response amplifies all spiritual experience. Just like a congregation verbally responds whenever a preacher is perceived to be touched by the spirit, you celebrate when the spirit touches your body to move. When you get to a big room with vastest sacred ground, voiced praise can become a shout or your body may tremble, shake, or dance. All the activity and emotion found at the highest spiritual temperatures sit on the ecstatic foundation of seiki movement.

From a spiritual engineering standpoint, what underlies the call and response dynamic is a mutually amplified interaction between verbal praise and body movement where the emotion in praise intensifies as movement becomes more spontaneously expressed. Add whatever metaphors and hallowed names further excite your emotional enthusiasm, and invite yourself to be more experimental and less judgmental about spiritual names. Allow seiki to not only change your rhythm and movement but also sweep away whatever you think about any and all names, altering your preferences and eradicating any spiritual name allergies. Seiki can spontaneously change the rhythm, the movement, the call, the response, the name, the named, and the one expressing it all. Explore the ecstatic influence of diverse names from a spiritual engineering orientation rather than regard them as a litmus test of your faith. On Monday call for seiki, then call for experimental names during the weekdays, with the eagle landing on Saturday, followed by calling for the Lord on Sunday morning. And if it helps loosen your mind, simply redefine the word "NAME" as an acronym for Nomenclature Assigned to Mystery & Ecstasy.

The biggest obstacle to mastering seiki movement is the temptation to spend more time thinking about it than actually doing it. It's time to give your head a break and move your body. Take a vacation from setting any other intention than to be moved by seiki, the vital life force. Minimize discussing spirituality, sorting out your thoughts, interpreting your present state, maintaining a gratitude attitude, or pondering a spiritual action. Act without precontemplation or post-reflection. Sit on the bench and call for seiki to move you. Give praise when your body moves in any way, and discipline your mind to allow nothing more than the call and the praise response. Zero in on the ecstatic ignition that lies beyond cognition. Ignore all mental hocus-pocus that takes you off a seiki focus!

The seiki movement call and response is the ground floor dynamic of Sacred Ecstatics, introducing you to the basic practice of generating circular momentum that amplifies emotion. The more you make the highest call and are ready to be moved when God responds, the more attuned your instrument is to the changes behind all creation. Get on board the fascinating ride of a moving body on a changing rhythm that is headed for ecstatic glory.

Ingredient 3: Tonal Alignment

The combination of the first two ingredients—fascinating rhythm and seiki movement—prepares your body to spontaneously move in synch with changing rhythms. You are rhythmically aligned as rhythm begets movement and movement effortlessly rides on rhythm. The third ingredient brings another alignment, this time with auditory tones. Here you imagine that your body is like a musical instrument that is both responsive to musical sounds and capable of producing them. Your body can function like any instrumental form from a drum to a violin, guitar, flute, horn, or piano. The musician Sun Ra captures this metaphor as follows:

> People are . . . like instruments because they got a heart that beats and that's a drum. They've got eardrums too, and they [got] some strings in there, so they actually got harps on each side of their head. If you play certain harmonies, these strings will vibrate in people's ears and touch different nerves in the body. When the proper things are played in each person, these strings will automatically tune themselves properly and then the person will be in tune.[29]

Gathering the third ingredient requires tuning your body instrument through a special way of connecting you to musical sound. As Sun Ra suggests, when the "proper things are played in each person," you will be automatically tuned. The body's utmost responsiveness to music is created when your physical movements are aligned with both rhythm and tone. When all three ingredients are present and in synch, you are ready to be physically moved by music in a more dynamic way, and this especially includes sacred songs.

Alignment of Body Movement with Sound

We have created a tonal alignment method that involves matching body movement with auditory tones. When a specific body area moves and pulses to a selected tone, the body instrument's mechanical vibration is aligned with an acoustic vibration. As a particular musical note is heard (we usually play a single key on the piano), you move a certain part of your body in an oscillating, vibratory way. For instance, when a bass note (such as a low C) is played, physically move your hips by alternately contracting and releasing, wiggling, shaking, or doing whatever movement you choose. Aim to associate this low frequency note with a physically pulsed movement at a lower location on your body. Next, do this for a midrange note, usually middle C, and respond with movement in the shoulder and upper chest area, anywhere near your heart. Finally, hit a high C note and move your head in response, doing so with a movement that is a higher frequency oscillation than the movements below. (It is typically easier to keep this head and neck movement small in scope to ensure a nice, effortless oscillation).

After these three notes are paired with different body movement sites, the musical notes can be played in different sequences. For instance, you can go from the bottom note to the high note without the middle note, as well as other patterns. The goal is to smoothly coordinate your body's different movements with distinctly heard tones. As body movement and external sound are well paired, two keyboards — one musical and the other somatic — become aligned with one another. Each localized body movement should eventually feel as if it is physically playing the acoustic notes of a real piano. Your three-note body keyboard can then be imagined as having keys at your hips, shoulders, and head.

When you first learn how to tonally align and tune your body, you begin with a conscious focus on what part of your body will move. How it moves pulses, oscillates, trembles, shakes, quakes, or vibrates, however, should be more spontaneous rather than willed. The more you respond to tone with effortless seiki-like movement, the better the tune-up.

Once the simple three-note body tuning is mastered, other notes can be localized on the body, enabling a musical scale to be performed and experienced. This is a more advanced body tuning. What remains most important is that auditory vibration (sound) is coupled with a mechanical vibration (movement). Following the activation of a full body scale, a melodic line can be introduced for your body to move in kind with its tonal progression. Your body then learns to be even more finely tuned as it advances from three notes to octaves and melodies, preparing you to be both physically and emotionally responsive to sacred music in a whole new way.

Socrates suggested that "rhythm and harmony find their way into the inward places of the soul."[30] Pythagoras followed this perspective and used musical sound to heal the soul with divinely inspired resonance. Your body is best prepared for a soul tune-up when body movement and musical sound are in accord. After this tactile-auditory alignment is thoroughly established and rehearsed, you are better able to imagine, experience, and operate a somatic keyboard that is analogous to an actual musical piano. Again, you may feel like different parts of your body serve as piano keys that produce musical tones when you physically move.

A laboratory setup can actually produce the latter configuration. Electrodes are attached to various regions of the body to register an electrical signal from muscular activity that, in turn, activates a musical tone on a nearby sound generator or digital musical instrument. In this way, the body's movements can literally play music. Another way of connecting the body to music involves converting acoustic vibration to electricity and administering the current to the skin. Brad dreamed that Charles Henry had done this in his laboratory. We were subsequently quite surprised to find that he actually did experimentally apply electrodes to a person and convert musical vibration to electricity. Rather than hearing the music, subjects felt a dispersed field of electrical activity on the body. They reported feeling the same kind of euphoric emotion they would have felt if they had listened to music.

If you practice and work out your body piano with the dedication of a concert pianist, your body will become so keenly attuned to acoustic vibration that there will be moments when you *experience* your own body seeming to produce the music you hear being performed by another musician. You will also often feel like the music is playing you—the tones of a song will literally feel like they are pulling, triggering, or moving various parts of your body. The more connected, aligned, and tuned your body movement is to a spectrum of sound, the more you will shift back and forth between feeling like you are both making the music and being performed by it. When this degree of coordination is achieved, it makes no experiential difference which keyboard — the keys of an acoustic piano or the keys of a human body — is the one playing the other. The loop connecting both is now one whole circle. When you are perfectly tuned, you will feel like your body is the instrument, the performer, the music, and all the produced vibrations.

Experiment with Tuning Your Body Instrument

We illustrated the three-note body tuning with keys that are located at the hips, chest, and head. Any other body locales can also be selected. For instance, you can wiggle the little finger of your left hand whenever a bass note is sounded. The thumbs can move for the midrange note while the little finger of the right hand is saved for the high note. You can even apply this to your toes. Experiment with different key locations for your body keyboard. Reverse their order as well, for example, with the head as the low note key and the hips as the high note key. Compare this to a yogi standing on their head and playing a keyboard upside down. The more experimental you are with playing your body instrument, the more tunable and skilled an ecstatic performer you become.

Whatever locations are chosen, the specific vibratory nature of the movement can also vary. Since low notes involve slower vibrations, you can wiggle that part of the body at a slower frequency than what you do for the higher notes. Also play with the different kind of movements that are associated with playing a brief and distinct tone (staccato) versus a long and slurred tone (legato). This could be enacted, for example, by vertical (up and down) versus horizontal (side to side) movements. Make sure you also experiment with the experiential difference found in moving from a low note to a high note when the movement is a staccato separation or a legato slide. When you slide from low to high, as well as high to low, pay attention to what takes place in between the notes. Is there a straight path or a wavelike trajectory between the notes? Also try squeezing or clenching your pelvic muscles when a low tone is played and then imagine "shooting" this vibration toward the high note located at your head. Again, does it go straight up or does it wiggle itself upward? Do both and see which way is more effective — a straight shot or a climbing wave. Explore whether each is equally good for tuning. As always, experiment and tinker, forming no unnecessary inflexible conclusion.

As you become more skilled in moving your body to the sound of a whole tone, introduce sharps and flats. Here, a particular note is bent a bit to raise or drop its pitch. What movement can embody this kind of alteration? Is it found in the space between two successive whole notes like you find on a piano keyboard? Experiment with how to flatten and sharpen your movements. You will likely have to catch the feeling for the bent note before you can enact it with a movement. If you are moving from one body spot to another, like the separate keys on a piano, will you land on a discrete body locale? Or will you slide your trembling fingers along your chest to slur the notes, like a trombonist making a bluesy tone that is in between the familiar notes? Are you filled with wonder when you ponder how a bottom note's flattening is always the upper note's sharpening, while remembering that a bottom note is also the upper note for the note below it?

Explore Different Sounds and Instruments

Listen to different kinds of prerecorded musical tones and find which classical instrument moves you the most — a French horn, trumpet, bass flute, piccolo, cello, viola, harp, clarinet, oboe, or bassoon. Try world instruments as well. How does your body like being a gamelan, mbira, mouthbow, juice harp, steel drum, zydeco rub board, tone bones, accordion, didgeridoo, harmonica, shamisen, marimba, erhu, or cimbalon? Try them all out to become a well-rounded, ecstatic musical aficionado.

If you are a musician, try moving your body to the different tones you make on your instrument. Play your flute, trumpet, violin, guitar, or tambourine while calling for spontaneous body movement. The more parts of your body that move, the more your whole body makes the music. It's a remarkably different experience to play the piano with your whole body than only your hands. Take another look at master musicians and notice how much of their whole body is involved when they produce extraordinarily moving music.

Also explore tuning your body while vocally producing the tones yourself. For the three-note tuning, you can sing each of the notes while moving to them. Remember that your voice can also imitate the sound of a musical instrument. Experiment to find which instrument sound brings a better tuning for you. Vary your vocal dynamics for each tone to see how it affects the body's corresponding action while also discovering how the sounds you make are influenced by different body movements. You will find that the stronger your voice's vibration is, the more it empowers the mechanical vibration of your entire body. An inspired quivering voice triggers the body's trembling rejoice.

Be open to other genres of music and try some experimental playlists. Get classically tuned, jazz tuned, gypsy tuned, rock tuned, folk tuned, and gospel tuned, to name a few of the musical possibilities. Also experience the same song played differently by multiple artists. For example, find twelve different renditions of "Fly Me to the Moon" and then take off on a flight where the more you experience the same song changing, the more spontaneously responsive to change you become.

You can also tune with another person, taking turns being the tone producer and the movement responder. One person can voice or play a tone while the other responds with movement. Anything you can imagine to couple sound and movement helps further tune your instrument, including coupling all of this with other human body instruments. In all the activities of tuning, assure you are making yourself ready for the reception of praiseworthy sound and the leaps of joy that are ready to explode when ecstatic emotion arrives. There is no end to what you can learn through changing sounds, changing movements, and the changing ways of linking them together.

Add Rhythm

More advanced body tunings add rhythmic variation to the pairing of tone and movement. Here you gain proficiency in moving your body in correspondence to toned whole notes, half notes, quarter notes, eighth notes, sixteenth notes, and so on. Experiment with diverse rhythmic forms for playing notes from triplets to arpeggios. Like learning to play the piano, the body piano begins by matching the keys to the tones and then builds up the scales to play a melody. Dynamic expression and rhythm are added to make it all come together for a more aesthetically inspiring performance.

Consider fantasizing a complete air drum trap set and imagine that you are surrounded by a bass drum, snare drum, tom toms, cymbals, hi-hat, cowbell, triangle, gong, and all the rest of it. As you make the body movements associated with playing this ensemble of percussion instruments, make the rhythmic sounds. This can generate quite an enthusiastic tonal alignment *and* a rhythmic alignment as the range of low- to high-toned percussive sounds are made from the boom-boom of the bass drum to the high-pitched swish of a cymbal, with a mid-toned snare sandwiched in between.

Notice the gaps between the sounds and appreciate that making music is as much about quiet, empty space as it is interspersing sound. The silence between the notes and the sound between the silences create the breathing rhythm that moves a melody. Without this alternating current between sound and silence, no song can emerge to stir the life force and ignite the soul.

With time and dedication every spot on your skin can learn to function as a low, middle, or high note. This ultimate instrumental flexibility enables the sounds of music to spontaneously play, move, pulse, and sound your body in endless ways. To reach this performance height, allow more emotion to come into your motion. This is the key to ecstatically playing the body keys. In First Creation, *everything must change* — not just the notes but also the location of the keys, the form of the vibration, the frequency of the tone, the rhythmic pulse that alternates sound and silence, the emotion and motion of the performer's call and response, and the whole instrument itself.

Sacred Transduction

The conversion of one kind of energetic vibration to another is technically called *transduction*. It takes place when a piano's hammers and strings convert mechanical vibration into acoustic vibration. The tonal alignment of body tuning also creates transduced vibrations—musical sound transformed into body movement and vice versa. The overarching engineering goal of ecstatic spirituality is to become so attuned to the divine that its vibrations are conducted and transformed in ways that benefit all who are within its reach. Transduction is the dynamic that enables the sacred vibration to be converted into embodied ecstatic experience. Here the divinely inspired acoustic vibrations from sacred music are transduced to mechanical tactile vibrations that are felt in the recipient's body. Sacred transduction is the process by which you "catch the spirit" that is carried inside heavenly music.

Ludwig van Beethoven had no choice but to find alternative pathways of transduction when he lost his hearing. He found that mechanical vibration preserves what is most essential about the vibrational phenomena of music, allowing it to be directly felt even without hearing its sound. After going deaf, the composer attached a metal rod to his piano keyboard and clenched down on the other end of the rod with his teeth, enabling bone conduction to occur. The acoustic vibrations of the piano were mechanically transferred to his jaw so that he could feel the vibration inherent in music. The extraordinary emotion behind the music of Beethoven's 9th Symphony was for him externally performed via mechanical vibration alone. A somatically felt pulse was aligned with the internally imagined music, bypassing the need to hear external sound. The transmission of sacred emotion can traverse diverse pathways, crossing internal and external phenomena with both real and imagined acoustic and mechanical vibrations as well as their transformation from one form to another. Transduction of aligned vibration rather than reception of a specific kind of vibration enables a human being to capture the sacred emotion of divine creation's composition.

The process of sacred transduction enables us to better understand how a Bushman n/om-kxao enhances the reception and transmission of vibration. She transforms the music performed by the community surrounding her into physical body movement while the inner body's felt vibration (the sacred vibration of n/om) inspires her own sound making. To put it in Bushman terms, a n/om song wakes up the n/om inside the doctor, who in turn transmits it through shaking, dancing, shouting, singing, and vibratory touch. Here sacred transduction builds a pathway for the mysterious transmission of n/om that is so unfamiliar to our time, though it now may be rediscovered in the dance of acoustic and mechanical vibration.

A Mystery Beyond Vibration

The "fire in the bones" that spiritually cooked ecstatics describe is, of course, more than simple vibration felt by bone conduction. This mysterious fire is a metaphor for the sacred vibration, something far more complex than a mechanical pulse. You can't just shake your body and presume you are having the same experience as a cooked ecstatic. As previously mentioned, the sacred vibration holds a special kind of sacred emotion that makes the tuned body feel incredibly alive in a spiritually uplifting way. This rare kind of spiritually heated emotion is far removed from any familiar sentiment and is not found in the taxonomy of psychological emotion. Without question, such emotion feels astonishingly "holy" and this is what makes the body shake with trembling joy and quaking wonder. Without emotion of the sacred kind, you are essentially a mechanical generator that rattles some cold, dry bones.

As the old spiritual goes, "Ezekiel connected dem dry bones" and brought them to life with a divine force. He administered the mysterious fire that gave ecstatic life to the recipient. What is it that persists and remains unaltered inside all the changing forms of transduced sacred vibration? What passes through the metal rod that allows someone like Beethoven to compose extraordinary music when he could no longer hear? What connects "dem dry bones" so the "word of the Lord" can be heard? Can the mystery held inside any vibration be traced back to that which gave origin to the first vibration, first pulse, first beat, and first breath of creation? Is the rope to God itself the long ancestral line of transformed vibrations, shifting from one carrier to another? Is the first vibration the first inspirational emotion that set in motion all of creation?

Consider these words of Sufi master Hazrat Inayat Khan as a response to our questions: "Music is the basis of the whole creation. In reality the whole of creation is music, and what we call music is simply a miniature of the original music, which is creation itself, expressed in tone and rhythm."[31] Sacred Ecstatics invites you to consider yourself and the universe as more like a song than a story. God communicates primarily through music rather than words, and this music calls for you to dance in order for its sacred vibration to be more fully felt. Make a joyful noise, sing an ode to joy, and wildly leap to meet and greet the Creator of the singing and dancing universe!

Technically speaking, from a spiritual engineering standpoint, any vibration is capable of taking you straight to the emotion, motion, and commotion of that which inspired its original creation. Whether the deep sound of a whale, the heartbeat of the beloved, or the high frequency wing beat of a bee, any and all vibration has the potential to awaken the emotion that inspired the divine to create everything, including you. If you can catch the vibration of a sound or a song, you catch the feeling that inspired the movement of larynx, wing, or other resonating thing. Spiritual engineering enables you to see that vibrational attunement through body alignment with movement, rhythm, and tone allows you to catch the emotion that inspired the original composition or the prodigious performance of music. In other words, we face the extraordinary profundity that spiritually cooked mystics, saints, healers, and shamans repeatedly discovered: when you catch a song, you catch its originating emotion. When the song is from God, you catch God's love. It is the sacred emotion of creation that matters most of all. Its vibe is what sets in motion all sacred ecstatic experience that follows.

When you go into the woods, a mourning room, or a prayer closet to pray for spiritual intervention and vision, you hope to receive the mystical rod or the rope of conductance that enables you to transduce a holy song and receive its sacred emotion. More of your body must be involved in order to hear the sweet pulsing secrets of the cosmos, whether given by a whistling bird, a singing Bushman, or the music of the spheres, all of which are born of the divinely immortal composer.

Tuning In to the Divine

Following a session of being introduced to the practice of tonal alignment, one of our mentorship students Hayley Merron Stevens had the following dream:

> Last night I dreamt over and over again that my body was a tuning fork. My legs were close together without a gap and served as a handle. My pelvis was the curve of the tuning fork's base and the sides of my body were the tuning fork's side prongs. The muscles running vertically up both sides of my spine were involved, but they somehow included the whole breadth of my body. My spine was the empty space between the fork's prongs, though it felt it was simultaneously physically present and absent.
>
> A tone was then sounded. I heard and felt its vibration, but I also saw it as a light. This multisensory experience is difficult if not impossible to describe, but it involved some kind of energy moving from the base of my spine to its

top, doing so over and over again. The sound I heard was clear and it felt cleansing to experience its movement.

Each dream was the same and started with seeing the tuning fork handle and the other involved parts of my body. It always finished with the sound, light, feeling, and energy that moved from the bottom to the top of my spine. However, with each dream, the sound became clearer and stronger.

I have never used a tuning fork before so I don't really understand how they work. Nonetheless, today as I walk and move around, I feel like I have that tuning fork inside my body. I have become a tuning fork.

Your body is a resonator, like a tuning fork, and good alignment is possible when you surround yourself with a higher sonic atmosphere—what Sun Ra called playing the "proper things." When appropriately readied, your instrument will catch the highest vibes. Prepare your instrument to be in alignment with divinely inspired music. Make sure you are attuned to masterful music of the gods rather than uninspiring elevator-like music that can't take you high enough to be close to divine mystery. Like a shaman or medicine person who needs a holy song to heal, you also need the kind of music that aligns you with the sacred.

As earlier mentioned, Pythagorean musical healing was a "tuning of the soul into consonance with the celestial harmony."[32] Music enabled Pythagoras to make "soul adjustments," tuning it to higher resonance.[33] You must do the same—tune your body keyboard to be maximally responsive to the sound of music that is divine—that is, a song that is emotionally inspired by a personal experience of the numinous, luminous, mystery, and love of the Creator. Anything less results in you being less attuned to the most important resonance.

In summary, rhythmic alignment requires rhythmic detrainment, boarding a fascinating rhythm, and the launch of spontaneous seiki movement. Tonal alignment requires a rhythmically aligned body to be additionally aligned with tone. Rhythmic and tonal alignment together comprise a whole body tuning, preparing you to be better moved by music and more likely to catch the emotion it carries. Go past any naïve and oversimplified attempt to tune your body with a singular tone or a simple sequence of tones.[j] Alignment with the divine requires a well-tuned and soulfully tempered body instrument that is capable of playing and being played by a sacred song. This requires the mutual alignment of rhythm, movement, and tone. While Pythagoras used songs to remedy ailments, that didn't go far enough. Your body must be tuned to physically move with the melodic tones, harmonies, and rhythms of sacred music that is on fire, something only heard in the big concert hall where spiritual heat brings syncopation, embellishment, and improvisation to renew the soul.

Emergence of the Ecstatic Dancing Body

Sacred Ecstatics invites the dance of everything — the dance of different body movements, different tones, different rhythms, and the different pairings of any and all of the above. When the body smoothly coordinates its movement with an ongoing progression of musical tones, a new kind of dancing body is made ready to emerge, one that is danced by the emotion and life force of the sacred vibration. With good spiritual engineering, anyone can experience being a dancer. All movement is beautiful and inspiring when it comes forth spontaneously and is inspired by the sacred.

The bodies of Bushman n/om-kxaosi (traditional doctors)

---

[j] For instance, tuning the spine, chakras, or spiritual body to tuning forks, vibrating bowls, and the like is not sufficient to tune the body instrument. Like a musical piano, more is needed than simply matching the strings to the frequency of a tone. Each note of the piano has multiple strings, and each of these strings must be tempered, that is, made a bit "off" with one another (rather than perfectly matched) so the enriched tone has the ring of soul.

are always moving in relationship with the clapping, drumming, swishing of percussive cocoons worn on the ankles, and other kinds of ecstatic rhythm making. Their bodies are also highly responsive to the tones, melodies, and harmonies produced by the singers. The fine-tuned alignment of body movement to rhythm and tone is what unleashes the power of spirited ceremony. The call of the African drum for bodies to respond requires such a high degree of attunement that the drummer feels as if the dancing bodies have strings or a force field pulling their hands to beat the drum. At the same time, the dancers feel that the drumming is yanking the cords of their muscles and limbs. The same thing happens in an old sanctified black church service where the shouts of the preacher elicit body responses. Hearing a shout becomes indistinguishable from feeling something mysteriously pull your body to move at the same time the sound is heard. The more that your auditory and kinesthetic senses are intertwined, the more likely you will catch — and be caught by — the spirit. If you truly want something spiritual to get a hold on you, then you must both hear and move in a spirited way.

The coordinated integration of spontaneous movement with tone and rhythm will also help you learn to be more in tune with other people. As Edward Hall suggests, "people are tied together yet isolated from each other by invisible threads of rhythm." [34] We are both separated and connected through coordinated movements and sounds that ride on a shared rhythmic thread. Like the musical movement between silence and sound, human relationship dances between separateness and togetherness. We go back and forth between expressing a separated staccato or the slurred, blurred blend of legato. The same dancing musical truth about being in relationship with others also applies to your connection with the divine. Be aligned with the beats and frequencies that bring God down to earth and inside your body as you move and sing with the resonance of divine emotion that is evoked by sacred song.

While we have introduced the gathering of ingredients as a process that passes from one ingredient to the next, the ingredients are actually never separate. Each one is always dancing with the others. They naturally coexist so that a change in one ripples a change through each of the others. For instance, both tonal alignment and a fascinating rhythm help release seiki movement. The latter spontaneity further enhances tonal alignment and being caught by a changing rhythm. Finally, clearing away monotonous entrainment and detoxing a soulless rhythmic field helps you have a good relationship with both seiki and tonal alignment. When you emphasize the dancing interconnectedness of these beginning three ingredients, you realize that any singular ingredient leads to them all.

Ingredient 4: Sacred Emotion

Of all the ingredients required for spiritual cooking, sacred emotion is the most important. It's what makes your heart rise, empowers the sacred vibration, and awakens mystical faculties—including the full blossoming of your body instrument. Being filled with sacred ecstatic emotion surpasses any realization of oneness, illumined "aha" moment, harmonic convergence of duality, or shift in consciousness. More than anything, sacred ecstasy is supercharged, heartfelt bliss—a joy so strongly felt that it pulses your body with vibratory elation, spiritual intoxication, and unbridled celebration.

In its fullest intensity, sacred emotion is a burning, passionate connection with your creator, a big love that touches your heart in a rapturous way. As Bushman doctor, /Kunta !elae, describes it, "The feeling is so intense that you feel your heart breaking and opening to everything in the world." [k] Saint Thérèse of Lisieux described the sacred emotion of divine love in this verse, which she adapted from Saint John of the Cross:

> Love, I have experienced it,
> Knows how to use (what power!)
> The good and the bad it finds in me.

---

[k] Personal communication with Bradford Keeney, 2002.

It transforms my soul into itself.
This Fire burning in my soul
Penetrates my heart forever.
Thus in its delightful flame
I am being wholly consumed by Love![35]

Remember that the ecstatic journey is a climb up the spiritual thermometer from being ice cold to spiritually on fire. Without a doubt, the single most important correlation with spiritual temperature is the degree of sacred emotion that is felt. When you are spiritually cold as an iceberg, thought reigns and emotion is diminished, sometimes even devalued as a lesser sentiment or nuisance. As you melt from ice to liquid, sacred emotion lifts and your body's fluidity increases, loosening both stuck thoughts and body knots. The Bushmen doctors call this temperature transition "waking up," the condition necessary for spiritual cooking. As you climb the spiritual thermometer toward sacred ecstasy, it is the higher emotion of your heart that awakens, not your mind or higher consciousness. Keep in mind that it is not enough to have your body filled with the power of rhythm, the beauty of tone, or the elegance of movement. Though these are vital ingredients of spiritual cooking, without sacred emotion you cannot climb to the highest degrees of spiritual heat and be cooked by God.

We are not saying that sacred ecstasy is the only valuable spiritual experience a person can have — there is something of benefit found at every degree of temperature. But a soul-igniting, emotional union with the divine is what distinguishes ecstatic spiritual traditions from all the others. Never forget that Saint Teresa of Avila experienced her body being speared by the hot flames of Jesus and was left trembling with rapture. It is no accident that the most spiritually cooked n/om-kxao of the Kalahari is called a "heart of the spears" because they are able to throw arrows, nails, and spears of n/om into others. For ecstatics this somatically felt pierce and burst of emotion comprise the ultimate spiritual experience, guiding direction, and true north compass setting for the mystical journey.

Inspired by Pascal,[36] we suggest that there are three kinds of human beings — (1) those who have been pierced or filled with the colossal trembling love that comes from intimacy with the divine; (2) those who are haunted by this missing emotional experience and are on a journey to find it, and finally, (3) those whose hearts do not yet have an appetite for it. Ask yourself: Are you a recipient of sacred emotion, a seeker of it, or someone who has yet to know that it exists? The Holy Grail offers you a drink of love from its holy cup. What are you going to do now that you know about this ultimate offering? Are you denying it exists or wanting to be nearer the fountain, actively on the hunt for the emotion that sets in motion what spiritually matters most?

Don't be shy about setting the highest intention that rises above all other goals — getting spiritually cooked by the sizzling flames of sacred emotion. Rather than ask for the sacred vibration, ask for its highest emotion, the divine love that leaves its mark as a newborn life-pulse within. Being set on fire by this love is the divine's will for your life. You must first be ignited and excited before you can fulfill your mission and make a difference in the world. Go ahead: wholeheartedly make a request to be spiritually cooked to assure both the divine and yourself that you are aligned with the highest purpose. Don't be wishy-washy; say it and act like you mean it by taking the necessary steps that bring you nearer the divine. There you will spontaneously fall in love with the holiest love. The only effort required on your part involves initially mobilizing yourself to have your body tuned and aligned to the right rhythm, tone, and movement — this makes you good tinder for sacred combustion.

The Final and Most Important Ingredient of Spiritual Cooking

Gathering all the basic ingredients is required for full-blown spiritual cooking to later take place. Once again, the previous three ingredients by themselves are not enough. You can be a master percussionist, a professional dancer, the world's best musician, and a prodigious tuner with perfect auditory and movement form, but without the ingredient of sacred emotion you cannot make the shift from creative performance to sacred ecstatic experience.

Sacred emotion is the horse that needs to be in front of the body cart. When you shake, move, sing, tone, percuss, or tune without sacred emotion, the sacred vibration cannot be activated and the spiritual temperature can never rise past a certain degree. We cannot say this directly, clearly, and loudly enough: it is your personal longing for an emotionally felt connection with divinity that marks your practice as sacred. You must both crave and surrender to a heartfelt relationship with the source of mystery to which all true prayers are directed, from sacred pipe holders to dancing Bushmen, singing healers, drumming shamans, and kneeling saints.

The essential ingredient of sacred emotion is too often found missing in today's contemporary spiritual practices. It's common for people to be embarrassed about desiring, feeling, and expressing sacred emotion, but the cost of looking cool is that you never get to experience the joy and fulfillment of spiritual heat. Again, it is the paucity of sacred emotion that contributes to global spiritual cooling and maintaining steady refrigeration of the soul.

Even among black churches, which have traditionally not been shy about inviting spirited expression, some have more emotion and cooking going on than others, making them susceptible to ostracism by those who claim that excessive emotion brings a drift away from "the word" or worse, that it is caused by "the devil's influence." What we see in the politics of emotion's role in the black church is another reenactment of "the routinization of the spirit." The original exhilarating experience is cooled down, conquered, and replaced by an overemphasis on text, belief, and institutional governance.

There is another dynamic at play for those who look down on ecstatic emotional expression. While others are receiving the sacred vibration, seiki transmissions, Bushman arrows of n/om, and baptisms of fire, some folks start to feel disappointed that they aren't receiving these spiritual gifts. Soon trickster arrives and whispers the lie that ecstasy is not that important and that it is wrong to desire the fire of sacred ecstatic emotion. These individuals then proclaim that people such as themselves who are not ecstatic are actually more in alignment with the divine. Sacred ecstasy and joy are thus devalued and traded in for the currency of sour piety.

Spiritual refrigeration is created by the turn that devalues spiritual burn and upholds holy word. Once sacred emotion disappears or is minimized, dictatorial law and order arrive to ban the heat. Spiritual temperature and cooking are forgotten in favor of the observational looking that fosters judgment, disqualification, and condemnation of others. Shaking is ridiculed and quaking is sneered on, as ecstasy, wild joy, spiritual intoxication, spontaneous movement, improvised song, and trembling dance are called hysterical and fanatical. The spiritual zombies then rise again from the dead and embalm others with a calm that prohibits the ecstatic balm and shaking medicine required for an awakened spiritual life.

We invite you to not follow what you may have been taught about avoiding overexcitement or excess emotion of the sacred kind. Both institutionalized religions and new age institutions don't want you to have an unmediated emotional experience of divinity because it would undermine their authority and verbal pomposity. Go for the biggest joy and care not whether others are jealous and throw the sticks and stones of pious words as they wallow in the misery that trickster one-upmanship promotes. Steer your ship toward the fire and join the Kalahari Bushmen and all the world's spiritual movers and shakers who have been cooked by the mightiest flames of love.

Sacred Music Is the Divine Love Elixir and Temperature Fixer

Confucius said, "Music produces a kind of pleasure which human nature cannot do without." Likewise, the most exhilarating sacred ecstasy simply cannot occur without music. While it is possible to experience a direct infusion of sacred emotion, akin to being struck by divine lighting, this is extremely rare. Transmission usually requires the magical potion or ecstatic elixir of sacred music to serve as a carrier. Music is the primary means of heavenly communication and ecstatic penetration, which is why a sacred song is simultaneously like a divine telephone line, a glass of holy love, and an arrow or spear that can pierce the heart. If you meet someone who claims to have spoken to God, ask that person to sing. If there is no song, then immediately flee and warn others to stay away. Music is "a higher revelation" (Ludwig van Beethoven), "the language of spirits" (Kahlil Gibran), and "the only art of heaven given to earth, the only art of earth we take to heaven" (Walter Savage Landor). It is "a magic key, to which the most tightly closed heart opens" (Maria Augusta von Trapp).[37]

The basic practices of ingredient 4 aim to stir up sacred emotion and help open your heart to its divine source by soaking you in a bath of sanctified music. The whole combination of rhythm, melody, and harmony that constitutes music carries more emotion than rhythm, tone, or movement alone. When you experience music with a tuned body instrument, the original emotion that led to its creation is received more strongly. When your whole body hears, rather than only your ears, we like to say that true hearing, rather than only "earing," takes place. Not only is the eardrum vibrating, so are your head, shoulders, hips, fingers, and toes. Experiencing music after your body has been attuned and aligned with changing movements, tones, and rhythms is the ultimate sonic mystery.

Sacred music from anywhere in the world is most beneficial when it physically moves your body in response to the emotion the music conveys. The creative source of such music is divine and leaves you singing and dancing with joy. As composer Joseph Haydn elaborates this experience: "When I think of my God, my heart dances within me for joy, and then my music has to dance, too."[38] Welcome all divinely inspired music no matter where it was geographically composed or what spiritual tradition subsequently held and honored it. If it holds sacred emotion, you may proceed to soak in it.

Directions for Gathering This Ingredient: The Sacred Music Soak

This practice arranges a time for you to strictly focus on absorbing the emotion of sacred music. When you soak in its sound, allow the tones and rhythms to penetrate you deeply. Hold back external movement for a while and focus only on feeling the emotion held inside the music. Once you feel it, proceed to imagine moving your inner body. Visualize this inner body as the original design for your divinely intended external physical form. Allow it to move with the music so that its perfectly imagined movements are smoothly coordinated with what is heard and felt. Do this while making sure that the song's sacred emotion is the center of your attention. When the coupled movement of your inner body and sacred emotion become elevated and intense enough, you are ready to release natural external movement.

"Being moved by music" figuratively means that your heart is pierced by music's emotion, and literally means that music is physically moving your body—acoustic vibration triggers or is converted into mechanical vibration. To fully feel the emotion in music, your body must move with its changing tones and beats. This sacred music soak aligns your body to the mysterious vibes of sacred emotion. If you find yourself giving too much attention to the movement of your body at the expense of catching the emotion of the music, then try restraining your movements or only moving your inner body until you feel sufficiently caught by the emotion to begin moving again.

Becoming a Sacred Ecstatics DJ

You need to regularly soak in music that stirs sacred emotion. With the help of spiritually cooked conductors, create a personal playlist of sanctified music. Know that the song that moved you today might be different than what will move you tomorrow, so let your playlist be diverse. If there comes a time when you receive a sacred song through visionary means, you can always rely on that song to awaken your sacred emotion. This is why such a song is so holy, mysterious, and powerful—for all practical purposes it *is* your rope to God and the Bushmen equate it as such.

Until you spiritually receive a sacred song, you can rely on the songs of others. Use the songs of your spiritual teacher or someone you regard as close to God who is also close to you. You can lean on your grandmother's favorite song, for instance, enabling your bond to her to connect you to her rope to the divine. You can also lean on the great song catchers themselves from Ludwig van Beethoven to George Gershwin, and especially the inspired hymn composers. We embrace the fact that some secular music from classical and opera to Tin Pan Alley melodies can carry sacred emotion, particularly when the songs are performed by master musicians and singers. Ingredient 4 provides an opportunity for you to roam around the musical landscape to experience how different kinds of music, but especially sacred music, can infuse elevated emotion.

It takes a great DJ to bring forth a great spiritual life. The art of being a DJ involves being able to discern what song needs to be played either to match the mood you are in or to elevate your emotion to a higher plane. Music must connect with your current mood but it also must do more—it must lift your emotion higher than it was when you started. A highly charged musical playlist and practical knowledge about when and how to change a tune are required. Rather than solely deal with a therapist or coach, seek an ecstatic, soulful DJ to help you wake up and move toward the heat beat.

A Sacred Ecstatics DJ collects the songs that are the most packed with sacred emotion. For instance, a gospel classic sung by the Mississippi Mass Choir has more sacred emotion than a barbershop quartet singing "Man On the Flying Trapeze." At the same time, it is wise to acknowledge that all songs are able to convey some kind of emotion. There is a time and place for every tune. One of the outcomes we find amazing about our intensives is that after we have all been spiritually cooked with sacred melodies and rhythms, we can switch to a Broadway standard like "Someone to Watch Over Me" and experience it being as holy as any hymn or medicine song.

In the spiritual heat, your heart is opened in ways not possible in the cold, and you will be able to feel the emotion held inside music in a new way. You may find yourself surprised to welcome a gospel hymn you never imaged being touched by before. Songs are the purest and surest carriers of emotion. Just as one song can be a bridge to another song, so one emotion can lead you to another emotion. In favorable spiritual climatic conditions, the love held inside a potent Cole Porter song can just as ably help you climb the rope traveled by all the inspired music makers. Let the songs take you up the spiritual thermometer one step, one song, and one emotion at a time. A master DJ facilitates the climb. If you want to go all the way, be mentored and led by a spiritually cooked ecstatic DJ.

Deejaying the Song Changes

Remember that *the changing* of First Creation underlies everything that is biologically and spiritually alive. This mysterious changing is the force of creation, the vitality of life, the process of transformation, the medicine of healing, the anointment of initiation, the mojo of mystical gifts, and the wonder working power of all miracles of any kind. You must not forget that the spiritual heat lives and thrives in the changes and this includes when songs are changed. It might take a New Orleans brass band or a mariachi singer to warm you up enough to catch the fire of gospel music. Or the latter may be required for you to receive the unexpected soul stirring of a folk song about the railroad or a country song that slays you with heartbreak. Change the music or nothing will change!

There is an art to making these changes that requires the same skills as climbing the mystical rope. This is why an effective ecstatic DJ must be spiritually cooked and anointed, knowing that changing a song provides a step up or down the staircase to heaven. Just like learning to respond to rhythmic changes, a DJ must learn when it is time to make a song change.

Even the most powerful spiritual song can go flat if it hangs around too long or is performed in the same way every time. Sacred music can grow stale and cold and turn you into a brittle ice cube if you don't occasionally take a break from it, switch tracks, or bring it back to life with improvisation. It is just as important to know when *not* to play or sing a song as it is to know when to play it. As always, serve the changing transformations rather than the fixing and solidifying of your preferences. A musician must change the way a song is performed or change the song, and a listener must change how he moves and is aligned with it.

As surprising as this may sound, it is more important for you to acquire a good song list than it is for you to have a drum, rattle, magical incantation, potion, medicine bundle, or prayer book. The better your song list and the more you learn how to discern when to make a song change, the more likely you will get cooked and stay cooked. Carry a device filled with musical recordings and regard this as your medicine chest of sacred songs. It is life-saving medicine and the strongest treatment because there is nothing like a song for injecting the healing power of sacred emotion. As Edward Lytton said, "The music, once admitted to the soul, becomes also a sort of spirit, and never dies."[39]

Encore: Never Forget That Sacred Emotion Is the Most Vital Ingredient

We cannot say enough that the changing rhythms, movements, and tones played on a tuned body instrument only fully come to life with sacred emotion. The extent to which the ingredients of spiritual cooking are skillfully infused with sacred emotion determines how easily you get cooked and how long the transformative heat can be sustained until it's time to cook again. As mentioned, nothing more effectively delivers sacred emotion than sanctified music. Songs are not only the tracks to God; they are envelopes that deliver the musical notes of divine love.

As Beethoven said, "music is a higher revelation than science or philosophy. Music is like wine . . . and I am the Bacchus serving it out to them, even unto intoxication." [40] He went further and specified, "Music is the electrical soil in which the spirit lives, thinks and invents, whilst philosophy damps its ardour by reducing it to a fixed principle . . . my whole nature is electric." [41] Music invites you to put your psychological and philosophical nature in its rightful secondary place while you step into being wholly electrical, a conductor of the emotional vibes transmitted by the divine resonance of sacred music. You need more than a good tune-up or shake-up. You require the music, emotion, and movement that collectively comprise a dance with divinity.

A good sacred music soak readies you for blending all the spiritual cooking ingredients with heartfelt emotion. Remember that throughout all the gathering practices, you are unlearning former habits that kept you in the cold, and learning new ecstatic means for awakening, tuning, and playing your body instrument. Hear that God is a song and feel that God is a vibration. Clear everything out of the way so that you can be touched by higher emotion and excited to move whenever sacred music strikes the deepest chords within and strums the strings of your heart. Kurt Vonnegut summarized the link of music with the sacred this way: "If I should ever die, God forbid, let this be my epitaph: 'The only proof he needed for the existence of God was music.'" [42]

Better than Wine

All the great mystics and saints agree that no lover of the divine can get enough of divine love. It is intoxicating, but it never turns sour or leaves you hung over the existential edge. Its ecstatic bounty is limitless. There is never a final satiation, for the more you drink of this cup, the more you desire its delight and the more you increasingly long for it. Yet the longing to be filled with this incredible emotion is as spiritually potent and fulfilling as its reception.

Divine love is better than wine. Speaking of this higher intoxicant, the nineteenth century English preacher Charles Spurgeon explained that "it has certain healing properties, it gives strength, it gives joy, it gives sacred exhilaration."[43] He went on to say that this extraordinary love is personal, forgiving, accepting, guiding, forbearing, providing, instructing, sanctifying, sustaining, upholding, enduring, and chastening.[44] Wine, the symbol of the richest earthly joy, is exceeded by the inebriating mystical love that is freely available to anyone who simply reaches out to receive it. It actually is not enough to compare this sacred emotion to either wine or love for it surpasses all familiar delight, satisfaction, joy, pleasure, and affection. Divine sacred emotion makes you both spiritually rich and ecstatically high. This is the pinnacle experience we call sacred ecstasy. It is freely available to you, but you must take action to receive it. Learn to gather the ingredients and build sacred ground, ensuring that the room is vast enough, your body tuned enough, your ego small enough, and your heart soft enough to drink from God's heavenly cup.

The Spiritual Cooking Checklist

We have now completed the basic practices for gathering the ingredients. Before you can raise the temperature in any spiritual work, from prayer to ceremony to a healing session, all of these four ingredients must be in your body. Here's a checklist to assure that you are somatically equipped for spiritual cooking:

_____   Fascinating rhythm
_____   Seiki movement
_____   Tonal alignment
_____   Sacred emotion

Once all of these ingredients are present, you should find yourself tuned rhythmically, kinetically, tonally, and emotionally, prepared to get moving on the sacred road formerly traversed by cooked medicine people, mystics, saints, and shamans. Again, these are the main ingredients needed to cook your life.

Flood your everyday with more awareness of the supreme importance of these cooking elements. We recommend that you make a space in a kitchen cabinet to hold four special bottles that are visually prominent every time you open that door. Label each bottle to indicate its ingredient: "fascinating rhythm," "seiki movement," "tonal alignment," and "sacred emotion." Make sure the largest jar is for sacred emotion since it is the most vital ingredient. You may also benefit from assembling a spiritual first aid kit or a doctor's medicine bag that has these four critically important ingredients. Find objects that symbolize each—perhaps a drumstick, a wiggly object like a slinky toy or a bobbing figurine, a harmonica for tonal alignment, and a special drawing or sculpting of a magical heart. Act like a good spiritual scout who is ready to hunt sacred ecstasy: *be prepared.*

STEP 2. BLENDING THE ECSTATIC INGREDIENTS TO EXPAND AND HEAT THE ROOM

The next section addresses the practices and dynamics of spiritual cooking. Until you master gathering and embodying the necessary ingredients, you will not be able to build sacred ground, strike a match, and sustain an ecstatic fire. The dynamic of spiritual cooking involves *blending* the four ingredients so the intensity of each is increased. This takes place through forming what we call a *mystical prayer wheel.* The spokes of the wheel include each of the ingredients. When they are blended through prayer, the wheel turns, expanding and heating the room. Once the movement of the wheel gains sufficient momentum and all the ingredients are amplified, the fire is lit and spiritual cooking begins.

As will be discussed, prayer can emphasize words, rhythm, melody, or movement. In particular, rhythmically chanted words, sung melodies, and improvised dances can shift from one to another. For this reason, it is more accurate to call the wheel a mystical prayer-chant-song-dance wheel. In the ecstatic turning, churning, and burning, the whole mystical wheel and its changing forms of expression provide a spiritual means of transportation that take you up to the big room fire of First Creation.

The mystical wheel also becomes the vehicle for "spiritual traveling" to the special ways and means of diverse ecstatic spiritual traditions and other mystical locales. The kind of traveling we speak of is nothing like the guided imagery or daydream fantasy taught in neoshamanic workshops. We are referring to experiential transport that takes you inside the rhythms, songs, and movements of other ecstatic traditions. For Sacred Ecstatics, these lineages and their highlighted contribution to spiritual cooking include African American sanctified singing, St. Vincent Caribbean 'doption, Kalahari Bushman healing and n/om transmission, and other First Creation destinations for God-driven expression. Spiritual travel destinations are not preplanned, nor are their boundaries clearly drawn. Traveling is led by a conductor and happens spontaneously during a Sacred Ecstatics intensive when the mystical wheel turns with sufficient momentum and heat. As you become more familiar with spiritual cooking you will find that every ecstatic cooking locale, lineage, and practice is more the same than different, and that in First Creation they easily morph one into another. You will also feel that "there is no place like an ecstatic home," as you remember that the heart of every home is the kitchen.

If you formerly were spiritually cooked and received the sacred vibration, you might be tempted to go straight to the sacred songs or dancing and skip the gathering of the necessary spiritual ingredients. Be warned that without mastering how to somatically hold all the necessary ingredients for spiritual cooking, whatever spiritual gifts and sacred emotion you formerly owned may fade. Growing your capacity to light a fire and sustain its heat requires mastery of all the ingredients. Even the saints did not always know that they needed to physically move, catch the right rhythm, tonally align their bodies, and receive fresh doses of sacred emotion through music. Everyone needs to develop greater skill in working with the ecstatic ingredients, whether it is to help you receive the sacred vibration, bring it back, enhance it, or grow it.

As a musician once said, "Don't practice until you get it right. Practice until you can't get it wrong." Beethoven took practice even further: "Don't only practice your art, but force your way into its secrets."[45] You benefit from practicing the art of Sacred Ecstatics, disciplining yourself to master the skills that enable the highest divine will to take over when it is time for you to be led further into spiritual mystery. Your instrument, like any musical instrument, is constantly in need of a tuning. As Pete Seeger commented, "When you play the 12-string guitar, you spend half your life tuning the instrument and the other half playing it out of tune."[46] As an instrument of the divine, you are no different so make sure you keep yourself tuned for God.

Although building sacred ground requires surrendering to divine will, there is a time and place for you to exercise your highest will, intention, and desire. You are the one who must act to gather the necessary ingredients, move yourself to the kitchen, and start blending. After that, the divine will take over and take charge of the cooking. Both you and God must each do your job. It is your responsibility to be tenderized, seasoned, and made ready for spiritual cooking, and it is God's duty to set you on fire and cook you. Make the highest spiritual request. You can't go wrong asking to be near the divine, longing for communion and union. Then, be as grateful for the gifts you are unable to perceive, notice, or recognize, as you would be if you received the most stunning miracles. The purpose of your life is this: getting spiritually cooked. Start asking for it and do what must be done to help make it happen!

Forming and Turning the Mystical Prayer Wheel

Prayer is the means for communicating with the divine, whether the latter is regarded as a personal friend, parental figure, guide, doctor, teacher, abstract deity, cosmic principle, the unknowable force behind all of creation, or some mix of these. Prayer in all its myriad forms is the foundation of every spiritual tradition that communes with the sacred, including the ancient indigenous religions. As Guarani shaman Tupa Nevangayu tells us, "The life of a shaman is the life of prayer. This is most essential."[47]

Sincerely calling on a hallowed name activates an emotional connection that pulls you toward an intimate moment with divinity. People all over the world pray to their dearly beloved Lord, God, Jehovah, Great Spirit, Allah, Jesus, Mary, Krishna, Big Holy, Creator, and all the names that are believed to be on the receiving end of a holy transmission line. Sacred communication does more than put you in touch with the numinous, however. It also builds a vaster context in which to situate your life — placing it on sacred ground as opposed to diminished living within the reduced limits of the secular and mundane. With devoted prayer your existential life expands, making enough room to feel God as part of your everyday. Remember: the bigger the room, the closer you are to the divine, the more sacred emotion you will feel, and the higher the spiritual temperature will rise.

The Spiritually Cooked Prayer Is a Mystical Wheel

The most valuable tool for gauging the strength of prayer (and all aspects of spirituality) is the spiritual thermometer. It enables you to determine whether prayer is limited to the lifeless repetition of words or whether it has any spiritual heat and ecstatic soul. A spiritually cold prayer fills your mind with all the presumed right words and beliefs, but fails to bring your heart closer to the divine. Generally speaking, too much chilly God talk distances you from the sacred walk. This disparity between creed and deed is found in all religions and spiritual ways that cherish cold discourse over spiritually cooked action, the latter being the truest indication of being touched by the divine.[1]

It is arguably better to *not pray* when you are spiritually cold because you risk a religious backfire — shrinking divinity to fit inside a small room and distancing your emotional relationship to all its heartwarming mystery. Perhaps your beginning prayer should be one that requests guidance on how to pray. You must learn to pray with all your heart rather than only your mind, something that requires gathering the necessary ingredients for spiritual cooking. Otherwise your prayer will likely end up as cold as the ice you are hoping your prayers will melt. Aim for a spiritually hot prayer. The great preacher Charles Spurgeon advised: "We cannot commune with God, who is a consuming fire, if there is no fire in our prayers."

In other words, from a spiritual engineering perspective, if you haven't gathered the required cooking ingredients and started to blend them, you are not ready to pray. You need to warm up before attempting anything spiritual, from prayer to song, dance, or scriptural reading. The history of religion is essentially a tale of how spirituality can move in opposite directions dependent on whether it is hot or cold. Spiritual ice pretends to be nice but sends you to word hell. There you find fundamentalists from all religions fighting over whose words and ideas are the best. Spiritual flames, however, belong to heaven and send you to the bliss that never misses the holy target. This fire resides in a vast space where there is room to ecstatically activate the sacred vibration, the power of which leaves you speechless.

The movement from small room ice to big room flames is experientially matched by the shift from calm spoken words to changing forms of excited expression. An ecstatic, improvised prayer requires a special blend of rhythm, movement, tone, and emotion. When these four ingredients are sufficiently mixed together, your prayers will have enough intensity to launch you

---

[1] For a more in-depth discussion of the spiritual thermometer, see chapter 2 in The Keeneys, *Sacred Ecstatics: The Recipe for Setting Your Soul on Fire* (Createspace, 2016).

to the big room. Avoid prayers comprised of repetitive rhetoric accompanied by a lifeless body, soulless rhythm, and unpleasing tone. Always remember the wisdom teaching that "in prayer it is better to have a heart without words than words without a heart" (Gandhi[m]) and that "prayer is an act of love; words are not needed" (Saint Theresa of Avila). When it comes to prayer, expressing a heart stirring rhythm, movement, tone, and emotion is more important than reciting clever words.

The dilemma is that you are most in need of prayer whenever you don't feel like praying — when you are too spiritually chilled to pray. Before rushing to voice some forced prayer words, gather the cooking ingredients. Then pray inside the rising heat. As the temperature gets warmer, so will the prayer and the one praying. As Soren Kierkegaard said, "The function of prayer is not to influence God, but rather to change the nature of the one who prays."[n] Raise the temperature of your prayer and your temperature will rise in kind.

Though your march up the spiritual thermometer must traverse a straight and narrow road, your advancement along the path requires a wheel of circular locomotion. Hildegard von Bingen envisioned human beings as a wheel encircled by a greater wheel of divinity. In between humanity and divinity is the middle wheel of prayer. When the mystical wheel of prayer is turned, it moves you into the greater wheel of divinity as it simultaneously expands the space of divine encirclement. The steady blending and amplification of rhythm, movement, tone, and sacred emotion is what makes the prayer wheel turn. Just as seiki movement introduced you to the circular call and response

---

[m] It is possible Gandhi was referencing the phrase by John Bunyan, "When thou prayest, rather let thy heart be without words, than thy words without a heart." From Nathan Whiting, *The Works of that Eminent Servant of Christ, John Bunyan: Minister of Gospel, and Formerly Pastor of a Congregation at Bedford*, vol. 1 (New Haven, CT: Nathan Whiting, 1831), 96.

[n] This quote is widely attributed to Soren Kierkegaard; however, it is actually found in his translated works as, "The prayer does not change God, but it changes the one who offers it." Soren Kierkegaard, *Purity of Heart Is to Will One Thing*, trans. Douglas V. Steere (Seaside, OR: Rough Draft Printing, 2013), 34.

between seiki and movement, we now invite you to create a call and response between all four primary ingredients of sacred ecstasy. This blend provides the fuel for moving the mystical prayer wheel that, in turn, enables your travel on the spiritual highway.

While many of us have heard of mechanical prayer wheels in Tibet, fewer folks know that there is a gospel song that mentions the wheels of prayer. It is found in the chorus of "Have a Little Talk with Jesus" written in 1930 by Reverend Cleavant Derricks, a black preacher who tried to compose songs that would help lift the spirits of poor black church members living in the Great Depression. As was often the case for black writers and composers, Derricks never received any royalties on his composition. It was stolen from him and recorded by Elvis Presley, Loretta Lynn, Brenda Lee, and many others. Here are the main lyrics to his song:

> Now let us have a little talk with Jesus
> Let us tell Him all about our troubles
> He will hear our faintest cry and we will answer
> by and by
> Now when you feel a little prayer wheel turning
> Then you'll know a little fire is burning
> You will find a little talk with Jesus makes it right

The United Methodist Church and other institutions later had difficulty with his mention of a prayer wheel, thinking it was unbiblical, pagan, and unnecessary. A Methodist committee considered changing the words to "feel the Holy Spirit churning," but elected not to after finding that former slaves and other African American worshippers used prayer wheels, as did some southern, rural white Christians.

Prayer is spiritually cold, lifeless, and static unless you "*feel* a little prayer wheel turning." We aren't speaking of turning the gears of a mechanical device, but the turning of sacred emotion with all the other ecstatic ingredients, bringing passionate energy and spiritual heat to the act of prayer. A prayer comes to life when there is sufficient sacred emotion and expressive body motion. What you feel is the spirit moving in your heart. Prayer is the beginning action and experience of spiritual cooking. With each turning of the prayer wheel you are moved further along, constructing an ever-expanding big room to hold the cooking of your life. As the room expands, the fire gets hotter, and you are led to the sacred songs and dances of God.

Getting Prayer Started Right

Here's some practical advice to help you operate a mystical prayer wheel. Begin with the fewest words of a prayer. For example, you can say, "God help me" or "Have thine own way Lord." Perhaps you prefer "thy will be done," "Great Spirit help me," or "Hail Mary, full of grace." You might simply say, "Thank you," inspired by the mystic Meister Eckhart who is often quoted as having said: "If the only prayer you ever say in your entire life is thank you, it will be enough." Limit yourself to the least and simplest words, doing so to help you stay more focused and concentrated. Martin Luther also is said to have offered the same advice: "The fewer the words, the better the prayer."

There is a traditional Chasidic story about the special prayer of a devoted Jew who wanted to pray but had not learned to speak Hebrew. He decided to recite the only Hebrew he knew: the alphabet. He faithfully said it over and over again with all his heart until a rabbi asked what he thought he was doing. The man told the rabbi, "The Holy One, Blessed is He, knows what is in my heart. I will give Him the letters, and He can put the words together."[48] The prayer wheel turns by the sound of the heart's devotion rather than the mind's phraseology. Keeping the words simple is a matter of practical spiritual engineering. Saying too many words at first can cause you to either mentally drift or go into a robotic trance that has no heart and soul. The least words help bring the yeast that makes the holy bread rise.

In the beginning of a word prayer, stay focused on the same words and only aim to blend in all the cooking ingredients.

Heating hallowed prayer words requires a lively rhythm, a good tone, a moving body, and heartfelt emotion. As the words start to warm up you will eventually notice a tug to improvise rather than stick to the original words. Allow a bit of improvisation — not too much and not too little. Wait until you are sufficiently heated for this to occur spontaneously and effortlessly. Stay with the same words at first, but when the spiritual heat is felt, allow the words to melt. Further vary their timing, tone, and your accompanying body movement, allowing room for more natural embellishment and change. For example, here's an improvised, temperature-raising prayer involving the repetition of a line from the Lord's Prayer, "Thy will be done." As you read it, try expressing it with rhythmic and tonal variation:

> *Thy will be done.*
> *Thy will, thy will, thy will.*
> *Be done, be done.*
> *Thy will, oh Lord, thy will.*

Now other short prayer words may be mixed in:

> *Have thine own way, Lord.*
> *Thy will, thy will, thy will be done.*
> *Have thine own way, Lord.*

What's critically important is that these improvised variations of prayer words are inspired by and "ride on" underlying changes in the cadence or rhythmic timing. Your body should also be moving as it automatically responds to the rhythm of your prayer and the emotion it inspires. Start by focusing on specific words and as you spiritually warm up, bring more improvisation to their expression with more fascinating rhythms, pleasing tones, and energizing movements. Vary the softness and loudness of your tone as well as alter its pitch. Welcome more surprising and celebrative body motion as something holy moves onto the altar of your heart. Remember that the amplification of ecstatic expression must be in relationship to authentic sacred emotion. The purpose of cooking a prayer is not to go wild for no reason, but to set your heart and soul on fire. Only a few prayer words thrown into the mix of the four basic ingredients for spiritual cooking are what bring prayer to life and raise the spiritual temperature. Move from frozen prayer forms to prayer jazz in order to bring home the heat.

The next practical advice for heating up a prayer is to remember that a prayer and song are not separate, even when they seem to be independent forms of expression. Prayer will move naturally into song as the wheel keeps turning and building up spiritual steam. Sacred songs, especially the ones that come to healers, mystics, and shamans, are always hybrid prayer-songs. They are prayers expressed through melody. Prayer fasts, from those of Native American medicine people to African American preachers and Caribbean Shakers, begin with constant prayer and the hope that the ritual will culminate with the reception of a sacred song. With the practical knowledge of spiritual engineering, you recognize that a natural process takes place in a prayer or vision fast — the more you heat a prayer, the more likely it is divinely converted into song.

To get that mystical prayer wheel turning, you are going to have to throw in new words, rhythms, tones, and natural body movement when the inspiration strikes. Sing when you feel music pulling you. Then come back to the spoken and rhythmically chanted prayer when it feels time to do so. In this back and forth along the whole spectrum of sacred expression, the mystical wheel turns. Encourage an internal "call and response" to take place as you voice a prayer. Say the words and then immediately have an internal choir sing or an inner drum beat a rhythm in response to your holy prayer line, or mix up all the forms:

"Have thine own way, Lord." (a spoken call)
Boom, boom, dee da, boom boom (a rhythmic response)

"Have thine own way." (now a sung call)
Ka ka a chee, ka ka a boom (again, a rhythmic response)

"Have thine own way, Lord" (back to a spoken call)
Boom da boom da boom da boom (another rhythmic response)

Make prayer an improvised sacred performance for the divine that is not limited to words. Alternate whatever expressive form is the call or the response. Include any and all elements of expression and never leave out fascinating rhythms, musical tones, a moving body, and the sacred emotion that makes it all come together as praise that can raise prayer up the vertical rope to God.

Keep On Turning and Transforming the Wheel

To keep on turning the mystical prayer wheel, be ready to shift the emphasis from the word to the rhythm, the melody, or the dance, doing so in any order, as long as they are calling and responding to each other to sustain the bounce that helps everything roll along. The wheel really starts to turn and the ingredients to blend when your words mount a rhythm and become a chant. The wheel can later change its gear so that melody gets on board the rhythm and song pours forth (with or without words). In all of this, your whole body is moving and spontaneously changing how it moves, whether it is trembling and shaking, or your hands are clapping, arms waving, or feet stomping. Keep in mind that when you are praying, your body movement will naturally be tempered by the need to keep your words, chant, or song on the rhythm.

Imagine that each form of a call and response serves as a spoke of the wheel. For instance, a tone that calls the body to respond with movement is a "tone-movement spoke." Other call and response spokes include the back and forth between movement and rhythm, rhythm and tone, emotion and vocalized expression, and so forth. When all the spokes come to life, the mystical prayer wheel is fully formed. Inside the wheel, each spoke not only amplifies the call and response it holds; it also calls on and responds to all the other spokes. The whole

THE SPIRITUAL ENGINEERING OF SACRED ECSTASY

prayer wheel is itself a "higher amplifier" of all the amplifiers within, a more encompassing circle that holds the smaller circles of call and response — another wheel within a wheel.

Mastery of using the mystical prayer wheel is the key to unlocking the secret to climbing the rope to God: it is the art of cooking a prayer. A dead prayer is cold, without a sacred pulse, missing an inspiring tone, absent of movement, and lacking emotional life — it can't take you anywhere except a collapse into frustration, boredom, or despair. However, a prayer infused with sacred emotion, uplifting tone, and rhythmic motion is alive as it continuously builds sacred ground and sets a fire within. It prepares you for an extraordinary miracle: when your whole-hearted and fully embodied prayer goes as far as you can take it, you reach a holy mountain top where God has been waiting to turn your whole life around. The mystical prayer wheel starts moving on its own because it is now in God's hands. It prays you, lifts you, places you on the higher floor of the vastest sacred ground, and sets your soul on fire. You find you have leapt from your prayer wheel into the greater wheel of divinity. Climbing the rope is making the leap from the mystical prayer wheel to the big wheel of God.

Trickster Mind Won't Go Away, So Keep It at Bay and Utilize Whatever It May Say

We now offer some additional advice for how to better work with your "can't live with it, can't live without it" one-and-only life partner, main squeeze, and co-conspirator in all matters: your mind. You will never be able to entirely block trickster mind from initial interference when you are in a small room. The more you try to stop your thoughts, the more your mind reminds you that it is here to stay and say whatever it wants. In truth, mind is the fifth (not so silent) ingredient in the room. It is present when you gather and blend the other vital ecstatic ingredients. You are going to have to learn how to not let your mind distract you from the higher purpose at hand by developing the skill that uses trickster thought production as a resource rather than a detriment. As the room gets bigger, mind's thoughts will no longer dominate because the other ecstatic ingredients become more present, active, and empowered. Later, in the big room, the only thoughts that arrive are those that help maintain the sanctified atmosphere rather than interfere with the ongoing expansion and heat.

When the spiritual temperature is still cooler, there is a simple trick that harnesses the tricky thoughts of trickster mind. Allow your mind to have its say, but only one thought at a time. After it has offered a thought, the rule of ecstatic law and order is that the other ingredients must immediately get their turn. After a thought, invite and enact a *change* in the rhythm, tone, and body movement. The emphasis here is on change, not doing more of the same. Don't just shift your attention to paying more attention to another ecstatic ingredient (because that is just more thinking). Change the ingredient itself—its volume, tempo, pitch, position, embellishment, or any other noticeable quality.

For instance, let us imagine that this thought pops into your mind as you proceed to gather, blend, and form a prayer wheel: "Should I get a tambourine rather than clap or sound a rhythm?" Do not allow a second thought to follow. Blow the whistle, stop the mind train, and turn to change the present rhythm, tone, or movement. You can even choose to vocally produce the sound of a tambourine. Only after such changes take place can another thought be given consideration. The action of altering the other ingredients makes thinking an equal partner rather than an overbearing tyrant.

It may help to develop the deep belief that every thought that arises during the ecstatic blending is a constantly changing secret message whose translated code always means "change the rhythm, tone, and movement." The other thing you can do is focus only on the most interesting word you find in the thought. In the previous example, it might be the word, "tambourine." Then express that word alone with changing tones, rhythms, and body movements until it changes into a rhyme or unexpected sound. *Tambourine, tam-tam-bour-bour-rine-rine, tam-tam, time-time, bour-bour, pour-pour, rine-rine, dream-*

dream, tambourine, time for dream, pour a dream; in other words, jam on the principal metaphor. Don't judge what comes forth; just enthusiastically ride and enjoy the changing, emphasizing natural spontaneity over cognitively evaluated aesthetic merit. This practice will not only help stop the drift of a free-associating mind but also amplify the ecstatic ingredients and help them blend.

In general, make trickster your friend, ally, and kitchen helper. Allow it to have one thought at a time; knowing each thought will always mean the same thing—a prescription for ecstatic action. Remember that each thought invites you to take its main metaphor on an ecstatic joy ride. Rise above the tides of thought that threaten washing away the big room and the mystical prayer wheel you are trying to build. Go beyond the reach of mind by showing it how to capture the metaphor whose altered tone, rhythm, and movement can lead to rapture.

The Art of Ecstatic Praying: Experimenting with the Mystical Prayer Wheel

Prayer has not been introduced until now because you need to initially gather the required spiritual ingredients to excite rather than only recite a prayer. Only then are you prepared to join with the spirit and request of Gerhard Tersteegen's prayer: "Draw near to my heart and inflame it. Touch my uncircumcised lips with a burning coal from Thine altar, that I may not speak of Thine ardent love in a cold or feeble manner."[49]

Below are some recommendations for exploring and experimenting with how to operate the mystical prayer wheel. Ecstatic praying always involves blending the spiritual cooking ingredients to form, turn, and transform the wheel. Though prayer is typically regarded as a largely linguistic exercise, ecstatic spiritual engineering reveals that hallowed words primarily serve blending the ingredients to expand and heat the room. Once the mystical wheel gains momentum, words can move in and out of prominence as rhythm, sung tones, and movement have their time in the spotlight.

Add a Fascinating Rhythm to a Simple Prayer Line

As mentioned, it is better to start with a simple prayer line — only a few words such as "thy will be done," "Do it Lord," or "Holy spirit, breathe on me." Make sure it is immediately placed on a fascinating rhythm and avoid falling into a trance where words are recited to a monotonous beat. Prayer must ride on top of a syncopated body pulse in order for it to experientially lead you somewhere. Note that such a rhythm can either be slow or fast. It's the syncopation, liveliness, and non-monotony that matter.

Again, cooked praying hosts multiple forms of call and response. The rhythmic bounce you carry when you begin working the mystical prayer wheel is the body's call for you to pray with an enthusiastic voice. The emergent chant heats and turns until it calls for a song to ride on its rhythm that is now ready to host a melodic line. As the rhythmic pulse of song is further cooked, its beat and heat jump into your bones and make you want to dance. A cooked prayer requires a cooked rhythm that invites more of you to pray with all the ingredients. Don't restrict prayer to speech alone. Pray with your feet, legs, hips, arms, and hands as well as with your rhythmic swing and tonal ring. Aim for a whole body prayer that excites emotion and ignites celebrative commotion. It begins by mixing a fascinating rhythm with a few prayer words and ends with the whole of you on fire with God's love.

Pray with All Your Heart

Never forget that it is not the amount or the cleverness of words that matter in prayer, but the intensity of emotion. Charles Spurgeon wrote: "Some brethren pray by the yard; but true prayer is measured by weight, and not by length. A single groan before God may have more fullness of prayer in it than a fine oration of great length."[50] Feel free to groan, moan, sigh, and weep for the divine because the "the essence of prayer lies in the heart drawing near to God: and it can do that without words."[51]

Heightened emotion inspires the motion required to turn the prayer wheel and bring you near the divine. In order to circulate this kind of emotion, your body must host the rhythms, tones, and movements that enable it to be expressed. Otherwise you may feel a spark of sacred emotion, but you won't be able to amplify it and use it as fuel for spiritual cooking. Sometimes a certain prayer line helps spark emotion, while at other times a heartfelt tone, soulful rhythm, or sacred song better ignites what words alone cannot. Make awakening, amplifying, and nurturing sacred emotion a priority in your life. Experiment with how you access and sustain it. The more sacred emotion you feel and can maintain, the more readily you can turn a prayer wheel.

Allow Rhythm and Melodic Tone to Alternate

Once a prayer starts cooking, it is made more ready to change its form. Sometimes rhythm will be primary, and other times melody will rise in prominence as your prayer leans toward song. This alternation is part of the journeying toward the divine. Allow prayer to shift, and don't feel it is necessary to get locked into either rhythmic or melodic dominance. Using a simple prayer line such as "The Lord is my shepherd," alternate between saying it on a rhythm and expressing it with more melodic tone. While there will never be a time when your prayer is absent of rhythm, you will feel the qualitative difference between chanting a prayer on either a slow or fast syncopated rhythm versus expressing it through melody. Experimental tinkering helps you from getting locked into one form of praying, which after a while can go cold.

Remember that spiritual power is found in the changes, not in the fixed forms. In a group gathering, an ordained captain or conductor initiates the change because they know how to read the spiritual temperature and follow higher divine guidance. When you pray alone, however, you will have to tinker and experiment with making the changes yourself. Always do your best to surrender too much self-consciousness or willful purpose, otherwise your praying will feel and sound too forced or contrived. Having a good prayer line and praying with all your heart both help in this regard. Rather than praying to put on a show for yourself, show God that you long for the fire of communion and union!

Make Sure the Body Is Moving

Again, you must pray with your whole body, not just your mind and vocal chords. If your words are riding on a rhythm and filled with emotion, then your body will naturally move as well. If your body is totally still, however, it is a sign that your prayer has little to no emotion or rhythm. Because all of the ecstatic ingredients are held together in an interactive mix, go ahead and move your body while you pray and experience how this automatically helps pull forth a rhythm and emotion. It is much more difficult to recite cold, flat words while performing a good seiki sway. Likewise, a simple rock, bounce, or occasional jolt helps keep the whole of you awake and inside the turning of the prayer wheel.

As another experiment, try returning to the basic call and response of seiki movement, now with the understanding that this exercise is another way to turn the mystical prayer wheel. Feel free to call for "seiki" or the "holy spirit, " or use a prayer line to make the call for divine mystery to move you: "Move, me Lord." Just like you did during the seiki movement exercise, emphasize spontaneous, effortless movement. Let your body get swept away in the ocean of motion and sacred emotion that is amplified and sustained by the call and response of the mystical wheel.

The more of you that is involved in prayer, the more interesting you are to God. Don't be shy to experiment with any imagined way to more wholly pray, transforming prayer into a laboratory for catching God's attention. Make yourself a good target and more attractive bait. If you want to be reeled in by the divine fishing line, you must wiggle and move. Consider what makes you attractive, interesting, and fascinating to God, and then prepare yourself accordingly.

Be Open to Interfaith Prayer Lines

Examine prayers from all around the world whose lines voice a true north compass setting and point you in the highest direction. With spiritual scissors, cut out the words that best indicate this orientation. For example, we boldface the compass settings found in these diverse prayers:

> **"Oh, Great Spirit** Whose voice I hear in the winds, And whose breath gives life to all the world, **hear me, I am small and weak,** I need your strength and wisdom."[52]

> **"Allow us to recognize Thee in all Thy holy names and forms;** as Rama, as Krishna, as Shiva, as Buddha. Let us know Thee as Abraham, as Solomon, as Zarathustra, as Moses, as Jesus, as Mohammed, and in many other names and forms, known and unknown to the world."[53]

> "Hear, Israel, the Lord is our God, the Lord is One. Blessed be the Name of His glorious kingdom for ever and ever. And you shall **love the Lord your God with all your heart and with all your soul and with all your might."** (Jewish prayer from the *Book of Deuteronomy,* chapter 6)

Discover how the holiest prayers are more alike than different in that they call forth a hallowed name and remind you that you are part of greater divine whole. Make the most important primary distinction in the construction of the holiest reality: your surrender to and intimacy with divinity. Choose the best corner-stone you can find for the big room hosting your involvement with God. You must first build sacred ground — step one of the Sacred Ecstatics recipe — and this operationally means that how you start points you toward where you will end.

Make sure you start right with the greatest choice of the first building bock, the one that enables a big room to be built.

Find the holiest prayers and focus on their holiest cornerstones. When this distinction, cornerstone, and compass setting is heated with sacred emotion, movement, rhythm, and tone, construction will commence and the big room will be successfully built. Call upon God's name and never stop calling upon it, distinguishing, indicating, reindicating, and framing your life with a big holy room where you can commune with holiness.

Make a Rhythm Prayer

Again, pay more attention to the rhythm rather than the words of prayer. The heartbeat of your prayer is its underlying pulse and without it, no prayer can come to life. To experience firsthand how true this is, try an experiment in which you abandon all words and only pray with a voiced rhythm. Concentrate on putting all your sacred emotion inside this rhythm prayer and discover how words are not even needed to bring you close to the divine.

You can't fully grasp what holy words are meant to say until they are cooked inside spiritual fire. Rhythm not only holds the lyrics of prayer, it also holds the music and dance of prayer. Rhythm is the prayer meter that sets the holy beat and turns up the spiritual temperature. Words do not become a true prayer until they are simmering with spiritual heat. Uncooked praying is just mumbo jumbo rather than spiritual gumbo. Start right with a good rhythm that is alive, captivating, and fascinating. On its tracks the holy train carries whatever prayer wishes to convey, transporting it and you to the hottest ecstatic locales.

Use Prayer for Tonal Alignment

The whole of prayer blends all the ingredients of spiritual cooking. Praying with every ingredient *is* spiritual cooking, and there are almost endless ways to mix and blend the four ingredients. For example, as you conduct a tonal tune-up, use a prayer word to make the tone. Sing the word "do" while toning a bass note and wiggling your hips. Then sing "it" for the mid-body movement and its associated midrange tone. End with "Lord" as the high note and headshake. All together now: "Do it Lord!" becomes both an integrated prayer and a fine-tuning of your body instrument.

Align movement and tone with your prayer lines and see how they bring attunement with divine resonance. Make yourself a holy instrument by infusing rhythm, tone, and movement into your whole body prayer. Bring all the elements of spiritual cooking together and get ready to turn your prayer into song and all the other changing forms of divine expression. Then return to experience differently the sacred words of the prayer you began with, discovering that you can't truly hear them until you are cooked. Only in the heat can prayer words truly lead you to the mystery that originally brought them into the world.

Making an Improvised Sound Prayer

Sometimes words need to be let go in favor of improvised tones that are unburdened by the weight of both denotation and connotation. We call this a "sound prayer" and it can be a simple sequence of separate or continuous sounds. While the quality of its emotion can remain the same or shift between sorrow and joy, this kind of prayer too must have the rhythm, tone, and body movement that make a prayer cook. As before, avoid a monotone and be open for the changing tones of a chant or melodic line. Even an improvised melody that is similar to a jazz singer performing scat singing may arise, enabling the spirit to scatter itself more freely about through the ongoing surprises of tonal, rhythmic, and movement variation and embellishment.

Poly-Prayer: Two Prayer Lines at the Same Time

After becoming a seasoned praying instrument, you will find that your praying can become so focused and emotionally involved that you spontaneously burst into praying two prayers at the same time. Here one prayer line keeps going while another line is added on top of it. This kind of praying is experienced internally where your imagination is free to do anything it wishes, including introducing multiple voices, diverse instruments, and different lines of prayer. Poly-prayer requires more concentration than a single line of prayer and can only be accomplished when you are sufficiently spiritually heated and infused with enough emotion to lift your performance to another level where multiple foci come into play.

As you learn how to make a double prayer, even more lines can be added until you have a symphony of prayer going on within you. One benefit of mastering poly-prayer is that it becomes easier to keep a prayer going inside of you as you move through the everyday events of your life. Here, prayer becomes continuous throughout the day and the night, like having an inner jukebox filled with God's greatest hits. This is what it means to really get spiritually cooked. You start living like the old saints, shamans, mystics, and cooked healers—with a constant song and prayer in your heart.

Mix It All Up

Constantly surprise yourself by not knowing how your prayers will start. They might begin with a beatbox performance of an unexpected rhythm, singing the line of a sacred song, moving your body in a spontaneous sway, or calling on the name of God. Mix it all up so that rhythm becomes a melody, body motion becomes felt emotion, and all the spiritual ingredients become a holy prayer. Go ahead and pray to burn the letter p off the word "pray" so you receive the holy ray. Emphasize vibrant mixing rather than wish for a fixing so your prayers remain charged with the changing, turning, and burning of the mystical prayer wheel.

Ancient rumor has it that God favors those who are playful children rather than overly serious adults. Don't just tell the divine what you want, show that you can play in the divine field of the Lord. Spend as much time skipping and leaping your prayers as you do expressing them on your knees. Try both moaning and making a joyful noise, but avoid the drone of being a monotone. Make sure the soles of your feet are as worn as your prayer seat. While there is a time to go into the prayer closet, there is also a time to come out of the closet and show God that you are ready to go outside and play underneath the heavenly sunshine where a shower of radiant blessings brings improvised abundance rather than another round of what's redundant.

What's My Line?

You need something more than a song list. You need a list of all-time prayer hits, especially the most holy lines that do not allow any room for unnecessary drift. Our own prayer list includes many of the lines we have already mentioned:

> "Thy will be done"
> "Help me, Lord."
> "Hear me, I am small and weak."
> "Take my hand."
> "Do it!"
> "Thank you!"
> "The Lord is my shepherd."

You only need one masterful prayer line to climb the rope to God, but feel free to add more. Don't make them up yourself until you have been sufficiently cooked to engage in well-tuned improvisation that is guided by wise discernment. Trust old and established prayer lines that have already worked for others and the prayers offered by truly spiritually cooked teachers, preachers, and spiritual pointers.

There was an old American television game show called *What's My Line?* where a panel had to guess a contestant's occupation (i.e., "line of work"). We suggest that this question also can be used to ask for your primary line of prayer. Ask yourself, "What's my line?" Know that your choice of a primary prayer line is the beginning of your mainline rope to God. If you don't yet have one, then you lack the necessary spiritual compass setting, primary distinction, or cornerstone. Again, turn to the tried-and-true prayer lines from any of the world's big wisdom traditions. Don't forget that your first and most important prayer line is the hallowed cornerstone needed to build sacred ground. Pray for the highest and vastest prayer line; work it and let it work on you.

Study the Ecstatic Praying of Others

We provide our students with video examples of ecstatic prayer. First watch and listen, allowing your inner body to move and pray along so that you catch the feeling, tone, and pulse of what you see and hear. When you are sufficiently moved on the inside, something will mysteriously pull the externalized clapping, stomping, and praying aloud out of you, doing so in a way that is totally aligned with the people in the video. Always make sure you stay in synch with the conductor leading the prayer in the video. Your voice should not be louder and your rhythm should be in time with the anointed group leader.

Recognize the practical truth that a lot can be learned from others who are seasoned and skilled in the art of cooking a prayer. Just as a good music, dance, or acting student studies the work of the masters and learns to adopt their good habits, so too do you benefit from learning to move, sound, and pray like the master spiritual cooks. Trickster will always find a way to suggest that you already have what you need and can skip learning from others to concentrate on letting your own unique forms of self-expression loose. We advise you to ignore that temptation and only concentrate on learning the art of spiritual cooking from those who do it well. Eventually when you make it to the fire in the big room, you will experience firsthand how all your expression — both that which is unique to you and that which echoes the performance of others — comes forth spontaneously and naturally with no effort on your part. Like a Bushman n/om-kxao, you will eventually feel like all the ancestors from the beginning of time are praying with you, around you, beside you, and inside you.

Spiritual cooking is often optimal inside a group. When more than one person gathers to pray, the fire is more likely to be caught and spread among everyone. Therefore when you watch a video of people praying, it's always best to pray along with them in a way that teaches you to blend in rather than stand out, just as you would if you attended a live service or ceremony. Spiritual cooking requires moving from the cold solo performance of trickster *egology* to the fiery harmony of sacred ecology. Embrace the practical spiritual engineering of this long-standing wisdom and your ecstatic life will soar.

Know What You Are Praying For: "What Do You Want?"

What do you long for? What do you want from the divine when you are standing, kneeling, prostrating, or dancing in the big room of prayer? Do you want "the joy, the fulfillment, the explosion, and the everything" described by those who are touched by the divine spirit?[54] Ask yourself what outcome you seek through prayer.° Before you answer, however, take your spiritual temperature. Don't just pose the question to your rational mind and answer it with small thoughts and cold words. Take it to the big room. Sing it on a soulful melody. Dance it, shake it, and stomp it out. Put this question on a fascinating rhythm and cook it. Let it simmer, shimmer, and tumble through you day and night. Hear it being asked by a

---

° Be aware that in the cold, you are more likely to freeze words into literality and duality. For instance, "thy will be done" can become literally interpreted as the notion that you shouldn't express your will so you (either humbly or piously) aim to be goalless and without needs or desires. However, "thy will be done" is itself a desired outcome and an expression of an orientation you hope to achieve. You simply cannot avoid having a goal, including the desire to not have one. Once you spiritually heat up you will not be so entangled in these trickster technicalities that only paralyze you from being able to turn the prayer wheel. Pay less attention to definitional meaning and the fuss it inspires while shifting yourself to performing the actions that actually get the wheel turning. If you drift into sideline hermeneutics or the interpretation of text, blow a referee's whistle and get back on the playing field where the spiritual action is.

chorus of angels, the old oak trees, in the grandest of cathedrals, and near the banks of the clearest stream. What do you long for? What do you want?

While it's true that you have to be careful about the pitfalls of being too outcome driven with your spiritual life, it's equally true that losing touch with the highest purpose of your efforts can get you sidetracked. You need to make sure that the spiritual path you are on is aligned with the outcome you seek. Be aware that there is a trickster falsehood hidden in the old truism that there are many paths to the same ultimate spiritual destination. Different paths can actually lead to very different places.

For example, if you want to spiritually cook, shake, and tremble like a Kalahari Bushman n/om-kxao, sitting on your meditation cushion will not take you there. Nor will listening to Alan Watts. Although we really enjoy Alan Watts' lectures, the man didn't know anything about the sacred vibration or the Kalahari recipe for cooking a spirited life. If you follow Watts' instruction, you end up with few spiritual kilowatts—a cool cucumber sandwich rather than hot baked Kalahari bread. If you're not clear about your spiritual target, you may find yourself following the wrong recipe. It's important to consider what your ultimate spiritual goal is because that will tell you what trail you ought to be walking on. Ask yourself: Whose tracks do I want to follow?

The Sacred Ecstatics recipe for setting your soul on fire follows the tracks of the Shakers, Quakers, rapture seekers, and spirited bakers from diverse traditions. We suggest not being shy about openly desiring the fire in your bones of sacred ecstasy. This longing is a rope that pulls you toward the path walked by the soulful mystics, song catchers, and shamans from Saint Teresa of Avila, to Lucie E. Campbell, Osumi Sensei, and the great doctors of the Kalahari. Are you here to get spiritually cooked, hooked, and lassoed by the Big Holy? If so, then it does no good to be wishy-washy about it. Only when you know your ultimate destination can you pray for the maps that help you find its treasure.

The Big Room Calls for Big Desire

As we wrote in *Sacred Ecstatics*:

> Introduce yourself to the truest spiritual law of attraction: big rooms attract profound wholeness and small rooms attract trivial partiality. As the room expands, so does the nature of your prayers. Hence you are protected from making petty requests as you move away from ego's shallow wishing well. Here we find that the new age/new thought belief in the power of thought, intention, and attraction simply makes a monstrous part–whole error. It is *the room* holding your thinking and action that attracts, not any particular thought found inside it. Divine-centered contexts attract sacred mystery and make your relationship to the numinous stronger, whereas self-centered contexts attract more inflation of your trickster mind while cutting off your connection to higher mystical gifts. Before making a prayer, make sure the room is big enough to receive a bigger and more wholesome reward.[55]

The cornerstone is the first stone set in the construction of a foundation, and all other stones are laid in relationship to it. Start with the right stone and you end up with a room big enough for sacred mystery. When you lay the foundation for spiritual activity, you must be both 100 percent congruent and 100 percent humble. Be sincere and clear in your prayers about your longing and desire to be near the divine. Saint Augustine even defined prayer as an expression of ultimate desire:

> For it is they heart's desire that is thy prayer; and if thy desire continues uninterrupted, thy prayer continueth also. . . . Whatever else you are doing, if you do but long for that Sabbath, you do not

cease to pray. If you would never cease to pray, never cease to long after it. The continuance of thy longing is the continuance of thy prayer.[56]

Get your feet walking in the same direction as the deepest desires of your heart and mind. Then follow that prayer with the humility that comes from feeling your smallness and fragility in the grand scheme of things. If for some reason you can't muster up some sincere humility, follow the advice of Carlos Castaneda's Don Juan and look over your left shoulder. There you'll find death waiting like a constant companion.[p]

Pure desire for the highest spiritual purpose must also hold hands with the sincerest dedication to the work required to help achieve it. This marriage of desire and commitment helps keep you from falling into either inflated apathy or exaggerated boast. The mission of your life is not accomplished alone. It is shared with God's mission. You are responsible for (1) gathering the necessary spiritual ingredients for cooking and (2) initiating the turning of the mystical prayer wheel. This is the creation of sacred ground, step one of the Sacred Ecstatics recipe for setting your whole life on fire. After your part is done, God takes over and is responsible for spiritually cooking you. Whatever God has in store for you in the big room, from small gifts to full-blown anointment, is up to God. Getting to that room is up to you. Do you want to get to the big room? If so, then say it, ask for it, and get to work moving toward it, continuously praying for divine help along the way.

Only God can bring you the higher wisdom you need. No matter how much book knowledge or street smarts you have, it won't help you when it comes to handling your most important concerns and affairs. Spiritual wisdom, power, and guidance is only granted when you make room to receive it, and that includes softening your heart and tuning your body to be pierced by God's arrows, nails, and spears. Make room for the

---

[p] It's widely known that Castaneda's Don Juan is a fictional character, which means we are free to be inspired by him the way we are inspired by any character in literature.

mystical prayer wheel, for God, and for the holy fire that makes your life truly matter. This is easier said than done. And it's never done.

Thy Will Be Done

We held a graduation ceremony at the end of our first mentorship program and gave each student the tiniest certificate that has probably ever existed. It was so small it fit in a matchbox (inspired by the first mystical prescription in our book, *Sacred Ecstatics*.)

Upon receiving it, everyone wept with joy, realizing the truth expressed by Raymond Moody: "the most powerful prayer is surrender." While everyone wrestles with willful intrusions, trickster confusions, and ego delusions, you have to be just as careful that you don't spend so much time battling demons that you miss the call to fall in love and in line with the divine.

The burning desire for heavenly fire is the ultimate life-giving force that pulls you straight to the source. You can't go wrong when you long for holy song, and you don't stand a chance unless you show up at the dance. Always explicitly or implicitly pray, "thy will be done," but don't let trickster piety dampen your hunger for the sweet sacred pie in the holiest sky. Go ahead and pray the mystic's prayer, as articulated by William Sharp:

Lay me to sleep in sheltering flame,
O Master of the Hidden Fire!
Wash pure my heart, and cleanse for me
My soul's desire.
In flame of sunrise bathe my mind,
O Master of the Hidden Fire,
That, when I wake, clear-eyed may be
My soul's desire.[57]

In the same spirit of Sacred Ecstatics, St. Anselm reminds us that you are in need of the fire that spiritually cooks you and that it is important to ask for it:

Pierce with the arrows of Thy love the secret chambers of the inner man. Let the entrance of Thy healthful flames set the sluggish heart alight, and the burning fire of Thy sacred inspiration enlighten it and consume all that is within me, both of mind and body.[58]

Charles Spurgeon joins her when he prays: "We must get rid of the icicles that hang about our lips. We must ask the Lord to thaw the ice-caves of our soul and to make our hearts like a furnace of fire heated seven times hotter."[59] We pray you will tell God what you want. Be neither hesitant nor fire resistant. Then add, "thy will be done," whether voiced in those exact words or abbreviated as, "whatever," said in a humbly, rumbly, and tumbly manner.

My Will Be Done (in the Cold) and Thy Will Be Done (in the Heat)

When the room is small and the temperature is cold, "thy will" cannot readily be done. In such a space and climate, *your* will must do something that makes the room big and warm enough for God to step in and take over. Your focus, goals, and motivation need to be adjusted and aimed at the truest and highest North so the right action can spring forth. Only then are you able to sweep away the clutter and prepare for the divine to make your wings flutter. Step 1 of the Sacred Ecstatics recipe — building sacred ground — requires your good will, determined willpower, and faithful action. Unless you make room for the divine to be near, "thy will" is far away, or more accurately, you are not yet able to notice and be influenced by it. When the spiritual temperature is chilly, you need to get busy altering the room. This requires real discipline and effort. When you build vast enough space, even if it requires turning the prayer wheel until you feel ready to collapse from exhaustion, God shows up to take over. You shift from cold to hot as your will is handed over to "thy will."

Do not use the wisdom directive concerning "thy will" to be a trickster excuse for your not doing the necessary hard work that helps higher power arrive. There is a time and place for your will to kick into action, especially when you are far removed or out of sorts with God. Trickster mind always wants you to be irresponsible at such a moment and will mumble in your ear some convoluted "ice advice" such as, "This should be God's will, not mine." As theologian Harvey Cox proposed, Adam and Eve's original sin was not eating the apple of the tree of knowledge, it was letting a snake tell them what to think and do.[60] Ignore trickster's twisted and spiritually inverted advice or else risk remaining in the same sinking, shrinking rut and becoming even more entrenched in whatever small room has imprisoned you. God's will is that you exercise your will to build sacred ground and light a fire whenever a cramped and chilly situation calls for you to take corrective action. When it is time for divine will to take over, you will immediately know it. In an instant, your action will feel spontaneous and have a soulful rhythm and tone. Divinity is the holy Tao of utmost spontaneity, the purest jazz on earth as it is in heaven's music and dance hall. Build it and "thy will" shall come and be done.

Target Practice

One of the Guarani shamans from the Amazon, Tupa Nevangayu, once told Brad, "To receive the sacred luminosity, you must pray every day and dance every night. You must prepare yourself to become available for this light."[61] Follow the advice of the strong shamans and make yourself ready and available for spirit to work on you. Every time you make yourself ready to pray, move, and sing, consider it target practice rather than spiritual practice. Know your target: heartfelt union and electric communion with the divine. Go ahead and pray with Sir Richard of Chichester to help keep you more aligned with what the saints desired: "May we know Thee more clearly, love Thee more dearly, and follow Thee more nearly."[62]

Follow the Bushman n/om-kxaosi and learn to track God. In the changing of First Creation you are the hunter, the target, the bow, and the arrow all at the same time. Aim all of your efforts at the supreme target. Know that as you do so, the gods are aiming their fire-tipped love arrows at you. Such is the reciprocity of sacred luminosity and the mutuality of on-fire spirituality. Ready, aim, *fire!* Because "the longing is your recognition of the deepest truth that God is love and that this is all you want. Every lesser desire melts when it comes near that flame."[63] Let your deepest longing, highest desire, and most dedicated hunt be your prayer.

A Mystical Prayer Secret: Increase the Volume Within

Your inner body carries none of the limitations of your physical form. For example, your inner voice can sing better than Pavarotti and dance better than Nureyev, as well make better music than any orchestra, band, or instrument. When you pray powerfully inside yourself, your body will feel it. Use this mystical secret to enhance sacred emotion. Pray with extraordinary amplitude to reach the highest mystical altitude.

We invite you to internally make a sound with a super human volume, a loudness that is not physically possible to achieve on the outside. Imagine making a beautiful sound that can be heard around the world, shattering glass and crumbling mountains. Again, don't be shy—go ahead and dare to release a cosmic scale tone. When you experience this kind of volume internally, emotion and vibration are kicked up several notches. Praying, shouting, or singing at this level of energized volume will help open the door to mystery. Here a more intense tone is able to better voice an empowered sacred emotion. Reverend Charles Spurgeon defined prayer's effectiveness by the intensity of its emotion: "Not length but strength is desirable."[64] Go for the super tone of incredible emotion to help send your message along the divine telephone line.

One night Brad tried an experiment and internally shouted out bursts of seiki and n/om sounds and prayers, imaging that he was releasing arrows toward our mentorship students all over the world. He made such a loud internal sound that he felt he might explode. It actually startled him. The night he did this, he told no one he was doing it. We woke up the next morning to receive this letter from Amy Priest, one of our students:

Dear Hillary and Brad,

I just woke from a dream that I would like to share with you: I was walking down a winding trail in the forest, coming back to join the mentorship group. I found Brad out there amongst the trees. When he saw me, I was shocked to experience my belly tighten as I doubled over. He grabbed my hand and it felt like I was shocked by a bolt of lightning that was more powerful than what exists on Earth. The experience seemed to last for- ever, perhaps for eons. I could see nothing and hear nothing as I was turned into a ball of light- ning. As the energy entered my body, I thought, "I'm gonna die, this guy is crazy." I wondered whether my heart was going to burst. At some point the intensity started to come down a little.

Brad then asked me to come join him. He was shooting arrows with a regular bow and arrow, but the arrowhead had a glowing red-hot tip. Brad explained that it was target practice time for him. The target consisted of a bent metal clothes hanger with two hanging figurines bobbling back and forth. Brad hit his target every time. He asked me to try. I barely grazed the target.

Then I heard Hillary's voice down at the camp—it was like a loudspeaker announcement in the forest saying "It's time to come back." This message made me giggle. We made our way back to the mentorship circle around the fire for it was now nighttime and everyone had gathered. I felt like I was spinning from what happened.

I'm now heading back to bed. It's 3am here. Much love to both of you.

In another experiment, Brad prayed with tones only, using the amplification method to make the sound internally louder than what is humanly possible. Before he went to sleep he sang two notes, bass and midrange tones, to our class. He did not sing the high note. The next morning we received this letter from someone in our mentorship program:

Hi Brad & Hillary,

Both of you were in my dream last night. We were gathered for an intensive. It was morning and not all the participants were there. They were trickling in after their breakfast. People started moving in a gentle rocking motion. You and Brad started singing with tones only. You oscillated the low tones and then moved to the middle oscillating tones. I then woke up. I understood that you were going to voice the high tones next and some things might happen.

A few weeks later Hillary dreamed she was praying with the super amplification of volume. When she hit the high note of her prayer, she actually made a loud noise out loud that woke us up. We invite you to pray and sing with all your lungs and at the top of your voice, making the loudest joyful noise within so it will spiritually wake you up. Do it to spark sacred emotion and get closer to the divine who hosts the fire and attends the wild of deep nature. Do this to tear down the walls of Jericho that prevent you from hearing and feeling the divine echo and its rhythmic knock at your door. Anything can happen when you ask with all your heart and request with all your might that a holy light come to fill your every night. Scream your prayers before you dream them!

How We Personally Pray

Our mainline rope is to the living, mystical Jesus whose light and love we experience as supreme, whether we are awake or in a dream. We call upon his name because, as the gospel song declares, it is "the sweetest name we know." This was always the case for Brad from the time he was a boy living next to his father's church and near his grandfather's church. He never drifted far away from his mainline connection to God, even though he repeatedly denounced Christians whose hearts profaned the name and teaching of the carpenter whose nails delivered ultimate n/om rather than icy judgment or meanness. Jesus brought Brad through the physical and metaphysical veil and was the cosmic egg that held all divine gifts. Hillary experienced the same emotional relationship with Jesus once she received a Kalahari n/om nail and a sacred song. Today we both say to one another in private that Jesus is our rope to God. We also say he is the big Bushman n/om-kxao whose n/om is the purest and strongest sacred vibration of all.

Consequently, the strongest songs that get our sacred vibrations going most are those that praise his name—the old sanctified gospel hymns. This does not mean that we have not received other holy songs and that even includes a Cole Porter tune.[q] We don't believe it is possible to truly experience or understand Jesus unless you are in the spiritual fire. In these ecstatic flames many mystics from every religion have found him, including Yogananda, Ibn Arabi, and Black Elk. Jesus is our main rope and we hold onto him as the bridge between flesh and spirit, earth and heaven.

We respect whatever other holy ones people choose to call upon in prayer, primarily because we are interested in spiritual engineering and temperature taking rather than spiritual naming. But Jesus is the main name we call upon. We call upon his name like a child would call for their best, truest, most joyful, and most loving friend, or parent, brother, sister, or mother, all combined. Jesus can take on any and all relational forms of unconditional love. We also often pray the Lord's Prayer (the King James version from Matthew 6: 9–13) because that is the prayer Jesus formulated for his disciples and that alone makes it special to us:

> Our Father which art in heaven,
> hallowed be thy name.
> Thy kingdom come, thy will be done in earth,
> as it is in heaven.
> Give us this day our daily bread.
> And forgive us our debts,
> as we forgive our debtors.
> And lead us not into temptation, but deliver us
> from evil: For thine is the kingdom, and the
> power, and the glory, forever.
> Amen.

We never pray, and this especially includes the Lord's Prayer, without our complete focus and attention riveted to the prayer itself. If we notice the prayer focus slipping and weakening—whether it is caused by distracting thoughts, a

---

[q] See our report of Brad's receiving the song, "Ev'ry Time We Say Goodbye," in a visionary visit to a spiritual classroom: http://sacredecstatics.com/home-is-where-the-song-is/.

mindless stupor, a disassociated trance state, or impassionate involvement—we immediately stop and start the prayer over. We often repeat a small line of the prayer over and over until it heats and permeates our whole awareness, deeply sinking into both surface conscious, deep unconscious, and higher conscious mind. We are especially open to making any kind of tonal, rhythmic, and movement variation as we pray, doing so to help lift sacred emotion. Only after we experience a powerfully focused absorption of a prayer line will we choose whether to stay with those words or heat the next line. We never know whether we will stay within a single prayer loop or continue on until the actual praying is occurring. Sometimes we heat one looped line after another until the whole prayer is sizzling.

There is a circus and vaudeville act where a number of spinning plates are kept spinning, each on top of a separate stick. The performer must keep going back and forth to keep each plate moving so it doesn't fall. We similarly may keep all the lines of the prayer hot until they are all pulsing with spirited hot expression. We jump from one line to another making sure they are all vibrant and heated at the same time. In summary, we want the prayer to be experienced like it is the first time we have ever prayed and to feel all the passion of our whole being involved. We can say from experience that when done this way, prayer becomes the strongest and most extraordinary medicine on the planet.

In addition, we sometimes draw upon the prayers of the saints who were in love with the love of Jesus. Hillary particularly enjoys saying the prayer of St. Nicholas of Flüe (1417–1487) because, as she likes to playfully say, it's an expedient prayer that gets right to the point and covers all the bases. Hillary also sometimes chooses one or two lines from this prayer the way we do with the Lord's Prayer:

My Lord and my God,
remove far from me whatever keeps
me from You.

My Lord and my God,
confer upon me whatever enables me to
reach You.

My Lord and my God,
free me from self and make me wholly
Yours.

Hillary often uses the first line from Psalm 23: "The Lord is my shepherd, I shall not want." Brad prefers saying "Lord" rather than "God" when he prays because that is what he heard his grandparents and parents say when they prayed, so this word has more sacred emotion and familial relationship attached for him. In general, both of us choose the simplest prayers that emphasize a familial and loving relationship to a personal father, mother, or Jesus figure we accept wholeheartedly and uncritically. Children's prayers are powerful to us as are the old prayers and way of praying with tone and rhythm found in the sanctified black church where we find the most masterful praying going on when it comes to spiritual cooking.

It is not always easy for us to speak about our relationship to Jesus because he seems to be the most polarizing and misunderstood of all the holy ones. Yet we agree with Joao Carvalho of Brazil, one of Brad's former spiritual teachers, who said that Jesus is "the Saint of saints." He is the sun light of God, the great comforter, the big doctor, and the holy pointing way. Jesus is a force of love and anyone who acts full of hatred and judgment toward others does not have Jesus living in their heart, no matter what they say.

The spiritual engineering of Sacred Ecstatics can help you cook any and all prayers with all hallowed names. It can also help you ecstatically awaken a personally felt relationship with Jesus. We find that the Jesus who hung out with the Catholic saints and the early Protestant preachers is the same one who dances down the aisles in old-school sanctified churches. We pray with all of these anointed ones by our side. We are on the same side with them and it is radically distinct from what the cold Jesus naming folks say, whose rhythm, tone, movement, and emotion just isn't right. We denounce their talk, but cherish the name they abuse in their pseudoconversion of holiness into human ice that is seldom nice to all people and all religions. We are not "know-it-all" Jesus hammers that pound on every head. We are "feel-it-all" n/om-kxaosi with nails of n/om and a Jesus rope.

Praying Ecstatic Shamans

Sacred Ecstatics offers an ecstatically hot shamanism that prioritizes the main divine rope over all other spiritual ropes. Absolute devotion to the Creator of all ropes through constant prayer puts us in relationship to divine will rather than our taking it upon ourselves to personally negotiate with derivative spiritual forms. Sometimes God points us toward a spiritual helper or guide, whether it is a plant, animal, ancestor, former saint, preacher, poet, musician, or rascal. However, you should always let God direct this horizontal rope connection rather than ask for such a thing on your own. We never pray to or ask help from any of the lesser forms—that too easily gets us lost and in trouble. When you pray wholeheartedly to God, you are more assured that whatever comes is something directed from above. If you have any doubt about a spiritual experience—whether it involves intuition, premonition, cognition, or vision—then follow Saint Theresa's advice to pay no attention to it unless God later makes it absolutely certain that it is holy and of divine importance.

Bypassing the Creator commits the part-whole error that maintains presence in a small room governed by too much purposefulness on your part. If you think you can receive and handle the spiritual power of the horizontal plane without the weak and meek surrender to the highest conductor, you are headed for a spiritual train wreck. The paradox is that if you have a strong vertical rope, you are more likely to meet a spirit but you will have less interest in it.

Be careful if you think you can both effectively pray to God and perform a neoshamanic ritual that calls upon lesser spiritual forms. These two orientations cancel each other out, meaning you cannot live in both realities at the same time. Such a two-handed, two-faced situation signifies you are in a room with funhouse mirrors built by trickster. What you typically have is a tiny idol of God in one hand and multiple idols, totems, and tokens of spirit in the other hand. This setup can only create more of the same — endless imitations held inside make-believe-it's-true mind. Every time you add a trinket, and this includes your God trinket, you get another shopping fix. In fact, you are only getting more addicted to adding more charms, paraphernalia, trinkets, and doodads to your charm bracelet, seeing spiritual magic, synchronicity, and gee-whiz fizz wherever you look. Give up all the fake imitations and pray to experience the authentic masterpiece. Do this to make your spiritual life more real and in touch with the Creator's never ceasing originality.

If you are worried that giving up your neoshamanic practices will take all the presumed spiritual magic out of your life, then your faith in God is weaker than you think and you have not yet surrendered to the highest divine source and force. There is no greater mystical power and ecstatic glory than experiencing an emotional closeness to divinity, which is what makes sticking only to praying on the vertical rope a liberating joy. Once you have tasted divine wine from the vertical vine, you will have no interest in continuing to drink neoshamanic Kool-Aid that is artificially sweetened. Go for God's rope rather than trickster's dope! Be truly fed and satisfied by the holy bread prayer can bring. We will be straight with you: it's possible that God will never put you in contact with a lesser spirit, whether animal or vegetable or ancestral in nature. But who cares because you will have a close personal relationship with your creator, the ultimate wisdom and miracle fountain from which all gifts and blessings flow. The question is: Do you trust God to handle your spiritual, mystical, healing, and shamanic affairs, or do you prefer to chase a trickster curiosity and take matters into your own hands?

Being a shaman for God rather than a shamanic practitioner for trickster mind requires that you primarily hold onto the main divine rope and pray to never let go. You don't ask or wish for fantasy journeys, nor are you so easily seduced to believe that magical helpers will follow your command. Don't even assume you will pick up a drum unless you feel your divine rope pull you to do so. Clear and free yourself so anything can happen, especially a sweet prayer. Whenever a ritual gets locked into a form, especially a standardized method, know that God, spirit, and all higher power are far away. After all, the divine rope is attached to First Creation where everything is changing. Therefore, when you have a divine hookup, expect improvisation to rule over memorization. When it's spiritually hot, a holy jam session happens; if it's cold, all remains more of the same old mind trip.

We want to make absolutely clear that we are not claiming or implying that the spirits that are less than their Creator are evil, nor are we suggesting that relating to them should be avoided at all costs. This is the misunderstanding of "trickster" that the Christian church and other religions typically perpetuate, converting trickster into a devil that is separate from God. Trickster is simply one inseparable side of God — the side that constantly changes, including its role as one that can help or hinder. Its shape-shifting quality renders it unreliable and in need of divine guidance. Don't ever call on or commune with spirit helpers; only pray and call on the trustworthy and stable side of God (what the Bushmen call the Sky God) and let the divine be in charge of all of creation, including you. After all, in the grand scheme of things, you, too, are only another trickster that constantly changes and is in need of God just like all the other unruly ancestors, fruit flies, crawly ones, bears, otters, and critters of spirit.

Always hold onto your divine rope and its mystical prayer wheel. If you are subsequently introduced to other spiritual forms of creation, it is then glorious and especially dear without any fear because God is in charge. In the big room you are the spirit helper for God, not the other way around, and this can only take place in a sacred space where the walls and pitfalls of mind have been removed. Rather than stick to a horizontal plane plan, think more vertically and head toward the big room where you become a hollow resonating instrument capable of receiving the sacred vibration of holiness. This is the alternative reality the Creator offers you. When your mystical wheel cooks prayer into sacred song, you are then able to truly spiritually travel, partaking on journeys to the divinely chosen spirit lands. You do so with the spiritual heat that defeats trickster mind's interference, static noise, and ego inflating wind.

A cooked prayer that blends word, tone, rhythm, movement, and emotion is the rope to God, the road itself, and the means of all communication and transportation. You are the drum, song, and dance that wake up a journey to the divine embrace. Please inform your trickster mind to not be disappointed—God provides far more mystery and spirit than any trickster rope can promise. More importantly, you will know it is real and not have to be concerned about whether you are lost and only making things up.

Brad has sung with the coyote, eagle, elephant, giraffe, leopard, snake, crocodile, and various birds, butterflies, bees, trees, plants, seas, mountains, skies, ancestors, celestial choirs, great pianists and musicians of the past, among many other spiritual forms—doing so while holding onto his main rope to God. This was always done in vast spiritual space and in relationship to elder shamans rather than within a shrunken shamanic protocol. The former assures building up holiness whereas the latter method is stripped of sacred context, relationship, ecstatic heat, and holiness. The art of handling the fire of sacred ecstasy is the highest shamanism and it always requires a big room with a blazing, amazing grace fire. Admission to the big room requires that you come holding the necessary ingredients. Get real with God rather than make a deal with trickster, accomplished by using your mystical prayer wheel to set in motion the ecstatic journey of a lifetime.

Praying in First Creation Church

As members of the First Creation Church where ecstatic shamans, mystics, saints, preachers, teachers, healers, yogis, crazy wisdom conveyors, and all other spiritual mavericks gather, we pray as our rope moves us to pray. We avoid praying when we are cold. We avoid God talk when words are chilly. We check our spiritual temperature whenever we are out of sorts in any way, whether we are feeling irritated, angry, or selfish. In truth, those latter feelings are themselves the spiritual temperature reading — they indicate that we have gone cold and are in need of immediately taking spirited action. We avoid all self-reflection, introspection, and psychological insight like the plague. Instead we gather the ingredients needed for spiritual cooking whenever we are tempted to digress along a trickster line of thought. When we have all the basic spiritual ingredients in hand and are heading toward the kitchen, only then are we ready to pray.

As we prepared the section on the mystical prayer wheel, we were delighted and surprised to discover that Charles Spurgeon previously wrote: "I know of no better thermometer to your spiritual temperature than this, the measure of the intensity of your prayer."[65] Spiritual heat is found in the cooking of a prayer and this temperature is measured by the extent of sacred emotion you are able to voice in your longing and desire for divine contact. All effective sacred practice warms the soul. Your soul is never lost and in need of retrieval. What is lost is spiritual heat. You simply get cold as you drift away from the divine and are in need of having your soul set on fire again.

Gandhi reminds us that "Supplication, worship, prayer are no superstition; they are acts more real than the acts of eating, drinking, sitting or walking. It is no exaggeration to say that they alone are real, all else is unreal."[66] A cooked prayer is what really brings you to life and makes you tall enough to grasp the heavens. Dwight L. Moody put it this way: "He who kneels the most, stands the best." [67] Francis of Assisi went further to suggest, "We should seek not so much to pray but to become prayer."[68]

More than anything, prayer is the main way to spiritually cook. Its operation is bidirectional: you cook a prayer so the prayer can get hot enough to cook you. The successful enactment of cooked prayer also builds sacred ground. As the room gets vaster and hotter, prayer changes its rhythms, tones, movements, and emotional intensity. Make sure you are an experimentalist rather than a fundamentalist with prayer, free to explore all kinds of praying, including starting with only shouting one word, using only tones, or allowing a rhythm or movement to improvise anything. Allow the heated expression of prayer to take you anywhere and everywhere in the spiritual universe. It is the means and the goal, the flying arrow and the target for cooking a spiritual life. Whenever you hear the name of "prayer," regard it as a pyrotechnical skill that is used to light up your life. See the word "prayer" and say "song" out loud so you recognize that in another dimension of temperature, its name changes. Similarly, see the name "song" and say "prayer" out loud. The stretch from prayer to prayer-song and prayer-song-dance extends your rope to God.

In the ecstatic fire, prayer and song melt into the emotionally felt umbilical cord to creation. It connects you to both the original mother and father and the whole family and community that reside in eternity. Pray to become an ecstatically cooked prayer whose ray of heavenly sunshine illumines and starts a fire when magnified. Pray when you long for the spirit to move you. And when the spirit touches and moves your heart, it will really make you want to pray. As the old hymn says, "Every time I feel the spirit moving in my heart, I'm gonna pray." Pray to pray with the shamans, mystics, saints, healers, and First Creation movers and shakers of forever changing prayer.

The Ecstatic Prelude: Gathering and Blending to Cook Throughout the Day

Make sure you set aside some time each day to practice your basic ecstatic skills from gathering the ingredients to blending them into a mystical prayer wheel. This is your opportunity to learn how to more effectively get cooked. Suspend accentuating belief and the pursuit of stress relief in order to learn how to better excite and ignite your life. In addition to scheduled practice time, we urge you to add something truly revolutionary to your life — a brief mini-ecstatic workout interspersed throughout your day before you perform any task. We call it "the ecstatic prelude." Also consider it "the ecstatic pray-lude" through which connection to the divine is enhanced and strengthened via rhythm, movement, tone, and music with some prayer words thrown onboard. This ecstatic prelude gathers and blends the ingredients into a mystical prayer wheel and turns it for an intense, brief moment. The ecstatic prelude needs to only last 30–50 seconds to be effective. It can be performed internally so no one else is disturbed when you stir the spiritual atmosphere.

Consider your everyday life as a sequence of a limited number of events that range from eating breakfast, to going to work, and every other episode that takes place, one after another. There may be anywhere from twelve to thirty-five such events in each of your days. We are going to ask that you introduce a 30- to 50-second prelude before each event. When you wake up, before you go to sleep, and everything that occurs in between should be set up and preceded by a powerful immersion into a fascinating rhythm, seiki movement, tonal alignment, and the sacred emotion from a song, all rapidly blended together to form and turn the mystical prayer wheel. Add your prayer line and turn it into the moving circle or wheel of prayer that turns your world around.

Yellowtail, the revered Crow medicine man, advised: "Pray continuously throughout each day." This is practically fulfilled by repeatedly conducting the ecstatic prelude, regarding it as the cooking of prayer that keeps you simmering inside. Doing this ensures that all the spiritual ingredients for cooking are blended and poured into each event of your life. The whole of you should remain inside prayer and every cell of your body should be involved. Live inside the bookends of prayer. Like Gandhi, appreciate how "prayer is the key of the morning and the bolt of the evening." It should also be everything in between. "Prayer is where the action is," to quote John Wesley. Its rhythm, tone, movement, and emotion are what make prayer strong, hot, and holy, so never forget to show up with all the ingredients. Never miss a beat when it comes to your time with divinity. As Paul advised in I Thessalonians 5: 16–18, "Rejoice always, pray without ceasing, in everything give thanks; for this is the will of God."

Start the ecstatic prelude with a quick shaking motion that is immediately followed by voicing a fascinating rhythmic beat, either internally or externally. Within 10 seconds, seamlessly move on to voicing three tones (internally or externally) to which you will tune your body through corresponding movement. Your spontaneous seiki movement should have already kicked into motion. After tuning, quickly move to recalling any musical line of a sacred song that delivers you a drop or more of emotion to help mix all of these ingredients together. In a matter of seconds, you will have gathered and blended the ingredients and then formed the mystical prayer wheel that is ready for you to throw in a few words of a hallowed prayer line. Now turn the wheel several times with all you've got. Make it really cook. Its divine expansion and spiritual heat are then ready to embrace and host the next episode your life, no matter its assumed earthly importance.

The Sacred Ecstatics Alphabet Prayer

You are invited to say the alphabet in a new spiritual way, making each letter evoke a special prayer moment. This ecstatic means of praying starts with the letter A, repeatedly sung out loud while continuously changing the pitch, duration, tremolo, and rhythmic pulse. Make sure you infuse the toned alphabet letter with sacred emotion and make the sound so intensely felt that it spontaneously triggers your body to move. Don't force your body to move by sheer intention or conscious will power. Vary the quality and intensity of your tone until it brings an involuntary body response.

Your goal is to keep voicing the letter *A* and moving with it until a hallowed word or brief sacred phrase unexpectedly pops into your mind. Once it does, tone the word or phrase one time or a few times, depending on how you feel. Don't consciously produce any of the words, but wait for them to ride in on your rhythm and tone, maintaining a "thy will be done" attitude. Your responsibility is to change the repeating tone; moving it across high, midrange, and low frequencies; changing its duration from long to short; adjusting its vibrational quality; and altering its rhythmic pulse to include any kind of beat, but especially welcoming rhythms that are more fascinating than monotonous. Sometimes you might hold the tone for a long time as if inspired by Tibetan throat singers, while at other times you might create a burst of successive, syncopated, staccato sounds like a jazz scat singer. Pour your sacred emotion into the tone and keep altering the expression of each alphabet letter until a word or phrase you feel is sacred arrives outside any mental contriving. It might be "amen," "almighty," "altar," "amazing grace," "at the cross," "anoint," "accept," "align," or any other hallowed name, metaphor, or formulation.

As you change how you tonally and rhythmically express a single alphabet letter, close your eyes and imagine the performance of a dancer within who looks exactly like you and is dancing beautifully to your sound. With your mind's inner vision, see yourself masterfully and creatively dancing to the alphabet prayer you are performing. You can even imagine being an extraordinary ballet master able to do what no other human being has ever done before. For instance, perform an unbelievable pirouette, spinning and whirling at such a speed that you launch into space. Or imagine holding a magical Mary Poppins-like umbrella that opens and gently lifts you above the floor where you hover and make tremendous gymnastic maneuvers. Let the crescendo of a tone pop the umbrella open and then glide, flip, and twirl in the air as inspired by the subsequent tones. Internally explore all kinds of impossible dance movements while you are toning each letter. Any kind of dance may be imagined from recognized genres to freeform improvisation. Keep at bay any other chanting habits or prayer routines that might interfere, hold back, or cool off your one-of-a-kind, freshly improvised alphabet prayer.

Keep externally toning and internally dancing a particular letter until a word arrives that carries divine resonance. Once a hallowed word arrives, tone it either once or a few times and then move on to the next letter of the alphabet. Before advancing, make sure the word or phrase actually brought a sacred emotional uplift. Let each hallowed word arrive in God's time and do not resist, modify, or subjugate its divine delivery. Always limit yourself to working with only a single alphabet letter at a time and abandon any personal concern over your ability to creatively produce words. This means of prayer sets you free from having to either memorize or improvise—that job is given to the divine linguist. You only need to be more like a child, ready and able to recite the alphabet one letter at a time.

Forgo all words in favor of a single letter that serves as bait to attract God's attention and as the target for a divinely delivered word. You are trying to catch a hallowed word from the holiest depth of the vastest sea. During this process your mind should only allow room for these prescriptive thoughts that mobilize specified action: (1) vary your expression of one alphabet letter; (2) hear and feel it build sufficient emotional intensity to inspire effortless body movement; (3) imagine and visualize an internal dancer that moves in synch with the external sound, and (4) wait for God to bring a holy word or phrase that begins with the particular letter at hand. Your letter represents the incomplete partiality of you that is in need of being made a whole and holy word.

As the experienced intensity of your tone calls your body to respond with spontaneous movement, and the changes of pitch, duration, tremolo, and rhythm help open and clear the sacred pipeline, God is inspired to make a house call and administer the words. In this way, each letter becomes a prayer and each prayer becomes part of an ongoing prayer string that holds a sequence of prayers. Go as far along the alphabet with this prayer string as you can, allowing you to build a stronger rope to God. You will recognize that weaving a prayer string is another form of turning the mystical wheel.

When you can naturally execute this version of the Sacred Ecstatics Alphabet Prayer, learn to do it in reverse. Now you externally move your body while you internally make the tones of each letter. Go for the impossible sounds and rhythms that can only occur in your wildest imagination. Sing it or play it on an instrument, doing so with such a volume that you imagine it can be heard around the world. Externally move in a way that is in synch with the changing tones and rhythms of each letter sung inside of you until a hallowed word or phrase arrives as before. Express the alphabet with more of you, from both the inside and the outside, as a means of learning how to effectively gather and blend the ecstatic ingredients of prayer. Notice how this ecstatic way of praying the alphabet functions as a *sacred word catcher* that spontaneously formulates and articulates prayers and builds prayers within prayers. Consider this practice to be a well-engineered way of learning the ABCs of ecstatic praying. Always remember that it is the changing of First Creation that makes a prayer cook — changing everything from a tone's quality and rhythmic pulse to changing the body's movements, as well as catching the changing words that show up to ride the prayer wheel in all of its changing forms. As you master these ABCs you are made better able to perform the "1, 2, 3" of the three-step Sacred Ecstatics recipe.

Morten's Prayer Bomb

This experimental form of praying is another way of performing the prelude. It spreads one single prayer throughout your whole day. We developed it for Morten Østbye, one of our mentorship graduates who teaches Sacred Ecstatics in Norway. He once expressed a desire to pray more often throughout each day. "Morten's prayer bomb" is a form of praying that is based on the idea that the intensity of your prayer is more important that its duration. Here, you voice one-word prayers from the time you wake up in the morning until you retire at night. Over the course of the day all the words combine to comprise a whole one-sentence prayer.

When you arise, immediately pray one word such as "Thy!" Then at lunch you offer the next one-word prayer: "Will!" At dinner you pray "Be!" And finally, at bedtime you finish with the final one-word prayer: "Done!" This enables you to live inside one single prayer line that is stretched across your waking day. Don't think about doing this; try it out and discover what happens. Experiment with it and truly experience it with your whole being rather than merely contemplate or ponder its meaning.

It is critically important that each single-word prayer is expressed as an ecstatic explosion — a prayer bomb. Gather the cooking ingredients quickly and stir them up as if you are preparing spiritual nitroglycerin, rocket fuel, or any highly ignitable and explosive substance. Pack it with as much sacred emotion as you can until it can't be held back any longer. Like launching a rocket or igniting dynamite, hit the switch and let it rip at full force. Your one word of prayer should explode and launch itself out of you, feeling like it is sent through the whole cosmos.

"Thy!!!" There it goes, past the clouds, the sky, the sun, the solar system, going all the way to God's target. The power of this prayer bomb should leave you reverberating with a sacred vibration for hours. If done with full spiritual force, you will find that you still hear it inside your head and feel all the concentrated emotion that exploded and launched it. Before you know it, time passes by and the next prayer bomb is ready to be launched at noon: "Will!!!" Now you start wonder if something *will* really happen. Two reverberations are rippling through you: one from your wake up prayer bomb and the other from your noon prayer bomb. Two sacred vibrations mingle and combine to further empower the inner tingle.

You are praying in a way likely never done before and its power can start a chain reaction, perhaps forming a chain or incredibly strong rope to God. At dinner, you are more prepared to eat holy bread when you explode and launch "Be!!!" Your body has given birth to a trinity of three powerful prayer vibes circulating inside you, enough to make a Pythagorean triangle that rings the tone of a sacred song. As you ring inside, God's telephone is picked up. "Hello!!" Tell God what you want. Do it! Say it! You are on fire so use the connected wire. By the time you lie down to go to sleep, all four of the prayer directions are ready to meet and cross one another, with all their distinctions, differentiations, juxtapositions, relationships, harmonies, cacophonies, contraries, unities, and trembling power. The prayer is soon done: "Done!!!" It is done: the prayer is done, you are cooked well done, and into the nighttime sleep you go, resonating with prayer that has aligned and attuned you to be caught by the four-cornered cross, the trinity, the holy duo of parent and offspring, and the singular source of creation from above.

As a bonus prayer bomb experiment, follow Morten's prescription and set your alarm every night for three o'clock in the morning. Wake up and pray with all your heart and soul either out loud or internally for 60 seconds straight. Make sure you include all the ingredients and choose a simple prayer line, preferably the one you spread throughout the day. Detonate this 60-second prayer bomb with enough spiritual power to reverberate throughout the universe. Imagine a bomb of divine love exploding with enough force to knock the books off the shelves in the Hall of Records, vibrate the strings of the heavenly harps, and make the cherubs jump. For one solid minute of eternity, express your longing to be near God with every fiber of your being. Experience how a prayer bomb unleashes a holy pierce, ecstatic shock, and fountain of joy that opens, awakens, and fills hearts with divine love.

Cook without Ceasing

The ecstatic prelude teaches you to place your everyday activities in the background and bring prayer to the foreground. Make prayer the main act and realize that intensity of emotion rather than density of abstraction fires up your relationship with God. Shoot your prayers like an archer releasing a bow. Ignite them like they are dynamite. We once drove by a rural church in Mississippi that was called Church of Holy Ghost Dynamite! Think of that place when you explode a prayer in your home space. Launch a prayer like a bottle rocket or better, a spiritually manned, ecstatically equipped flight to the outer edge of the galaxy. Pray so hard and so intensely that you think you might explode. But make sure all the ingredients are within and that all your body is trembling. Hopefully, you will explode and launch the birth of your spiritual being that will journey into the spiritual universe. We have been launched by prayer and sent in vision to explore what is beyond the earth, sun, and stars. So, too, have others who have been powerfully charged and discharged by prayer. Osumi Sensei was spiritually shot inside her own body to mystically learn anatomy. Preachers, teachers, prophets, and healers have been prayer-propelled to classrooms where they were taught, equipped, and made ready for a special mission. If you want to go to heaven in this lifetime, then know that prayer is required for the ecstatic flight.

Pray so tenderly that it generates spiritual nuclear energy. Pray to implode the self and explode a dispersion of holiness. Pray with wonder and pray with thunder, making a mysterious sound within that can spark seismic activity, earthquakes, typhoons, hurricanes, floods, tidal waves, tsunamis, wildfires, avalanches, and parting of the seas, all of the holiest kind. However you pray, concentrate it so it can burst into a holy fireworks show and intersperse it so it stretches across time and space. Pray in the least amount of time in order to launch a rocket climb. Pray like there is no tomorrow yet with expression that is sweet, soft, and tender. Make morning, noon, and bedtime your whole eternity, your whole life. Make your prayer a good time to die and a good time to be reborn.

As you become better at creating ecstatically powerful preludes and prayer bombs, the aligning, tuning, and cooking they offer will empower and sanctify the activities that follow. At the end of the day you will have walked from one prelude to another, each a step up the rope. With these preludes, you infuse the holy force of creation into every moment of your everyday, turning your whole life into a revitalizing and improvising performance rather than the same old memorized routine. Don't forget to prelude, for it shapes both how you pray and how you get through the day on the wings of prayer.

Ecstatic Spiritual Traveling

The initial Sacred Ecstatics practices involve gathering the specific ingredients required for spiritual cooking. Each ingredient is held inside a back-and-forth interaction and can serve as either the call or the response—your body either calls or responds with spontaneous movement, vocalized tones, or rhythmic beats, all infused with sacred emotion. These ingredients must be further blended and amplified in the next phase to create and turn a wheel—the mystical wheel of prayer. Here is found the circular dynamic for constructing sacred ground—expanding the room and striking a match. Once the spiritual fire is burning strongly, the wheel transforms again and becomes a means of mystical transportation. But before this can occur, you must work the wheel of prayer. In other words, prayer is your ticket to ride and without it you are unable to go on any real spiritual journey. Ezekiel regarded the mystical wheel as a "chariot," though it can be any First Creation form, whether a ship, plane, car, bus, horse, or mule, to mention a few. As old cooked parishioners say, "Get on board!"

"Spiritual travel" takes place when your body steps into the rhythms, movements, songs, emotion, and ways of ecstatic devotion and celebration associated with a geographical site's local spiritual tradition. Among the Spiritual Baptists in St.

Vincent, people may dream a certain locale, including Africa, China, India, and other places. In the vision they receive the sounds, songs, or movements associated with that destination. Later during a worship service, if a spiritual leader begins singing the song or making the movement or instrumental sounds received in the vision, it is regarded as taking a spiritual journey to that place. Others are invited to hop on board and travel with them by joining in with the same kind of expression. Similarly in the Kalahari, a n/om-kxao who has climbed the rope to God in spiritual vision may later physically enact that climb in the dance, which is regarded as taking the whole community on a journey up the rope to God. Spiritual travel, whether in St. Vincent, the Kalahari, or at a Sacred Ecstatics intensive, is not preplanned but arises spontaneously once the mystical wheel is turning with enough heat and momentum to take everyone on a ride.

In this section we give you a glimpse of the mystical spirit lands, particular travel destinations where the spiritual temperature is extremely hot. In the African American sanctified church you find the gift of a singing heart that helps you fly away to glory. Next, the Caribbean offers an ecstatic form of expression largely unfamiliar to our time — the spirited embodiment of ecstatic rhythm and musical sounds called 'doption that turns you into a drum or musical instrument. Moving on to the Kalahari, you find the hottest ecstatic expression in the Bushman ways of healing and transmission of the sacred vibration. There you are a hunter of n/om with mystical arrows and spears. Finally, we mention other possible destinations for spiritual traveling, some familiar and others yet to be discovered.

Instructions for Experiencing Each Ecstatic Locale

In addition to listening to our ecstatic travel tracks, we invite you to play audio and video recordings of gospel music, 'doption, and the Kalahari that we provide from our collection.[r] Let the conductors in the recordings lead you on a journey by tuning into how people embody the ingredients, blend them, and turn the mystical wheel. When you begin, refer to our instructions in Part One for engaging your inner body. The initial goal is to feel and absorb the sacred emotion in their expression rather than be in a hurry to move, clap, shout, or sing along. Don't do the latter until you have been sufficiently warmed inside. Allow your inner body to catch the emotion, hear the music, mirror the movement, and pulse the rhythmic beat. Once you reach sufficient inner resonance, your external performance will spring forth naturally when it is time. Don't force it. You must own the feeling for ecstatic expression before it can resonate the strings of your body instrument.

When it comes to gospel songs, primarily attend and be responsive to the soulful rhythms and tonal embellishment rather than only focus on the lyrics. Go for the "ecstatics" rather than the "semantics." Only later, when your body instrument is well tuned and able to smoothly move in synch with this kind of music, can your heart be sufficiently lifted for a hymn's lyrics to appropriately enter your mind, charge your body, and feed your soul. Moving with a sanctified melody, harmony, and rhythm helps the lyrics become holy bread, ecstatic cake, divine manna, and spiritual nourishment. Stated differently, you and the words both need to be sufficiently cooked before you can partake in a spiritual meal. Only then can you receive the sacred vibration that scripture was designed to convey rather than experience the spiritual indigestion that interpretation alone often brings.

---

[r] Although you can find many videos of African American gospel, Spiritual Baptists (Shakers), and the Kalahari healing dance on the Internet, not all recordings represent potent, cooked expression. Fortunately, one can still find audio and video recordings of traditional gospel on the Internet if you know what to look for. Videos of strong 'doption or authentic Kalahari healing dances are virtually nonexistent on the Internet, and the ones we provide to our mentorship students via our YouTube channel were shot during Brad's visits to St. Vincent and the Kalahari.

While observing a sanctified performance of song, 'doption, or a Kalahari healing dance, make sure that you clap, move, and sing along in the way that is shown on the videos (again, first doing so with your inner body until you catch the vibe enough to recreate it externally). Allow spiritually cooked folks to teach you their way of ecstatic expression. That's why you are visiting a spiritual locale—to learn from others. Again, this kind of spiritual travel is not about daydreaming that you are having an out-of-body experience or sending your soul to another dimension. It is about catching and absorbing the feeling for the movements, tones, melodies, harmonies, rhythms, and sacred emotion of people who are spiritually cooking. This lays the right tracks for your continued ecstatic development. The whole purpose of spiritual engineering is to teach you the skills that have been long proven to nurture sacred ecstasy: blending the primary ingredients and turning the mystical wheel. Tuning into the cooked expression of others will help grow your spiritual engineering chops.

The emergence of the whole body instrument comes to life through (1) sanctified singing; (2) embodied rhythm and sound making; and (3) spontaneous body movement that triggers, amplifies, and sustains trembling, quaking, and shaking vibration. In terms of spiritual engineering, your body learns to serve as a transducer and resonator of acoustic vibration that is aligned with somatic mechanical vibration. For example, a vibratory body movement can inspire you to make a sound that emits an ecstatic vibration, and this pulsing tone further inspires more movement. This is the body keyboard in action that Charles Henry envisioned, with its acoustic and tactile vibrations aligned and mutually influencing one another. More than anything else, this kind of tone and movement (music and dance) performance awakens the sacred emotion that ignites a fire in your bones. As the fire moves through your entire spiritual circulatory system, you are further tuned, aligned, and regulated as a divine instrument whose form may change from a singing voice to a drumming percussion instrument to a grand piano concert (and other variations), ready to be masterfully played by higher hands. The shift from vocal performance to making other instrumental sounds takes place in the spiritual locale of the Caribbean, something we will discuss later.

As always, if you don't feel enough sacred emotion and movement to awaken your external expression, then back up and gather more cooking ingredients and restart blending the mystical wheel. It won't help to force sanctified singing, rhythm and sound making, or vibratory movement because you can't will it. "Sanctified" means that divine will has taken over your expression. The mystical wheel must gather enough momentum to spontaneously turn in order for sanctified singing and other cooked expression to naturally arise. Don't try enacting in the cold what can only take place in the heated big room—that's only a posture that blocks movement toward the vast green spiritual pasture. Again, only use willpower and disciplined action in the cold to initially get the wheel turning that takes you to the crossroads. Once you pass through the gate and find yourself on a moving mystical prayer wheel, give everything up and allow God's will to cook you well done. Do your part in the cold zone so the divine can do its part in the hot zone.

Your experience may change each time you travel to an ecstatic destination. Sometimes a particular song will instill so much spiritual power that it feels like you will be shot out of a cannon. On another day you may experience the same song differently—it might make you soft and tender, ready to weep rather than shout. There is no need to analyze or explain this changing phenomenon. Always arrive at every mystical locale as if it is your first time, every time. Hand over your body instrument to higher playing and conducting. All the experiential outcomes taking place in the big music room are chosen by God.

African American Sanctified Singers: The Singing Heart

The first stop in our spiritual itinerary is the experiential locale of an African American church that gives voice to sanctified singing. This music is extraordinarily saturated with the sacred vibration and its elevated emotion. Though other things of spiritual importance take place in the sanctified church, our main interest is to accentuate its most notable contribution: the conversion of a heated prayer into a cooked gospel song. Here the mystical prayer wheel may heat hallowed prayer words until an ecstatic threshold is reached where vocal expression shifts to melodic song. You transition from a prayer-chant to a prayer-song and this intensifies the sacred emotion in your heart. This kind of singing triggers further body vibration and shaking at a higher frequency and stronger amplitude.

Sanctified singing is the experience of being sung by God. "The Lord God uses your vocal organs, and words come out without your having anything to do with it." [69] Stuernagel describes this special kind of singing:

> The Spirit-filled believer will also be "making melody in the heart." He will have a singing heart. Not everybody can sing with the voice, but everybody can have a whole music-box deep down in the soul. Besides, the vocal song must cease at intervals, but the heavenly heart-song can go on forever. It is the new song of heaven wafted down to Earth which will continue through countless ages.[70]

Receiving the sacred vibration is indistinguishable from the installation of a music box in your soul and activation of a singing heart. When spiritually cooked, not only will you feel called to sing, you will also hear and feel music playing inside you day and night. Living an ecstatic or cooked spiritual life is living a new kind of musical life. Whatever happens to you, no matter how extreme the drama, you are held by the sacred rhythms and melodic tones that make you musically and spiritually whole. It is no surprise that the great composers from cultures around the world so deeply knew and profoundly heard that music was the aural bridge between heaven and earth. God is a singing God and a cooked prayer eventually becomes a singing prayer that is most pleasing to divine ears.

Even people who traditionally have an allergy to the names of Jesus or God are sometimes shocked to find they suddenly and unexpectedly relish these old cooked sacred songs because of their undeniable soulfulness. In the cold you might even think you are an agnostic or atheist but later, in the heat, find yourself rocked by the spirited vibe these songs contain. It matters little to us what you *think* beforehand about God, Jesus, Mary, or Ezekiel and his wheel. What matters most is that these songs, when heard inside the big room, are *felt* as powerful carriers of sacred emotion. This requires that your "heart rise," to use a Bushman phrase. Only then can the ecstatic power of these songs resonate within you.

We have found that the genre of sacred music traditionally performed in the African American church is arguably the spiritually hottest music on the planet. Something truly magical happened when the African way of holding and expressing the spirit doctored the old church hymns with n/om. Spiritual engineering enables us to now see that Africans were long familiar, perhaps from the beginning of humanity, with the need to gather the ingredients of spiritual cooking before launching a ceremony. With all the ingredients in hand and body, throwing a hymn into their blended mix gave birth to the sanctified singing of the church. Approach this kind of music as a powerful conveyor of sacred vibration and liberate yourself to absorb its rhythmic pulse, tone, somatic movement, and strong emotion. You might get lucky and feel the explosion of spiritual dynamite within!

Keep in mind that some of the strongest gospel songs are the slow tempo ones that are sung with the most passion. Don't assume that faster rhythms always bring a stronger sacred vibration. By the time you get to this ecstatically hot locale, you should recognize that it is primarily sacred emotion that amplifies the strongest vibrational current. Once you arrive through the church door, allow its songs to place you on an ecstatic God-driven magic carpet ride that lifts you to higher ground.

The Cooked Way of Learning to Sing and Play an Instrument.
When you are spiritually cooking in a gathering or inside a
vision, you may receive the gift of sanctified singing. You then
find yourself suddenly singing in an ecstatic, vibratory way,
even if you never sang before or don't believe you know how to
sing. Something will also be noticeably different about the
sound you now make—it will have more vibrational power and
emotional purity. This is one of the most surprising outcomes of
sacred ecstatic experience. Even more shocking are instances
when people find themselves suddenly able to play a musical
instrument. Though this is a very rare experience, it has
happened at the hottest sanctified church meetings.

For instance, during the Pentecostal movement that took
place at the Azusa Street Gospel Mission in Los Angeles during
the early 1900s, there were many reports of songs and music
spontaneously arising in the services. Consider this example
from Jennie Moore, a young African American woman:

> I sang under the power of the Spirit in many
> languages, the interpretation of both words and
> music I had never before heard, and in the home
> where the meeting was held, the Spirit led me to
> the piano, where I played and sang under
> inspiration, although I had not learned to play.[71]

Here is another account of divine musical intervention taking
place:

> While they were praying in regard to going to
> Africa, the oldest daughter, Bessie, went and sat
> down to the piano, and soon called to her mother
> to bring a pencil and paper, that the Lord was
> giving her a song.[72]

One of the lead vocalists of a well-known African American
singing group from Minneapolis that won a Grammy Award
told Brad an equally amazing story. When she was young, she

dreamed of a large keyboard in the sky. She saw Jesus in the clouds and he invited her to skip along the keys while holding a song in her heart. To her surprise, she found that she could play the piano by ear the very next morning though she had received no earthly training.

These stories suggest that there is a unique and seldom discussed way of learning, acquiring a skill, or finding a talent that is brought forth under ecstatic conditions. Whether under the influence of a divinely inspired visionary dream or the sacred ecstasy felt while fully awake, it is possible to be "rewired" or transformed to do something you previously were unable to accomplish. This type of spiritual learning takes place through sacred emotional absorption and installation of its vibration. It is the classic way that ecstatic mystics and shamans acquired their art and craft. Such higher learning usually occurs in the visionary spiritual classrooms where you are able to experience new ways of musical expression that include learning how to play a musical instrument. Or it may happen in the heat of an old-fashioned church meeting where ecstatic miracles abound.

Our book, *Sacred Ecstatics*, includes a testimony that Zora Neale Hurston collected from a parishioner in Beaufort, South Carolina, who received the gift of a musical instrument:

> I begin to call Jesus too, and that's how I got the Holy Ghost. I wasn't calling Jesus ten minutes before I was gone away in the spirit. I went to the east under beautiful shade trees and the green was like a carpet on the ground. There was a band of people. They all had different musical instruments. . . . I stood outside the ring. The director, he was a man marching time, giving the measures to the music. He just handed me a box (guitar) and didn't stop beating time. I played it. (Ecstasy — "Glory, sweet! Better felt than told! Glory!") I just went to play and went to laughing. Came through in the holiness, laughing, and

shouting in the bed. That was the glorious time of
my life. That was the day![73]

One night Brad dreamed that he was taken to an old country
black church, a small wooden shanty somewhere in the United
States. There a morning service was in full steam. The preacher
was old, dressed in a white suit, and he walked with a cane as
he spoke. He came up to Brad and prayed as if possessed by
God. As the old preacher worked himself into further spiritual
fervor and ecstasy, he lifted his cane toward Brad and its tip
touched the tip of every finger on both of Brad's hands, one at a
time. The congregation was shouting and carrying on as the
preacher did this. The whole scene was electrifying and other
worldly. Brad then walked to an upright piano in the dream and
started to play and sing gospel songs he had never heard before.
They were all composed on the spot, one after the other. The
service was on fire beyond description. The old preacher and his
cane had sanctified and anointed Brad's fingers to bring down
sacred songs. Brad woke up and continued receiving the songs
for what seemed over an hour until he fell asleep again.

Playing a musical instrument in the spirit feels the same as
expressing your singing heart, the voice of your soul's music
box. Your heart sings the piano, the drums, the horns, the strings, or
whatever instrumental form passes through your hands in First
Creation. There is nothing but heart singing in heaven.

Hillary spontaneously and powerfully received the gift of
sanctified singing during a Sacred Ecstatics intensive in Brazil.[s]
She had never sung in public before, and the vibration became
so strong inside her that she could hardly hold the microphone.
Once she began singing she couldn't stop, and she sang the
entire day and on into the evening. In the big room, and this
includes the smallest country praise house or a humble hotel
conference room in Brazil, anything musically magical can
happen. Rejoice for you were made to be an instrument of praise

---

[s] We share the full report of Hillary's experience in our book, *Sacred Ecstatics: The Recipe for Setting Your Soul on Fire.*

for the Lord. Go to sleep singing to better assure that heaven's bells are ringing for your arrival to the visionary classrooms.

When you are spiritually cooked enough, you automatically become an instrument for the musical performance of sacred song. Here "the only artist singing is the Holy Ghost," as a choir director once told us. An old spiritual reminds us that a spiritual life is about having a song:

> I got a song, you got a song,
> All God's children got a song.
> When I get to heaven I'm gonna sing-a my song.
> I'm gonna sing all over God's heaven!

If you want to feel what a sacred song can do for you, head to the sanctified singing of an old-school African American church. Make sure you bring all the cooking ingredients that enable you to be moved by the songs in the deepest way. Remember that it is the prayer of the wheel now turned by God that is singing and its motion sweeps you away on a mighty ride.

St. Vincent Shakers: The Body Drum and Musical Instruments of 'Doption

The St. Vincent Shakers (also called Spiritual Baptists) practice a syncretic mix of Christian and African spiritual traditions. They represent one of the most active ecstatic cultures in the world, and access to spiritual and healing knowledge is open to all of its practitioners. St. Vincent is one of the Windward Islands, located 190 miles north of Trinidad and 100 miles south of Barbados. It is lush with vegetation and contains a volcano, Mt. Soufrière, whose previous eruptions have caused extensive damage and loss of life. Unlike the mix of African religion and Catholicism that characterized the formation of Santería in Cuba, Candomblé in Brazil, and Vodou in Haiti, Shakerism in the Caribbean island of St. Vincent was a blend of African traditions with the Protestant church, particularly the Methodist church.

In the earliest appearances of the Shakers, the practice was rather wild, with shaking bodies and loud shouting. It caused such a commotion that it frightened a governor's horse, causing the man to fall to the ground. Governor Gideon Murray then immediately ordered the faith illegal. In 1912, an ordinance was passed "to render illegal the practice of 'Shakerism' as indulged in the colony of St. Vincent," stating that "a certain ignorant section of the inhabitants" was gathering and carrying on with practices "which tend to exercise a pernicious and demoralizing effect on said inhabitants."[74] In a speech made by the colonial administrator who advocated the ordinance, he described shaking as a "relic of barbarism."

Persecution had actually begun with the raiding and destruction of the early Methodist ministers' homes, and many years later, those found shaking were sent to prison. The ordinance was not repealed until 1965. In the early days, they and their tradition were called everything from Clap Hands to barefoot religion, candlelight religion, Believers, the Penitent, and Tieheads (because of the bands they wrap around their heads), while a few were named Jumpers. In spite of constant persecution and lack of respect, the Shakers physically survived and spiritually thrived. Their praise houses are spread throughout the island and meetings, often lasting four to five hours, are held regularly. The shaking religion was also developed in Trinidad, where practitioners were originally called Shouters. Other Caribbean groups that closely resemble their practice are the Revivalists of Jamaica and the Jordanites of Guyana.

Their ceremonial gatherings begin with a time for purification, spiritually cleaning the praise house to be free of any unwelcome spirits. They ring bells, pray, sing, and sprinkle water in every corner and entrance of the house. This part of the liturgy is a cool period. After the space feels appropriately prepared, the songs will change as the Holy Ghost is invited into the church. Things immediately become spiritually hot enough for shaking and quaking to take place. Grunts, shouts, hand clapping, drumming, and speaking in tongues, among other ecstatic forms of expression typically occur.

In the beginning of spiritual cooking, a Shaker makes connection with the Holy Ghost so it can do its work. This is when the body feels somewhat out of control as the transition is made to being filled with the spirit. Body movements and sounds are more likely to appear random and chaotic with spontaneous jerks, unexpected shouts, sobs, hisses, and other unintelligible sounds. The next phase of heating up takes place when the spirit moves into the body and better establishes control so it can now provide deeper ecstatic experience. Body movements and sounds become more rhythmically organized and brought in synch with the group. At this time, a strong form of overbreathing may take place where the person alternately sucks and releases air with a grunting sound. This is called 'doption and it marks the beginning of heightened spiritual cooking.

'Doption and Becoming a Drum. Rather than using the drums, as in the Vodou or Shango religions, the Shakers usually "use their voices to produce drum sounds that are sometimes classified into seven different forms and rhythms known as 'doption."[75] This is one of the greatest spiritual gifts you can receive and it refers to being "adopted" by the spirit. Called trumping or groaning in Jamaican Revival, it pairs rhythmic sound and movement in a powerful way. Shakers have called this guttural sound "the Song of God in man."[76] The 'doption comes up from energy in the belly and sounds like a drum beating from the chest. It may also take a musical form of tone and sound like a trumpet coming from the throat.

'Doption offers an ecstatic ride on concentrated waves of energy. When strong shaking arrives, the Shakers suggest that you should "work it out," "jump spirit," "work penitent," or "work the spirit" and transfer the spiritual power associated with shaking into 'doption. When this happens you still shake, but it becomes concentrated in the belly and chest. 'Doption is the principal way the original Shakers communicate with spirit. They justify its Christian authority by referring to Romans 8:15 and 22, which refer to the whole of creation groaning, waiting for the adoption of the spirit. Speaking of 'doption, Mother Sandy explains:

> If you go deep into the spirit you can get the experience of 'doption. It hits you in the belly, tightens you, and pumps your belly up and down. Move when the spirit adopts you. Walk it out. Stomp your feet, swing your arms, and let the sound come out. It will sound like a drum beating inside your chest. 'Doption can show you something. It can bring you a vision or even take you on a spiritual journey.[77]

When the 'doption first brings an extreme tightness in one's belly, it's tempting to be worried and concerned. Mother Ralph advises, "When you feel it, don't get scared. Don't hold your belly and sit down. Stand up and let your feet stomp the ground. You must walk it out, stamp it out in a dance for the Lord."[78] Until you are spiritually gifted with 'doption—something that is installed in the ecstatic fire of vision or in the spirited interaction with an anointed transmitter—don't try faking it. When you imitate a more advanced spiritual gift, you only learn habits that exterminate the possibility for authentic reception. When you watch or listen to a recording of 'doption, your goal is to absorb its powerful sacred emotion. All ecstatic expression in the big room requires making the shift to spontaneity and involuntary control on your part, inspired by surrendering to higher control. Again, you get there by first turning and then riding the mystical prayer wheel.

Mother Samuel speaks of strong 'doption as what happens "when the spirit gets into your body." In one of her spiritual journeys, she came to a fork in the road, where

> [a] spirit was standing at the middle of the two roads and I asked where 'doption came from. He pointed to the ground and the Earth began to shake. He showed me that the stomping of the feet

and the shaking of the Earth sent a pumping spiritual energy into the belly. That energy is then pumped up the body, with percussive sounds coming from the mouth. It was so powerful that I went into a top number one 'doption right there.[79]

Though elder Shakers believe that 'doption originally comes from Africa, in the spiritual classrooms it is taught in Zion, a place synonymous with Jerusalem, regarded as their most important locale. The original 'doption is also called "number one 'doption," "'doption number one," "one-foot 'doption," or "working the pump." It evokes the strongest expression of this kind of ecstatic performance. Some scholars hypothesize that during the time when enslaved Africans were prohibited from making drums and instruments, they discovered how to have their bodies make similar sounds. It is equally possible that it was the other way around — the body drum may have preceded the later development of percussion instruments that imitated the sounds and beats of 'doption.

Along this line of thought, Bishop Magna Atherly proposed that 'doption was brought from Africa and is a kind of "groaning in the spirit."[80] This groaning made the slaves strong enough to endure the punishments of a cruel slaveholder. "When the slave master met them groaning, they would beat them with a whip, but the power of God was so strong that the whip would fall to the ground." Atherly also reported an account about a slave master whose son became extremely ill. When his wife asked one of the slaves to use his spiritual power to heal, the slave reportedly "went down in a prayer and groaned," and then went out to procure a medicinal plant that provided a cure.[81]

The oldest Shakers who Brad met told him that there was only number one 'doption in earlier days and that "it was all we needed." However, as other spiritual classrooms and their locales were visited in vision, the sounds, rhythms, and movements of 'doption were altered to better fit and represent each place. A unique 'doption arrived for China, for India, and for every other place found in their expanded spiritual journeying.

Most of today's Shakers believe 'doption isn't as strong as it used to be. In the origin of their faith, 'doption would bring immediate spiritual gifts and instantly transform the person performing it. Later it became more of a purposefully orchestrated way of making socially learned rhythms and sounds. For it to be anointed and spiritually authenticated, however, it must be received in a vision, especially one taking place in their most important ritual, called "mourning" or "taking a spiritual journey," "a pilgrim journey," or "going to the secret room." There the spiritual gift of 'doption is either transferred to an initiate by an elder who has been appointed and anointed to do so, or it takes place inside a spiritually cooked dream.

Spiritually Receiving a Musical Instrument. Brad once dreamed that we were both with an elder master teacher in a room filled with musical instruments. Many of the instruments were unfamiliar. Brad was handed the gift of a musical instrument, a horn about one meter long. The bell of it was quite large and appeared like the top of the old metal Japanese lanterns Osumi Sensei had in her garden. The horn was made of a silver-like substance whose finish was flat rather than polished. We assumed the instrument was supposed to be blown like a trumpet.

> To our surprise we were shown how to rest the horn on our extended left arm and play it with a mallet, doing so like an African marimba. After I was given a mallet, I started to play the instrument automatically, making a series of triplet notes, each on different areas of the horn-marimba. Every place I tapped had a different tone. What was unusual is that it made the sound that comes from blowing a brass horn though I

was tapping it with a mallet. We then discovered that by simply imagining the tone, the instrument would sound. Hillary leaned over to place her ear near the end of the horn so she could more fully absorb its sound. I made sure that the tone wasn't too loud because I didn't want to hurt her eardrum. I played a low note for Hillary and its vibration went through both our bodies. We were amazed at the vibrational qualities of this spiritual musical instrument. With fullest sincerity we prayed for everyone in our mentorship class, playing a series of percussive tones, loud enough in the dream to be heard around the globe.

After the dream our research revealed that the shape of the visionary instrument has been called "Torricelli's trumpet" or *hyperbolicum acutum,* a geometric surface that has infinite surface area but finite volume. This object is something that is impossible to physically construct and is regarded by mathematicians as the perfect imaginary musical instrument. It is also known as Gabriel's horn, angelically used to announce that the divine is ready to communicate, ready to answer a call. Pythagoras brought humankind the geometric principles regarding the material world, but Torricelli's trumpet, "with its mind-bending combination of infinite and finite dimensions . . . describes an interpenetration of the ideal and the material, and invites us to imagine a music at the intersection of the impossible and the real."[82] The horn dream illustrates how you may even receive an impossible musical instrument in vision, a gift that provides a mystical means of revealing how music can bridge heaven and earth.

This otherworldly horn is similar to the horn that is received in visions of the St. Vincent Shakers. Consider this account by Mother Ollivierre:

On another journey [spiritual vision], I found myself walking down an ocean beach. I saw a man with hair from his eyebrows covering his whole face. I was scared and ran away. The pointer told me to go back and find that man. I went back and received a musical instrument, a horn that was buried under the sand. The man with the hair over his face taught me how to play it.[83]

After you receive this kind of gift, you find that whenever you get spiritually heated the sound may come through you while in 'doption. You make hornlike sounds that provide a tonal rhythmic accompaniment to the singing in a worship service. The spiritual horn of plenty also can send a prayer to heaven, doing so with the right tonal arrow and sonic release that hits the musical target. The same is true for all sweetly sounded prayers that convey the aural sincerity that pleases God's heavenly ear and, in turn, removes all your earthly fear.

Just as some people receive a horn, others receive a drum. Here is the late Mother Samuel's account:

I remember my first [visionary] journey—although I was praying with my eyes covered with bands, I saw the whole place lit up with light. Then my spirit began travelling to places I hadn't even learned about. And in these places, I spoke to people I had never met. I first traveled to Africa and heard the drums. Afterwards, I found I could beat the drums in spirit, though normally I couldn't beat them. When I talk with spirit I can beat the drum.[84]

You are a one-of-a-kind musical instrument that God made to communicate in a special holy manner. You do not need to sound like a perfect horn or drum; you only need to sincerely wish to sing or make a pleasing tone for God and the needed sound will come. Its vibration will travel upward and your call will be transmitted, received, and answered through the musical hotline.

The morning after receiving the horn in vision, we received an email from a student, Amy Priest:

Dear Hillary and Brad,

I want to share a dream I had last night. I dreamed that I was given a violin bow and I started playing it on my left forearm, as there was no violin present. It still sounded like a violin. The song that I played was "Twinkle, Twinkle, Little Star". I was in childish awe that I knew how to play it. And when I woke up, it felt like somehow I had been branded by the bow where I had played.

We responded with celebration and instruction:

Dear Amy,

This is wonderful news! You received a mystical violin as a special spiritual gift. You can now use it when you pray. Imagine that you are playing and hearing it as you did in the dream. Pray with it, allowing the musical sounds to voice the words of your prayer. Congratulations! You are truly blessed with this gift.

When you receive a musical instrument in a spiritual classroom, something that is mystically familiar to the Shakers of St. Vincent, it can spiritually empower all of your spiritual life from prayer to song and all other forms of divine communication. It also enables you to embody that form of musical instrument in order to make a joyful sound for God. Don't forget that your inner singing voice can make the sound of any instrument ever heard and even those never heard before. The more musically inspired and equipped you are, the better you are able to fulfill divine communication and communion. Trust the music that will carry you from fear to peace, transform suffering into joy, and transport you from mundane blah to supreme awe!

Playing a Duet with God. Brad also dreamed that we were at a performance hall where he performed a concert on a most unusual instrument—a piano with two keyboards. One was horizontal like a typical piano while the other was placed vertically at a 90-degree angle to the other keyboard, so the two formed an L-shape. In the dream, both keyboards were played at the same time. This visionary mystical instrument brought a teaching about the spiritual engineering setup required for being musically adopted by the spirit. The double keyboard enables you to simultaneously be in touch with heaven via the vertical keyboard and earth via the horizontal keyboard; the divine plays one keyboard as you play the other. When your body instrument is played as a double keyboard, you simultaneously receive and transmit sacred tone and rhythm that is heard and felt by others. You and God perform a duet on the keys of your body and the keys of heaven.

The vertical keyboard of your body piano is under God's musicianship and it transfers divine resonance directly and immediately to your body. As you hear, feel, and express sacred music, God does the same—each keyboard transduces and transfers its vibration to the other instrumentalist. You and God are in synch, playing both the vertical and horizontal keyboards of your body piano with mutually coordinated sanctification. 'Doption is one way this duet takes place—you and God are in a call and response of sound and movement with one another as you open your heart to let God's emotion come in. This is how you receive the highest bliss of sacred ecstasy.

This dual keyboard mystical piano can play, sing, drum, and make the sound of every percussion, string, reed, and brass instrument. It can even sound like a choir, symphony, brass band, string quartet, instrumental ensemble, or jazz trio. This sanctified performance sonically and tactilely touches the instruments of all involved—you, others, and the divine.

In St. Vincent, visionary visitation to a spiritual classroom may result in the installation of such a dual musical instrument, making 'doption possible—you and God adopt one another. You adopt God as a heavenly master musician and you are adopted as a divinely tuned instrument. In the spiritual fire you discover that you are mystical in order to become musical and musical to become mystical, a double ecstatic instrument for producing a sacred song, the supreme vehicle and main ventricle of the sacred heart that transmits the pulse of divine love.

'Doption Moves You along the Song Lines. The St. Vincent Shakers regard 'doption as the power that moves you along a song line. A spiritual journey requires a song that is also the passport, ticket, means of transport, and the navigational chart to the spiritual lands. The titles of some of the songs mention places like Zion, Canaan, the Valley, and Beulah Land. Each spiritual land has a song and anyone who has graduated from a particular spiritual classroom receives its music as well as its associated movement or dance for traveling.

Old-school shamanism also knew about the musical know-how required for healing and spiritual journeying. Truly cooked shamans needed a sacred song to connect the human body with spirit. They understood that healing takes place when the healer is adopted by the rhythm and melody of a sacred song previously gifted by spirit. As Ted Gioia wrote: "The shaman is the quintessential music healer, the prototype and antecedent of all later sonic therapists."[85] The German poet and philosopher Novalis (the pen name for Georg Philipp Friedrich Freiherr von Hardenberg) best summarizes this spiritual understanding of sacred music's power to heal: "Every disease is a musical problem. It's cure a musical solution."[86]

Music is also the truest measure of spiritual wealth. With many sacred songs you are prosperous, strong, and anointed; without a song you are poor. As a Navajo man once said, "'I am very poor. I do not own one song.'"[87] Old medicine people used to say when things heat up in a ceremony, "the songs are mounting."[88] Above all else, a medicine person lives by the axiom, "I sing; therefore I am strong." [89] Spiritual power, prosperity, and blessings arise with a prayer that becomes a song and everything else is secondary and usually sedentary.

The ecstatic singing, drumming, and instrumental playing of the musical heart and vibrational body provide a direct passage to holy transformational experience. Throw all your longing for God into a sacred song. Allow the tremors of your voice to shake your whole body free from whatever holds you back from musical, mystical ascent. In a matter of time, the sky will open and you will step inside the big room. Become a "song catcher" who is open to receive a singing heart and inner music box.

In the big room where spirit abounds, anything encountered can give you a song. A tree, a lark, a stone, a mango, an unseen voice, or another person's spirit can bring a tune of divine attunement. When you receive such a song, your body will tremble, quake, and shake when touched by its heightened emotion. Its sweet melody rhythmically sweeps away your psychological state and makes you spiritually weep with gratitude. A sacred song born and delivered in spiritual fire provides a line of direction that can take you traveling somewhere. It is also the ship that carries you and the key that opens the gate to a spiritual land's classroom. There, in the heat of the sacred fire, you are adopted by the holiest spirit and made an instrument for carrying out a divine mission.

The Kalahari Bushman Dancers: Somatic Vibrations that Pull and Transmit

The world's oldest living culture—that of the Kalahari Bushmen—holds the most enduring ecstatic know-how found anywhere. On their dance ground we find awareness and reverence of the ultimate importance of song as the highest gift from God that awakens the sacred vibration of n/om. Such a song unlocks the door to First Creation mystery. Without a song as your personal connection or rope to the divine, you remain spiritually asleep, unable to travel, and without access to the big room and its spiritual bounty. The Bushmen value a sacred song above all else and their performance of it is always freshly improvised with melodic and polyrhythmic embellishment to ensure its vitality. All the spiritual cooking ingredients of Sacred Ecstatics are found most fully activated in Bushman music and dance. These ecstatic roots remained alive and well in the global spreading of the African diaspora. The seeds of blues, jazz, and gospel were already sown in fertile African ground before musicians held brass horns, hollowed reeds, and gut strings of later instrumental forms.

What marks the Kalahari as different from ecstatic traditions elsewhere in Africa and throughout the diaspora, however, is its means of transmitting n/om, the Kalahari equivalent of the holy spirit and sacred vibration. A n/om-kxao can go past 'doption and shift another ecstatic gear to further elevate the spiritual temperature. This results in skin-to-skin contact with others, fostering a simultaneous experience of mechanical tactile vibration and acoustic vibration. A cooked Bushman uses vibratory touch for two main purposes: (1) to *pull* out a dirty "nail" of n/om that is presumed to be the cause of sickness, or (2) to *transmit* a clean nail of n/om to promote vitality. Recall that "nail," "thorn," "needle," and "arrow" are metaphors for the way n/om is experienced as something that can penetrate the human body. Only a cooked Bushman shares sacred vibration in this manner. Other people in the community participate by singing, clapping, and sometimes drumming, but do not put their hands on one another. As always, the n/om-kxao's ecstatic touching is not purposefully willed — it spontaneously happens like a pure seiki movement that is completely involuntary.

N/om can be transmitted through the acoustic vibrations of singing and shouting, as well as through the tactile vibration of touch. Skin-to-skin contact is an integral aspect of Bushman healing, and also one of the primary ways that n/om-kxaosi initiate other doctors and give each other nails of n/om. This kind of touch is largely absent from the African American and St. Vincent Shaker traditions that rely on singing, shouting, movement, cooked preaching, and other forms of vocal expression to wake up the holy spirit and help it circulate. It wouldn't be accurate, however, to suggest that touch is entirely absent in the African American church or among the Spiritual Baptists. The "laying on of hands" for both healing sickness and helping someone receive the holy spirit has historically been present among both groups. In general, however, physical touch is approached with caution among Christians, whereas in the Kalahari, n/om transmission more readily takes place through vibratory touch with the hands as well as full body contact between doctors.

Before ecstatic somatic interaction begins, a Bushman n/om-kxao experiences the sacred vibration concentrate in the belly in the form of a strong pulsing tightness. As the intensity of n/om builds, a new body motion emerges with a continuous alternating dynamic that is like an internal pump. This is similar to the Shaker's 'doption. The body feels like it has an internal piston pumping from the lower gut all the way up the higher chest — raising the energy from the belly to the heart. The Bushman's ecstatic body pump also shifts the main experience from one of raw physical power to the gentler though more powerful experience of a higher, heart-centered emotion that ushers in the next stage of spiritual cooking.

As the ecstatic pump is activated, its up and down movements are in synch with the stomping feet of the n/om-kxao and a hotter ecstatic dance form emerges. A Bushman dance usually begins with social dancing where some folks, especially the younger ones, perform to strut their stuff, but that only occurs before cooking begins. As the singing heats up, a n/om-kxao's movement shifts to the pump within, rather than any showy external display. Outside observers might not even recognize a dance form at all as heated movement becomes more of a walk, stomp, or march accompanied by whole body trembling and shaking. The body now only moves in ways that further amplify the sacred vibration and its ecstatic energetics, while stabilizing the dancer to not fall. Stomping helps the sacred vibration become further concentrated, intensified, and circulated while stabilizing an upright position.

Soon tremors are pumped upward into the vocal cords where sounds are made spontaneously — the tonal drumming, groaning, and snorting of 'doption. At first the sounds may be noises of the wild — screams, grunts, snorts, howls, barks, bird whistles, and other identifiable and unidentifiable noises. With more learning and acquired familiarity, the sounds transform into a soulful rhythmic performance. The sound is like the human voice imitating drums. Again, this gives us pause to wonder whether this particular ecstatic experience — rhythms pumped and expressed in a shaking ecstatic body — was the originating source of African drumming.

As the body moves in synch with the energized voicing of rhythm, the community recognizes that the n/om-kxao's ecstatic dance has truly begun. More than anything else this "dance" is movement that stomps and pumps the sacred vibration or n/om, accompanied by a plethora of improvised sounds. This is the Kalahari dance that holds transformational efficacy, readily distinguishable from the more entertaining choreography around the fire familiar to anthropologists and tourists. In the more ecstatically hot dance, the n/om-kxao must hold on and not topple over from the intensity of rising heat. Advanced somatic learning is needed to learn how to keep pumping while releasing the movement, rhythms, and tones in a natural and effortless manner. You may now appreciate why, in the reverse engineering of ecstatic experience, we instruct you to de-emphasize "dance" as it is usually understood. When the body is filled with sacred vibration, it is moved by a force that is stronger and wilder than, and less associated with, the typical choreographies of dance. Therefore, focus on catching the feeling in music and learn to surrender to spontaneous movement. This prepares your body to later be moved by the special vibration of heightened sacred emotion.

The Pulling of Healing. When a n/om-kxao trembles, shakes, stomps, and pumps, the sacred vibration starts to boil and the body may feel drawn or pulled toward someone who seems to unconsciously call for healing touch. Ecstatic healing in the

Kalahari is regarded as "pulling" sickness, that is, pulling out dirty arrows and nails from another person's sick or tired body. The n/om-kxao makes contact with the other person's body with shaking fingers, hands, arms, or the whole body. The surface contact area is where mechanical vibration is administered to the other. As both bodies now pulse together, the doctor's pump conducts the pulling. All of this takes place while the n/om-kxao expresses a heightened kind of sound making that is a hybrid of rhythmic 'doption and heart singing or an alternation of the two. These intense sounds are in synch with external body trembling and internal ecstatic pumping. Here acoustic and mechanical vibrations are synchronized, each amplifying the other. At the crescendo of this escalating energetic buildup, a very loud shrieking sound is released — this is the moment when sickness has been pulled out and disposed.

To a Kalahari Bushman, the idea of quietly holding your hand over another person's body without making physical contact would be evidence of a lack of healing know-how. Ecstatic healers do not presume to work with a subtle and invisible energy but a strongly felt spiritual energy that comes through mechanical vibration and a loudly heard acoustic vibration that are in synch to amplify emotional excitation. From the perspective of spiritual engineering, the absence of body movement, rhythm, tone, and emotion indicates no connection or resonance with a higher power. For spiritual cooking and the sacred vibration to be in operation, all cooking ingredients must be present, awakened, moving, circularly interacting, and amplifying. This is what makes the room big and hot enough for healing to naturally occur.

Engineering-wise, the Bushman n/om-kxaosi encourage more blending of ingredients and turning of the mystical wheel to take place than their ecstatic counterparts. Their bodies build up and store more voltage than those who pass out or are "slain in the spirit," which discharges rather than further charges the sacred vibration. The ecstatic height of spiritual cooking includes climbing to the top of the temperature scale where the body is transformed into a pulling doctor of the highest degree.

Again, this is not something you can personally choose to accomplish, and like all ecstatic capabilities, it is nurtured over time by being cooked in a community ecstatic gathering. Ecstatic pulling is something mysteriously involuntary that grabs hold of your body, not something you visualize taking place in your mind. The rope must pull you to pull out sickness. In this pulling you also pull out your own sickness, tiredness, selfishness, irritableness, and the rest. True ecstatic healing always feels invigorating after it is completed.

Transmitting the Sacred Vibration. The next ecstatic gearshift takes you even higher up the thermometer. You go past pulling sickness to transmitting heightened wellness—releasing fresh, clean arrows, nails, or spears of n/om—the metaphorical carriers of the sacred vibration. You are able to pass, transmit, and shoot the sacred vibration into the bodies of others as long as they are soft and ready to receive it. For those ready to be shaken by an ecstatic pierce, they will start shaking when touched in this manner. Keep in mind that the Bushmen believe that those who don't shake when touched still receive the benefits of pulling, although they aren't yet ready to fully receive an installation of the sacred vibration.

In the transmission of the sacred vibration, both transmitter and recipient physically tremble and shake together. Mutual trembling that is powerfully in synch creates a higher order vibration where the trembling of each person somehow mingles to create another kind of vibration that belongs to the whole interaction rather than the n/om-kxao alone. However, in the midst of this combinatorial vibration, the transmitter experiences an inner energetic buildup that starts in the belly and is released like an arrow from a bow or a projectile from a cannon. At the peak threshold, spontaneous release comes with a shrieking sound like it does in the moment of pulling. This time, however, you feel something has been *shot into* rather than pulled out of the other person. It is a euphoric, blissful experience when this occurs. At the climactic moment the body jerks or jolts, appearing like something was released. Saying that an arrow has been released is an excellent metaphor that fits the phenomenology of what the n/om-kxao physically experiences.

A n/om-kxao completely hands all body motion over to the mystical wheel, including the pumping action that enables transmitter and recipient to share a mutually felt sacred vibration. Like all ecstatic experience and expression, transmitting the sacred vibration cannot take place unless all the cooking ingredients are present and blended to form a turning ecstatic wheel that has sufficient momentum to raise the spiritual temperature. In the Kalahari, the blending and turning of the wheel begins with singing, clapping, and dancing, but does not involve the chanting of spoken prayers. The mystical wheel must continuously turn to amplify the ingredients— rhythm, movement, tone, and sacred emotion—enough to activate and circulate n/om in the doctors' bodies, which then intensifies the clapping and singing of the community. The sacred emotion in the singers' expression is both a call for the doctors' nails of n/om to wake up and become highly charged as well as a response to the doctors' becoming spiritually heated, which is signaled by their altered movement and vocal expression. Once the doctors' nails of n/om become extremely hot and their hearts have risen high, the hearts of everyone else rise in kind and everyone is touched, renewed, and transformed by the experience.

Using the Rope to Bring Down Heaven. The strongest n/om-kxao is able to stand in the hottest ecstatic fire and not fall, but continue climbing. He holds onto the rope as he moves onward to the sky village. Furthermore, he is able to bring the sky and all the ancestors back with him upon his return. Others at the dance recognize that this is taking place because they see the ecstatic emotion on the journeyer's face and the enthusiastic body movements, sounds, and rhythms. This is the strongest moment in a Bushman healing dance. When the ancestors come down, a moment of eternity is experienced. Here, everyone enters First Creation, the highest outcome of the dance. With no difference between past, present, and future, there is no partiality, incompleteness, sickness, or death. All the beloved ancestors are brought back for an ecstatic homecoming, made possible because hearts rose with singing that longs for and is pulled by the utmost love of creation.

Elder Bushman /Kunta / Ai!ae told Brad that the rope to God consists of one Bushman ancestor on top of the back of another ancestor, all the way back to the very first Bushman. When a person is teaching someone to climb the rope, the initiate is sometimes literally laid over the back of the dancing teacher. A strong shaman is said to be able to "carry many healers on his back."[90] The image of stacking one Bushman shaman on the back of another in a line going straight up to the sky was /Kunta's way of explaining the divine rope. Experientially, the line connects all ancestors through the generational links of an ongoing, reborn love. As you love your parents and grandparents, you can further feel how they loved their parents and grandparents, and on and on until you get to the first ancestors and the family of God. This is a love line — the singing, loving rope to God.

The Stages of Learning to Cook. When the Bushmen hold a n/om dance, the shaking n/om-kxaosi touch those members of the community, from infants to elders, with whom they feel pulled to share the sacred vibration. Receiving the vibration is a shaking medicine for both curing sickness and the maintenance of health. People don't ask to be touched; they trust that the rope will pull the n/om-kxao to another body if and only if it is necessary. The pulling of the rope determines all cooked action within the dance.

A Bushman n/om-kxao who becomes fully spiritually cooked goes through several stages of learning and transformation. In the beginning she learns how to start an ecstatic fire with the skills that gather and blend rhythm, tone, and movement with sacred emotion. No wheel can form or turn enough to burn without singing and dancing a special kind of song. Accordingly, the next stage of development involves the introduction of the stronger longing and pulling of sacred emotion that a sacred song provides, something that empowers more turning of the ecstatic wheel. As a Bushman n/om-kxao learns to sing in a way that makes the heart ascend, the inner body pump activates and intensifies until the pulling of healing commences. In the most advanced stage of learning, sacred emotion is exceptionally felt to create the ultimate existential melt where longing for and being pulled by God's love includes all living and departed relatives, ancestors, creatures, and the whole of creation. The n/om-kxao feels a love that is spiritually hot enough to burn away fear and hatred of any enemy. This is the highest level of transformation where the ropes to God are felt, smelled, heard, and seen.

At the highest spiritual temperature that surpasses any conscious, unconscious, or altered state, the Bushman ecstatic learns to lose awareness or interest in physical form, while perceiving and receiving all of nature, including one's own, as a vibrating cloud, fog, and mist of mystery. Like all ecstatic, mystical phenomena, this vibratory dissolve is not a visualization that takes place in a meditative state, but something somatically experienced by the strongest doctors cooked at the highest spiritual temperature. As Bushman doctor Motaope Saboabue summarized for Brad, "You may even forget that you have a body and think that you are a mist or a cloud. This is the way it must be."[t]

Similarities and Differences across the Main Spiritual Hot Zones

In addition to the three locations we have so far mentioned, we also frequently visit the Japanese tradition of seiki jutsu.

---

[t] Brad has personally experienced all stages of development as a n/om-kxao. The descriptions of Bushman ecstatic spirituality are drawn from both interviews with other doctors as well as our own personal experiences dancing with the Bushmen as n/om-kxaosi. For more information and first-person testimony from Kalahari n/om-kxaosi, see our books, *Way of the Bushman as Told by the Tribal Elders: Spiritual Teaching and Practices of the Ju/'hoansi* (Rochester, VT: Bear & Company, 2015) and Bradford Keeney, ed., *Kalahari Bushmen Healers* (Philadelphia, PA: Ringing Rocks Press, 2003).

Spending time on the seiki bench is a powerful way of gathering the ingredient of spontaneous body movement. Seiki also helps interrupt and restrain overzealous ruminating from taking you off course. Its bare bones minimalism of theoretical or theological ornamentation helps curb runaway cognition as your body constantly moves to sweep the sacred ground. What seiki doesn't bring, however, is the kind of heart singing, rhythms, and body movement found in the African diaspora. However, from the seiki jutsu perspective, all the latter are simply regarded as pure forms of seiki—they are spontaneous forms of body expression awakened by the higher power of the universe.

When you experience the heart singing of traditional African American gospel music, you are baptized in the echo of Bushman n/om songs, now enriched by subsequent musical and instrumental invention. We regard sanctified gospel songs as a natural extension of what began in the Kalahari thousands of years ago—a First Creation musical form that changes whenever folks from another time and place gather to cook. We also find that the 'doption of the St. Vincent Shakers is similar to the ecstatic pump among the Kalahari n/om-kxaosi, but it is something typically not experienced in the sanctified African American church. The church does not set its thermostat high enough for the spiritual temperature to get sufficiently hot for 'doption to emerge. Ecstatic singing is the church's typical pinnacle spiritual expression. While it may spill over into what is called a "shout" where "holy ghost dancing" erupts to fast instrumental music, the parishioners quickly dissipate spiritual energy rather than amplify and sustain it. 'Doption is required to take a maximally heated song to the next level of spiritual cooking, keep you on your feet, and increase your capacity for spiritual voltage and body trembling.

One, however, shouldn't generalize that a Shaker meeting is always spiritually hotter (or better) than a sanctified gospel service. There is a time and place for all ecstatic expression. What we should not forget is that a sacred song is what matters most for inducing spiritual cooking. Sanctified heart singing can arguably raise the temperature more than any other form of ecstatic expression. This is why we find the sanctified church, at its musical best, so ecstatically effective in lighting a spiritual fire. What is missing in the church is additional know-how regarding what to do with the higher spiritual voltage when it arrives. A trip to St. Vincent demonstrates how any advancement to a stronger spiritual charge must be placed under the next level of higher control — the ecstatic gear shift and transition into 'doption. You become adopted by the holy spirit's advanced regulation that can further amplify, sustain, and direct ecstatic expression.

The St. Vincent Shakers altered the primary form of the Kalahari ecstatic pump. The Shakers made 'doption and its body rhythm making a musical art form, pulling it away from its original emphasis on pulling and transmitting spiritual power through body contact. In the islands of the Caribbean, additional vocal instrumental expression was added that includes making the sound of a trumpet. Other movement choreographies, associated with diverse spiritual lands, also appeared. The primary, original 'doption is found in the Kalahari. We can speculate that the differentiation and elaboration of gods, melodies, rhythms, dance forms, and the like are all part of First Creation's ongoing march of changing forms. The evolution of additional forms, however, comes at the cost of devolving the primary form. This implicit understanding is held by older Shakers of St. Vincent who still remember to respect their oldest African ancestors, the ones who had the number one 'doption from which all others flowed. Their return to this 'doption in visionary dreams brings renewal through an ancestral homecoming.

From the Kalahari view, the more a religion elaborates its ritualistic forms, beliefs, names, and texts, the more trickster is involved. Trickster's presence can either be a good or a bad thing, or neither, depending on the situation and temperature at hand. Before the differentiation of divinity into distinct subclasses such as orishas (a Yoruba word), or loa (a Vodou word) for example, there was only the sky God of creation and the changing side of god that came in ever-changing forms. When names and specific characteristics were attached to God's changing forms, they became more real, solid, and permanent than they were meant to become. Frozen naming stops God's divine changing that keeps the spiritual world and physical world alive and in harmony. All the little gods and spirits, too, must be cooked and brought back to the source from which they came in order to start the world all over again. The same is true of the holy trinity, quaternary, four directions, pentad, hexagram, kilogram, and any other stabilized and measured sacred size or shape. Throw it all in the sacred fire so that you, the gods, and the source and force behind it all can remember that we are one in the big room. This returning brings the spiritual burning that replenishes the continuance of sacred circulation, heated perspiration, and divine respiration.

Although the Kalahari hosts the original 'doption in the form of the ecstatic n/om pump, it wouldn't be accurate to say that the Bushman dance is always spiritually hotter than a Shaker or African American church service. In the Kalahari, however, you can find the practical know-how that can host the highest upper range on the spiritual thermostat. Whereas 'doption is the hottest a Caribbean Shaker gets, a Kalahari n/om-kxao knows how to go further. In a Shaker praise meeting, when 'doption reaches its utmost height, the Shaker may pass out and fall. This is often a bewildering and confusing experience that results in cooling down to regain stability. Accompanied by gasps, groans, sighs, or shouts, the Shaker recuperates from breathlessness and dizziness, returning to the same kind of behavior that characterized the beginning stage of spiritual cooking. The Shaker will either remain cool or start heating up all over again.

Similarly, in the sanctified black church (and other charismatic churches around the world), parishioners typically faint and fall when their spiritual temperature gets too hot. Some parishioners even mistake this fainting as the highest peak of ecstatic worship, because they don't know that they can keep standing and allow 'doption to take place. Instead, they fall over and proclaim they are "slain in the spirit." St. Vincent Shakers also get "slain," though the fall occurs at a higher temperature threshold. Shakers also do not know that after 'doption has reached its height, there is no need for the body or the temperature to drop.

More ecstatic experience and spiritual cooking are possible on the Kalahari dance ground because a Bushman n/om-kxao has more tacit spiritual engineering knowledge. Whenever someone looks ready to fall, he will be physically held and encouraged to stand by others and prompted to go further. To drop is to fall short of going all the way to the highest heat. Of course if a doctor is overheated or has been cooking too quickly, he may have to be cooled off and then start the journey again. The goal is to walk and climb into the heavenly sky village while being upright and pulled by a straight rope. Furthermore, a n/om-kxao's healing capacity to pull dirty nails or arrows and transmit clean ones requires that the doctor remains heated while the rest of the community contributes to keeping the temperature high. The stronger the singing and dancing, the further the healer can climb and the more intense the cooking is for everyone. The Kalahari would likely cook even stronger if the heart singers of the sanctified church and the 'doption instrumentalists of the Caribbean were also a part of the chorus.

Be assured that seiki jutsu also knows how to gather and blend the ingredients of aligned rhythm, tone, and body movement for cooking. When a seiki master becomes ecstatically hot enough to transmit seiki to another person, we see Sacred Ecstatics in full blossom. The seiki master gathers the seiki in the atmosphere by banging the wall like it's a drum. She also makes loud shouting noises and tonal glissandos that amplify the seiki in her body and in the atmosphere. This tonal and rhythmic expression is done with such fervor that the body moves ecstatically in kind. When seiki is brought to a hot enough temperature, it is poured into the top of the head of the recipient, another spontaneous seiki movement accomplished outside of voluntary control.

When Brad showed Osumi Sensei a film of the Bushmen shooting n/om into one another at a Kalahari dance, she shouted, "Seiki!" Later when he showed the Bushmen a film of Osumi Sensei giving someone seiki in her treatment room, the Bushman elders shouted, "N/om!" While each ecstatic tradition has a different name for the ultimate force and vibration of life, all gather and blend the same essential ingredients to make the temperature hot enough for things to cook. The same spiritual engineering applies to all ways and means of ecstatic spirituality, but each locale varies its thermostat setting and differs in the practical wisdom concerning how far they know how to go. In addition, each owns a special resource that potentially has something to offer all the other traditions that cook.

Each ecstatic lineage can learn from the others, just as we can learn through ecstatically traveling to each place. When the St. Vincent Shakers and African American church parishioners are burdened by excessive scriptural interpretation, we can appreciate how Osumi Sensei is ready to help by instructing them to solely turn to the body and ask it to move without need for words. Osumi Sensei, in turn, can benefit from receiving a sacred song that would inspire her body to be even more moved by seiki. At each locale we are blessed by whatever advanced know-how is offered that complements or enhances the others. Spiritual engineering enables us to discern the action that matters rather than get lost in comparing names, beliefs, and interpretations. This pragmatic focus also enables us to see that every human body, regardless of the culture or religion into which it was born, comes equipped with the necessary tools for experiencing sacred ecstasy. You belong to the First Creation Kalahari, the Caribbean, and all other spiritual locales of the world.

Other First Creation Destinations

Sacred Ecstatics and its spiritual engineering provide a trail-blazing journey to any and all the ecstatic lineages, including syncretic blends of each, helping you learn the best of what the global wisdom in spiritual cooking can offer. As a spiritual engineer, notice the sweeping body at the seiki bench and how it empties you to make room for a First Creation flight to the church pew. Now hear the songs that heat the soul and awaken the heart to rise. On the wings of sanctified song, you may be transported to the Caribbean where you are more easily caught by the higher degrees of ecstatic rhythm and musical sound making. Finally, the praise house walls may dissolve so you are dancing on Kalahari sand underneath the infinite canopy of stars, taking an ecstatic stand for a higher temperature ascent rather than bending or falling to the cooling ground.

Sacred Ecstatics sets up a whole world tent, underneath which any geographical or theological borders disappear. It welcomes anything that can help a community get cooked by God. Circulate seiki so you are made ready to find your soul's music box and singing heart. Wait for the ecstatic pump, the body drum of spirit, and all the First Creation instruments to come, helping you climb further up the rope where the longing and the pulling bring you closer to the divine. Do all this to heal any divide between heaven and earth, bringing together each lineage and generation of humanity within the infinity of ever-changing divinity.

Follow the Songbook Rather Than the Storybook. Sacred Ecstatics embraces songbooks rather than storybooks. Songs open the door to whatever soulfully expresses life. In this vaster and more inclusive space, you find that the swing time of jazz is packed with vibratory soul and that the composers of Broadway musicals are more shamanic than any hallucinatory tonic. You also find that inside Beethoven grows a burning musical bush while Count Basie and Frank Sinatra can fly you to the moon. Sacred Ecstatics especially values the music that can trigger, amplify, or sustain the sacred vibration. Furthermore, when folks gather to cook others, the songs and song locales must change to keep us inside the big room of First Creation. Everything about music must change — genre, instrumentation, tempo, key, tones, rhythms, body mechanics of performance, and the overarching inspiring mood that words alone elude.

169

Follow the songs and don't fall for another story that only talks about ecstasy rather than sings it into an ecstatic reality. Forget *altered conscious states* and remember that you are more in need of a *soul-altering musical dynamic* that changes a deadbeat drone into a melodic tone with a fascinating beat. This is the mystical wheel that turns life into a song and dance performance. Life becomes more than a recycled tale whenever a song springs forth, lifts the curtain, turns on the lights, and converts your everyday into a mystical musical. In other words, ecstatically move along a melodic line and avoid being snared by a story line. Rather than comparing and sharing a narrative, get onboard a musical train that sings and dances you into eternity. Your world, with all its hills and valleys, must be filled with the sound of music for mystery to rise again. A hallowed word cannot ring its truth unless you sing it to life.

A New Kind of Syncretic Spirituality. Sacred Ecstatics brings a brand new kind of syncretic spirituality: one that can change its visionary locales, metaphors, tones, rhythms, movements, dances, and songs at a moment's notice, steered by the rope to God. The rope becomes stronger, softer, wiser, more absurd, more creative, more rigorous, more flexible, more harmonic, more dissonant, more stable, and more open to change —all aspects of the complex divine—whenever people spiritually cook. However, the rope turns brittle and breaks—disconnects from the creator's creating—whenever you hang out too long in the cold where the same story is always told. When the rope is pulsing with vitality, get out of the way and let it swing you wherever it wants. Your life won't mean a thing until you get that divine swing. All else said is simply more doo-wop.

We are open to traveling wherever God may send us in the vast universe of visionary classrooms. Bow in appreciation for whatever is offered and welcome all that God has in store, allowing it to become part of your ecstatic performance repertoire. Don't feel that you ever have to emotionally dilute a song, water down a koan, dumb down a shamanic ritual, temper a prophetic message, explain away a mystery, hush a cymbal, interpret a symbol, calm a movement, quiet a joyful noise, settle down a shaking ecstasy, edit the divinely absurd, distill infinity, or chill divinity. When you get happy and religious, shout with the loudest of the old timers. Also cook yourself to a char with n/om musical bars, joining voices and hands with the Kalahari dance troupes. With equal fervor, get adopted by the same spirit that has rocked and rolled all the shakers from England to the United States and the Caribbean. Hold nothing back in order to bring back the oldest ingredients that help anything and everything find its way to the spiritually ecstatic cooking pot. A beginner's mind, newborn heart, and everlasting soul are assured whenever you step into the big room where all is recreated for the very First Creation time.

We have spiritually traveled to Mount Zion, the river Jordan, ancient bookstores, old praise houses, the original tree of life, the four palm trees of the Amazon, the sensation laboratory of Charles Henry, the New York City apartment of Tesla with his vibrational inventions and mystical pigeons, the shaking tents of noisy spirits and shaking rattles, Ezekiel's classroom, William Blake's drawing room, and the classrooms, prayer rooms, and music rooms of saints, circuit riders, shaking shamans, forgotten mystics, gospel hymn writers, Beethoven, Liszt, Erroll Garner, Chet Baker, Cole Porter, Wendell Berry, Gregory Bateson, and Warren McCulloch. Visionary tracks have led us to encounters with eighteenth-century London preachers, spiritual healers, sacred pipes, whistles, flutes, trumpets, drums, keyboards, esoteric books, herbal roots, glasses of love, magical masons, Tibetan rain makers, root doctors, mojo doctors, holy medicine doctors, pointing and shaking fathers and mothers, Caribbean clappers, Bushman huggers, sanctified shouters, holy rollers, crazy wisdom jumpers, Diné sand painters, Lakota prayer tiers, Amazonian canoe travelers, Balinese gods, wheat fields of the Zohar, critters, insects, flowers, and endless shapeshifting First Creation forms of every size and shape, prayer, chant, song, tone, rhythm, movement, and sacred emotion.

Welcome to the never-ending travel destinations of Sacred Ecstatics and all its reversals, alterations, transformations, and changing. Pack lightly because nothing is needed except a willingness to leave behind everything except the ingredients for spiritual cooking. Let's rock and roll and shake and bake as we sing and dance ourselves to the praise house of creation. Hold on to the rope because anything can change, including the name of God, the big room, and the song that moves the universe along the longing to return home again and begin anew.

STEP 3. REENTERING THE EVERYDAY

After a round of spiritual cooking is finished, you descend the thermometer and reenter the everyday. You don't want to cool off and come down too quickly because that would be disorienting, and even worse, it could dissipate the spiritual heat you are meant to bring back. Keep the fire alive inside of you for as long as possible, doing so while your conduct shifts to better fit the spiritual temperature on the other side of the ceremonial door. The whole purpose of getting cooked is to get a transfusion of the sacred vibration, a divine recharge, and a musical-mystical empowerment that circulate holiness throughout you and into those you meet upon your return.

Sacred ecstasy involves an ongoing cycle of death and resurrection from cramped lifelessness to expanded soulful vitality, the most incredible thaw and awe ecstatic experience, and up and down the divine staircase ride. Returning from the spiritual fire requires just as much spiritual engineering know-how as your initial journey toward the ecstatic flames. Learn to embrace your life as a circle that moves through different seasons and temperatures rather than a straightline march toward a fixed endpoint. When you have mastered the gathering and blending of ingredients, the turning of the mystical wheel, and how to sustain the heat upon your return, you will have found the practical secrets to cooked ecstatic living.

Back and Forth through the Gate

While we were preparing to write this section about the spiritual engineering of reentry, Brad dreamed that we stood in front of a Japanese entrance to a forest with a shrine.

> In the dream, I recognized the path as leading to the Japanese lineage of seiki jutsu. Hillary and I both felt Ikuko Osumi Sensei and her ancestor Eizon Hoin were present on the other side. I saw the same gate I photographed when I visited the shrine with Osumi Sensei in Japan
>
> As Hillary and I stood transfixed in front of this mystical gate in the dream, we were suddenly hit with a powerful gust of seiki wind that brought more teaching about spiritual engineering. I was reminded that getting spiritually cooked always involves a crossing, passage, and a journey.

You never know where you will land or how hot the temperature will reach when you gather the ingredients and blend them into a mystical wheel. As we have said before, all you need to know is that you must faithfully execute the initial work of gathering and blending. Face the gate and prepare to move toward it. With spontaneous movement you automatically create a rhythm and make a tone. When all your body expression comes together with sacred emotion, the wheel turns and you feel the wind of movement that can carry you to the other side. Trust the movement of the wheel to remove psychological rust, lubricate spiritual gears, remove lesser wants, and throw you into higher mystery.

You must pass through the door, gate, portal, or entrance to First Creation to become spiritually cooked. And you must pass through it again on your way back, this time entering Second Creation as if for the very first time. We suggest that you say your name or verbally mark your return.[u] In St. Vincent they often say, "I return to myself," after each spiritual journey.

Carry the image of the gate shown here with you. Look at it from time to time and remember that the passage is equally important in both directions—leaving and returning. You face the gate whenever you head toward the big room, and you face it again when you come back. The successive returns enact one of the most important teachings: the more you cross, the thinner the line of division between the big room and your everyday reality becomes. The ultimate spiritual goal is not only entry through the gate but also the ability to more easily make the crossing again and again. Each time you enter the big room fire and then bring God's warmth back with you, the room of your life gets bigger as the sacred ground on which you walk grows stronger. With good spiritual engineering you are able acquire excellent ecstatic traveling habits that make future crossings easier, as you also reduce the separation between you and God's spiritual universe. This makes heaven more earthly and earth more heavenly until all that was distinguished, named, and separated are melted together as one.

In and Out of the Bottle

Shortly after dreaming of the gate, Brad received another visionary lesson about crossing in and out of the big room.

> In a particularly bizarre dream, I sat down at a café table with the famous American performer Bob Hope (1903-2003). We had a conversation about song, dance, humor, and acting—the

---

[u] In the Bushman puberty rite, a girl is considered passing into First Creation during her first menstruation. When the bleeding is over, she is given her name again as if for the first time to mark her new beginning in Second Creation. See Bradford Keeney and Hillary Keeney, "Reentry into First Creation: A Conceptual Frame for the Ju/'hoan Bushman Performance of Puberty Rites, Storytelling, and Healing Dance," *Journal of Anthropological Research*, 69 (2013), 65–86.

cornerstones of Hope's show biz career. In the middle of the table was a bottle the size of a wine bottle. Inside it was a well-formed peach. Mr. Hope mentioned that it was the secret to his long life — drinking this peach several times a day. "It's very expensive and rare, but I make sure I always have it on hand." Bob Hope, by the way, lived to be 100 years old.

I stared at the bottle and a voice whispered, "You are looking at the ultimate koan of life: how do you get a whole peach into and out of a bottle?" [v] I fell into a suspended state trying to think through this odd question. I was not aware that putting a whole peach inside a bottle is an old trick: a very young and small peach is placed inside a bottle while still attached to its tree branch, enabling the fruit to grow from inside. However, getting the peach out again is not so obvious.

In the dream I then heard the voice say, "Gather the ecstatic ingredients and get yourself out of the bottle." As I began to move to a rhythm, I remembered that Bob Hope began his career as a funny song and dance man on the vaudeville circuit. He had a dancing cane and could tap it along with his feet to the rhythm of a song. I started dancing as well and sang endless crazy rhymes such as, "shake the bottle, don't be timid, the peach longs to be a liquid . . . the cane can stir the peach and help it reach the bottle neck that sings it through . . . look at hope and bob not for an apple when a peach is within reach." This absurd hilarity lasted for a long time until I was flooded with the truth that higher passage can only be found in the giggling and wiggling of the

---

[v] In our book, *Sacred Ecstatics,* we describe the movement from cold to hot spiritual temperatures as moving from a small existential glass or bottle into the vast and boundless sea.

body rather than the restriction and contraction of abstraction.

When I woke up from the dream, I laughed and sang myself to my computer, curious about whether Bob Hope ever had anything to do with peaches. To my surprise, I found that California Cling Peaches hired Bob Hope to advertise its peaches in the late 1940s. Starting in 1950, and up through the next year when I was born, Bob Hope was featured in an advertisement published in magazines that circulated across America, featuring his recipe for peach upside down cake.

The dream's crazy peach wisdom suggests how to get yourself out of any small existential container. To get to the big room, pass through the eye of the needle, or exit the neck of the bottle, you must laugh, sing, and dance yourself into spiritual liquidity. You start as a solid peach trapped inside a bottle and the only way out is to shake, heat, and melt, enabling a fluid passage. Your highest essence needs to be *poured* rather than talked or walked through the gate. When you come back to the cooler world, you again solidify, but this time in the form of a sweet upside-down cake fresh out of the baker's oven. In First Creation all is reversed, making transitional change possible: solidity is liquidity, flesh is spirit, the seen is heard, the eye of the needle is a sacred ear, impossible physical passage is a song-and-dance routine, and a solid peach is also liquid gold and sweet cake.

For no reason other than honoring the spiritual fruit tree from which you came, treat yourself with a slice of peach upside-down cake. Enjoy it to remind yourself that a climb up the sacred tree is meant to bring back spiritual fruit in all its changing forms. You should come back poured into the world as a freshly baked sweet treat to share with others. The fruit we speak of is you, a First Creation peach that passes in and out of a bottle, pouring back and forth through the gate, baking and delivering holy cake and pie from the heavenly sky.

The Spiritual Engineering of Reentry

One of the most surprising outcomes of entering the big room and getting spiritually cooked is that you now realize you live in two contrary realities at the same time. Your true home is the big room of mystery and yet you are also a peach who lives in a bottle. You are an ecstatic traveler who can be poured through the gate to enter the spiritual fire, and yet most of your daily life will continue to take place at cooler temperatures. The spiritual engineering of reentry involves more than instructions for descending the thermometer and bringing the mystical wheel to a halt. It's about learning to transition through all your forms — from an ice cube to warm liquid, boiling steam, and back again as a sweeter, warmer human being. You also learn to live in relationship with your new experiential reference point: the big room and its spiritual fire. You want to make sure that all of your gathering, blending, and cooking bears fruit and transforms it to feed yourself and others in all the rooms and temperature zones of your life.

Though you can't avoid cooling down and resolidifying inside a bottle, your aim is to come back staying sweet and warm for as long as you can. Make sure upon your return that you keep the cooking ingredients close at hand. Above all else, add a prelude to every activity in your day. Sacred Ecstatics isn't about having a one-time cosmic explosion or big-bang enlightenment, but rather about developing new daily habits that help keep the room vast and the temperature simmering. Very spiritually cooked people around the world have one thing in common: their bodies hold all of the ingredients and they can turn the mystical wheel and cross through the gate easily and often. Each time you make the crossing, the more the wall separating heaven from earth crumbles and the more the line of demarcation erases. When it is almost gone, the small bottle practically disappears and you find yourself an indivisible part of God's changing creation.

When it comes to bringing a daily workout, prelude, or other cooking session to a close, aim to naturally and effortlessly let the mystical wheel slow down and come to a halt. This typically involves a slowing of your body movement and a cooling/ quieting of your vocal expression. You do not have to preplan this process; just let it happen on its own. The main thing to remember is that when ending any ecstatic session, you should avoid stopping your movement and expression too abruptly. Doing the latter throws you back into cool temperatures too quickly, which can make you feel out of whack when you go back to the rest of your day or evening.

It is good practice to close your session with a short, spoken prayer. Any prayer that reminds you to walk on sacred ground will work, including a simple, "Thank you, Lord." Because you are reentering cooler temperatures you can feel free to make this prayer longer than your initial prayer line, but it doesn't need to be. The best time for words is when you are sliding back down the thermometer and suspended between heaven and earth, in between the hot speechless realm and the poet's quarters where words still carry mystical warmth. This is the time to wordsmith a prayer if you are so inclined. In the slide down the rope you will find the right place and temperature for creating a word-linked bridge that joins heavenly sky and earthly ground.

Once you cross back through the gate to Second Creation, your goal is to keep the sacred fire burning and the mystical wheel turning within. You want to make sure the ingredients are held inside your body so that you can reach for them whenever you find yourself feeling cold, whether it's experienced as stress, crankiness, listlessness, anxiousness, anger, jealousy, ennui, lack of inspiration, or any of the other zillions of names for being spiritually chilled and out of touch with your rope to God. Make your sacred commotion inside more prominent than any outside disturbance. Have ceremony, church, and heavenly praise going on inside you while the world does its thing on the outside. Here, you find the real spiritual battle: trying to maintain and sustain the holiness within to remain in a bigger, warmer room no matter what the situation. Spiritually cooked ecstatics know what it means to be a good fire keeper. If life starts to cool you down, then gather the ingredients and return to turning the wheel to heat it up all over again.

You are in need of constant sacred music, rhythm, tone, and movement whose magical blend helps keep you near the threshold to the big room fire. In addition to the four ingredients, keep your prayer line close at hand. It will help you stay small and humble, ever ready to ecstatically tumble. Reaching for your prayer line keeps your ego at bay while your soul remains onboard the holy ship.

It requires a wheel-turning ride to get to the big room on high. On the way back down, the ride becomes a slide as your spiritual steam cools down and you return to everyday town. How you hold on to whatever was received in the heat will determine how you meet and greet others upon your return. You were sent to come back bearing spiritual fruit for others. From thaw to awe and back to the cool, you must arrive home ready to generously share rather than show off any newly acquired flare. What was given to you in the heat must be given away to others in order for it to remain strong inside you. If you felt love, then act lovingly and make things "loverly." If you felt joy, do something that will bring joy to someone else. If you were gifted with a new melody, a new lyric, or new inspiration of any kind, then compose, write, paint, sculpt, dance, or make it. All spiritual gifts received must be metabolized in order to keep the cycle of ecstatic life turning. By all means don't end any experience of Sacred Ecstatics with a trickster analysis or evaluation of your experience, including a lament that you didn't get as hot as you wanted. Doing so scatters the ingredients you gathered and puts you back inside the cramped bottle of self-obsession rather than big room ecstatic combustion.

When you return to your everyday after spiritual cooking, recall the four general directions of ecstatic spirituality: word masonry, creative art, absurd performance, and launching the next ascent.[91] Mind needs its time and place as does creativity, absurdity, and religiosity — all interdependent spokes of the everyday existential wheel. All spokes and wheels must turn within the higher mystical wheel, as they call on one another, serve one another, and participate in the inclusion of all ways and means of being alive.

Remember Bob Hope's long-life peach elixir and make sure you include time for a joke, a silly song and dance act, and a big moment of absurdity. Make yourself and others laugh in service of the crazy wisdom that is only wise in the big room. Change whatever is solidifying too quickly as you put some change in your inner music box, for without a song, the heat won't last long. Be a minstrel whose musical powers overcome babbling towers. Be a clown whenever your face has a frown and drown away fear with the tear of a holy fool who laughs when others cry and quietly weeps when others toot their own horns too loudly.

Clowning around must share equal time with your making whatever you are inspired to create after your creative faculties have been charged. Come back from the fire as a whole and contradictory human being, allowing the big wheel within wheels to make you simultaneously reverent and irreverent, logical and absurd, earthly and heavenly, all the other contraries necessary for spiritual progression in both the ascents and descents taking you up and down the rope. Not surprisingly, poet William Blake chose to symbolize God's action of creation as that of a blacksmith, smelting the crude ore, consuming the slag, and casting the molten iron into new forms. In First Creation, God is the blacksmith and you are the one being transformed into a tool that serves creation.

Finally, don't forget that trickster is a necessary part of creation. Be a true mystical thinker, scholar, and conversationalist whose use of language lays sacred foundation stones rather than litters the world with trickster trash talk. Bathe your words in an illumined mind filled with heavenly sunshine. Talk right in order to walk, melt, smelt, pour, and flow right. A few years ago Hillary dreamed she went to a spiritual classroom where she received a lesson about words:

> Brad and I were in a small old church with
> unpainted wooden walls, floors, and pews. I was

sitting in the pew right next to Brad, and everyone was rocking in their seats as women prayed. A woman was going around with a wooden bucket filled with holy water and a ladle, offering everyone a drink. When it was our turn to receive the water the woman said, "Be sweet to each other with your words."

When our words match the love we feel for God and one another, they and all forms of expression serve as life-giving bread and spirit-giving water that quench everyone's spiritual hunger and thirst. Get spiritually cooked in order to become the sacred water bearer, holy bread baker, mystical music maker, rocking rhythm shaker, and all other changing forms that allow you to be a well-tuned instrument of God's creation. Practice good spiritual engineering that assures the ingredients are present throughout each day and night. Make yourself the fourth dimension—the holder of the trinity of tone, beat, and motion that serves utmost sacred emotion. Come out of the cooking pot dancing and singing to demonstrate that you are ready to play. The trumpet calls, the keyboard is jamming, and the cosmos is tuned to include your instrument as a vital part of the sacred band.

Hunting Hare and Singing with Larks

The night after dreaming Bob Hope, Brad surprised himself by blurting out a specific request in prayer voiced in the middle of the night, "What mission do you wish Hillary and I to now pursue?" He reports:

> I fell asleep and then dreamed that a voice responded with these words: "Hunt hare." It was so shocking to hear this bizarre answer that I woke up in a state of bewilderment and wonderment. As I pondered those words, I recalled how the hare or rabbit was the animal

that symbolized trickster for many cultures throughout the world. Here we find the African American Brer Rabbit, the English Peter Rabbit, the Chinese moon rabbit, the Zambian Kalulu, the Aztec Ometotchtli (Two Rabbit), the Ojibway Mishaabooz (Great Hare), the Egyptian goddess Wenet, the Celtic goddess Cerridwen, and Hittavainen the East Finnish Karelian god of hare hunting, among others. More importantly to me, there is an old Bushman tale about the hare that is often told by Bushman elders:[92]

The Moon wanted to send a special teaching to human beings about death so she sent a messenger to earth. Her message was as follows: "As I die and come to life again, so shall you." One man, upon hearing this, started to argue with the moon. He had just lost his beloved mother and was so overcome with and defeated by sorrow that he could not believe that his mother could come back to life. His argument with the Moon escalated until the Moon became so upset that she hit the man on the face, cleaving his lip with the blow. She then cursed him, saying, "You shall always have this cleft and become a hare on the run."

The hare in the Bushman story is human trickster mind that refuses to accept that we may pass into First Creation with no separation of earth from the heavenly moon. Instead, doubting humanity is doomed to the insanity of trickster profanity where lips spew the cloven divides and dualisms of construed cognitive imprisonment. The Bushman tale inspires us to regard "hunting hare" as tracking trickster mind's ways of impeding and diverting us from ecstatic passage through the gate. Remember that trickster wants to convince us that we are more solid, heavy, and square than we are liquid, light, and circular.

You must discern and unlearn whatever habits block you from moving to the vaster side of things. In other words, your spiritual learning first requires unlearning whatever inhibits you from learning how to spiritually cook. Spiritual pointing, discernment, and prophetic announcement — the operations of hunting trickster hare — help you identify what must be unlearned. Without this kind of detection, your compass will forever spin and you will never know which direction gets you to the light of the mystical moon.

The spiritual engineering of Sacred Ecstatics helps fulfill the mission of finding and clearing trickster impediments, doing so through a pragmatic, down-to-earth approach. Make only one intention that creates an inner tension for sacred ascension: aim to come closer and closer to God. Only step out of the way when the wheel forms and turns, allowing divine will to take over and pull you through the open gate.

In vision I was reminded of the need to track, hunt, and call out the trickster traps found lurking everywhere. After thinking about the need for the unlearning that precedes higher learning, I asked another question in a second prayer voiced later that night. My question this time was, "What is the mystery Hillary and I are now serving?" After falling asleep again, I dreamed the same voice, this time responding with a loud and clear tone, *"The white lark of heaven."* The sound woke me up as before.

William Shakespeare wrote the famous literary line from Cymbeline, "Hark, hark! The lark at heaven's gate sings!" This line later inspired William Blake to suggest that the lark's song is the key to opening all twenty eight gates of heaven. The lark is one of the few birds known to sing when it flies. You carry a similar engineering: to make the flight from one side of the gate to another requires a song. Truly, it is song that courts the gatekeeper of heaven's gate. Song's emotion can melt anything, including you and the gatekeeper. You must wholeheartedly sing with all the saints and shamans for your holy pour into the vast sea. Song is the master key to opening all gates and hearts in the mystery kingdom of divine eternal joy where rhythmic release and musical peace liberate us from the reign of trickster's hare-brained knowing.

Further south than merry old England, we find the dune lark with its white belly as the only bird endemic to Namibia. It is most readily found in Bushmanland (now called the Nyae Nyae Conservancy). One of the ancient Bushman tales speaks of it being the bird that joyfully brings the first song to each morning. The lark was also a friend of the ostrich who in the beginning did not know how to sing. Inspired by the lark, it finally let out a song that sounded like "part lion's roar, part foghorn, part old man trumpeting into his handkerchief."[93]

You were born to be on a mission to arrive at the gate to eternity, the holy city, heaven, the sky village, First Creation, the infinite spiritual cosmos, and the big room. Once there you need a song to open the gate and pour yourself through. Unlearn trickster ways of spiritual obstruction through over-solidification as you learn the basics of divine deconstruction and reconstruction — the spiritual engineering of Sacred Ecstatics. It teaches you to follow the sound of the lark whose song can even teach an ostrich how to sing. After the gate opens its door, all else will naturally pour. When it is time to return, make sure you bring the song back with you and keep it going.

It takes a song to open the gate, travel, cook, and have a successful return. We invite you to get on the song trail, but beware of hares that only want to talk rather than take the sweet cake walk. Keep your eyes and ears on the singing lark. Pour its notes in and out of your heart.

Travel List for Reentering the Everyday

Make sure that you never forget that the spiritual descent is as important as the ascent. You are cooked in order to come back changed in ways that help others change. Don't put on your old hat or run back to your shrunken habitat with all its cold habits the moment you exit the big room. Come back slowly, bringing the big room with you because you want to remain in the vast space and its warmth for as long as possible. We have forged the spiritual engineering wisdom into a brief travel list for making a good return. Keep the following "how to exit" summary with you every time you conduct a home workout, attend a group intensive, or receive a private session.

1. *The Japanese Seiki Gate* – Your whole body must move past personal mind control and be under higher control of the ultimately nameless mystery. This is the essential lesson of seiki jutsu, Taoism, and all other high spiritual teaching. Carry the image of the Japanese gate you face on your way to spiritual cooking, which is the same gate you meet on your way back to the everyday. Whenever you find yourself feeling lifeless or stuck, simply take a look at the image of the gate to remind yourself that you are in need of another crossing into the big room. The same gate will be waiting for you upon your return. Equally value and appreciate the experiences offered in the passage through both sides of the gate. In this back and forth movement from one side to the other is found seiki, the pulse of pure movement and life force that brings health, vitality, and spiritual renewal.

2. *Upside-Down Cake* – On each side of the gate exists a world that appears upside-down to the other side. Any truth on one side can become its opposite on the other side. The loving big God of the big room becomes a judgmental small trickster god when frozen inside trickster's ice-cubed ego. Talk of weakness, meekness, and surrender can feel punitive when spoke in a small cold bottle, but instantly feels liberating and joy inducing when heard by vast room ears. Make sure you occasionally eat some upside-down cake or at least imagine doing so, reminding yourself how things reverse in the shift between hot and cold. No matter how sour, bitter, and distasteful you may have been before you were spiritually cooked, you return as a sweet peach upside-down cake that instills joy and hope in others. The same is true for other people in your life. Rather than go to war, work to bring everyone through the big room door. It helps to be more like a vaudeville act whose song and dance brings some laughter and tomfoolery to voicing the sacred. What looks crazy and foolish on the surface is now guided by sacred wisdom that resides within and exudes throughout. When you return, stay focused on the whole of the sweet and soft peach inside and give less attention to the bottle that holds it. Get trickster poor and spiritually wealthy so your opposites are better aligned, making you easier to pour into abundant mystery.

3. *Keep on Cooking on the Inside* – No matter how cool and tough you need to appear to others on the outside, keep on cooking your soft and peachy soul on the inside. The mystical prayer wheel must never stop shouting, chanting, singing, and dancing, enabling divine expansion and heat to reach every corner of your life. Stay on sacred ground when you come back. Don't be in a hurry to think and shrink when you can still sing and expand. When you carry the heavenly sunshine within

you, its rays are emitted and transmitted to others who feel that you truly have something that makes you spiritually sweet, warm, soft, and light. Draw and carry a picture of a mystical prayer wheel with you, making sure its spokes look like the rays of the sun. Also draw a little musical note at its center to remind you that holy music is what makes the heavenly world go round.

4. *Releasing Hare Tales and Catching Lark Songs* – Avoid falling into the same old rabbit holes and resist being repeatedly distracted by trickster tales about your past, present, or future that impede the gathering and blending required for cooking. Come closer to the lark's song that waits to pour your tones, rhythms, and movements through the gate of divine expression and celebration, bringing you forth anew as a better instrument that voices the tune that spiritually attunes. Be a musical instrument that bypasses the storyteller. Go for the wings of musical glory rather than get rebottled by a manmade story. If you must, carry two hand-drawn musical notes as a note reminding you to sing with the lark.

5. *Ride the Melt* – When you are cold, you appear solid as ice. When you are cooked, you liquefy and pass through the sacred portal on your way to becoming spiritual steam, the ecstatic dream that naturally rises to the sky. Make sure that you regularly visit your kitchen, open the freezer, and stare at an ice cube. Look at it and say, "This is my situation." Then place one ice cube in an open bowl and set it in a window where sunshine comes through. Act like you are uncertain whether it will melt or remain solid ice. Do this as a theatrical performance to please the gods. Here's the secret you should not show that you know: the ice will melt in the heavenly sunshine and so will you. Upon seeing the ice melt say again, "This is also my situation." Come back transformed after every trip to

the divine kitchen's spiritual cooking, ready to pour holy water and serve holy bread in all its changing forms.

Own the feeling that the gate is nearby, so the peach of you is ready to reach beyond the bottle, go past the branch, and even traverse further than the tree so you find the whole garden and the one who planted every seed of life within it. Only a song and dance, along with some wigging and giggling, can get you through the bottleneck. God likes to play in the field of the Lord. Shake the peach out of the bottle and send your soul through the gate. Be ready for the slapstick pratfall that requires a joke to drop a yoke and finally evoke the greatest mystery show that glows in the dark. We invite you to enjoy each ecstatic return performance as much as the initial exit. Ascend in order to descend and fall in order to rise. That's what it means to bake a holy cake and find you're upside-down and sweet as a bird singing to the rising sun.

The spiritual engineering practices of Sacred Ecstatics, including your post-cooking return to the everyday, help you live closer to divinity. Your initial entries into the big room fire mark the beginning of a spiritually reborn ecstatic life — one that walks, talks, shouts, rhymes, chimes, chants, sings, sounds a joyful noise, dances, trembles, and shakes with the saints, mystics, shamans, and spiritual ecstatics of the past, present, and future. There, all spiritual gifts may be sent down the rope, from spontaneous healing to optimization of your body instrument that goes beyond well-being and includes radical transformation, indescribable mysticism, life-altering anointments, and the wonderful bliss of extreme divine love.

In other words, the basic practices are designed to help bring you closer to supreme holiness, the source and force behind it all. They help alter how you are engineered, wired, and composed, transforming how you feel, see, hear, smell, taste, physically move, act, and interact with others. When you are in alignment and attunement with creation's original vibration, something gets a hold on you and shakes you up. The sacred vibration cracks your heart wide open, making you more of an empty cup, a hollow vessel, and a tuned body instrument through which divine resonance can be expressed.

Forget most of what you've been told or sold. Seek the fire-in-the-bones and ecstatic ignition that come from being nearer your Creator. Discover once and for all that the purpose of your life is to become spiritually cooked and made an instrument in the divine band. Life will take place more effortlessly and have more joy when you surrender to being tender tinder for God's fire. The daily practices develop good chops for participating in divine expansion and spiritual heating, bringing the utmost performance of your life. Have a workout with God and feel the bliss that you will otherwise miss. Sacred Ecstatics and its spiritual engineering invite you to be the song and dance you were born to perform.

PART THREE

ENGINEERING TIPS FOR PARTICIPATING IN SACRED ECSTATICS

The basic spiritual engineering skills of Sacred Ecstatics are important for two reasons: (1) they help you unlearn habits that detune, dampen, quiet, and still your body instrument; and (2) they introduce new habits that prime your body instrument for sacred ecstasy and empower your rope to God. Applying good spiritual engineering—whether in home cooking workouts, group intensives, or private sessions—puts you on the path of the old-school spiritually cooked mystics, saints, shamans, healers, and other singing and dancing ecstatics who shake and bake. These three formats will be briefly defined and followed by a list of practical tips for applying the basic skills of spiritual engineering in each.

THE SACRED ECSTATICS HOME COOKING WORKOUT

The Sacred Ecstatics home cooking workout enables you to exercise your body instrument and develop your ecstatic skills while strengthening your mystical rope. In addition to basic practices for gathering and blending the ingredients, the workout includes special "ecstatic travel tracks"—audio and video recordings that invite you to spiritually cook at home, either alone or with others. These tracks combine all the spiritual engineering practices in creatively fresh ways, providing a unique ecstatic spiritual voyage. Diverse cooking venues of the world come to life underneath the vast canopy of the big room. You may feel experientially transported to the Kalahari dance ground, the Japanese seiki bench, the Shaker praise house, the theatre of absurd revelry, the always changing musical mystery show, the experimental laboratory for sacred pyrotechnics, as well as other yet-to-be-invented forms that serve to raise the spiritual temperature and make more room for the mystery of divinity. Perform all your daily workout practices and follow the specially created ecstatic travel tracks to strengthen your big room spiritual cooking.

THE SACRED ECSTATICS GROUP INTENSIVE

Our group intensives provide an always one-of-a-kind combination of spirited ceremony, tent revival, and Life Force Theatre. Each intensive puts you in contact with the heartbeat, soulful sound, unleashed movement, and indefinable inspiration of mystery. Everything that takes place is entirely improvised and born in the moment. The atmosphere crackles with creative vitality and spiritual electricity, priming you for an immersion in the sacred vibration—the divine force behind ecstatic healing, transformation, and mystical experience.

When you come to an intensive ready to participate with well-honed spiritual engineering skills, you are more able to have your body infused with the sacred vibration, your heart lifted by ecstatic joy, your mind pointed toward the infinite, and your soul set on fire. You return home from this mountain-top experience as a well-tuned and regulated spiritual instrument ready to bring ecstatic vitality into your everyday work and play. To keep the fire burning at home, make sure you keep gathering the ingredients and turning the mystical wheel to sustain and further empower your relationship to the big room fire.

THE SACRED ECSTATICS PRIVATE SESSION

There is no session quite like a Sacred Ecstatics session—it brings new action and experience into the world, uniquely invented as you and your whole reality are spiritually cooked. Fueled by the sacred vibration and guided by the mystical rope, we welcome whatever the divine source and force has in store for you. That's why each session is a completely original experience every time.

What can happen in a session? Surprising metaphors and unexpected creative themes for your life may arise, as well as spontaneous rhyme, syncopated rhythm, evocative sound, magical song, mystical movement, vibrational touch, or a newborn spiritual ritual. In other words, a session provides another opportunity for spiritually cooking. Whether you come for healing or spiritual growth, the Sacred Ecstatics recipe is followed and its transformative power is best received when you arrive with some spiritual engineering know-how.

As conductors (we prefer this name over healer, shaman, medicine person, or spiritual coach), we emphasize tracking divine mystery wherever it may be found, whether it's in a forgotten joy, a repressed miracle from your past, or an unexpected here-and-now ecstatic blast. As you are brought closer to the big room of mystery and all the creative change it exudes, the session comes to life and spiritually cooks. Every session is an opportunity for you to take a ride inside the mystical wheel, so come to each session with all the ingredients already humming inside your body and be prepared to keep blending them in the hours and days that follow.

PRACTICAL TIPS FOR THE APPLICATION OF SPIRITUAL ENGINEERING

Here we provide a list of practical spiritual engineering tips for maximally effective participation in all the cooking forms of Sacred Ecstatics. These tips, like all instructions in this book, are a result of reverse engineering the oldest ways of getting spiritually cooked. Follow them to assure that you are doing your part to help raise the spiritual temperature, set your soul on fire, facilitate reception of the sacred vibration, and empower your rope to God.

Follow the Ecstatic Conductor

A spiritually anointed conductor or leader, called a spiritual captain among the Caribbean ecstatic Shakers, is required to help keep everyone in line with the same rhythm, song, and movement. Without such anointed steering it is difficult to establish the social coordination needed for a collective call and response. Describing it in spiritual engineering language, un-coordinated and random expression dampens or extinguishes the acoustic and mechanical vibrations because each competing vibration and rhythm cancels out the others. When all resona-tors sympathetically vibrate together, enhanced amplification naturally occurs. Get tuned to the conductor and follow their beat as well as the changes in tempo and dynamics they initiate. Do this with the recordings at home and with the live conductor at a session or intensive.

A conductor is like an ecstatic DJ for God who knows when to change the music in order to keep the temperature hot. She can discern when any kind of change is needed, whether it involves moving the emphasis from rhythm to melody (or vice versa), changing a song's tempo, or shifting the words of a prayer, among other forms of alteration. Follow the conductor's changes. When you are at home following an ecstatic travel track, make sure you move, pray, chant, or sing with what you hear or see on a recording or film. Follow the navigational course that has been set in motion for you. You are able to climb higher, sail further, and plunge deeper in matters of spiritual mystery when you follow the lead of someone who has experience steering the musical ship and changing the tunes.

Serving as an ecstatic conductor or DJ is an anointed rather than self-selected role that is checked and confirmed by other cooked elders. Unless you are both fully spiritually cooked and anointed to steer the ship, oversee the kitchen, and have the discernment to know when to make an ecstatic shift, learn to enjoy following the lead of a qualified conductor who is there to help everyone go farther. A spiritual voyage requires as much if not more specialized expertise and preparation as flying a plane, driving a freight train, or captaining a ship. Respect this practical wisdom or risk never getting off the ground, going off the rails, or having a total crash.

Togetherness is what makes the social alchemy of Sacred Ecstatics work. Unless you feel *and* act in synch with a greater community, the sacred circle of connection is broken and the mystical wheel is unable to turn and go anywhere. Always watch, listen to, and follow the conductor whose job it is to make sure everyone is traveling on the vertical rope to God.

Synch and Coordinate Rather than Do Your Own Thing

Spiritual cooking, whether done with two people or two hundred, involves aligning everyone's expression to more powerfully turn the mystical wheel. This requires that you tune into what is going on around you to synch and coordinate your rhythm, movement, and vocal expression with those of others and the conductor. You do not come to an intensive to be a passive audience member or to have an individual experience *alongside* others; you come to contribute to turning up the spiritual temperature so that everyone can get cooked.

Take advantage of the way joining a group rhythm, chant, and song is a lifeline that rescues you from drowning in individual mind chatter. You don't want to zone out, trance out, or become dissociated from the spiritual current coursing through the whole collective body. Instead, learn to become more adept at tuning in to the acoustic vibrations (music and ecstatic sounds) and the mechanical vibrations (body movements) around you. When each person plugs in, everyone gets plugged into the highest power station.

Make sure you "stay within your gift" — the unique and resourceful contribution you are able to contribute to the whole ensemble — no matter what it is. If you can't keep a beat, then don't play the tambourine and throw everyone off. If you have a natural talent for showing excitement when someone else sings beautifully, then use it to lift up all the singers. When you are in the big room and the temperature is high, you will really feel, rather than just abstractly know, that everyone is an inseparable part of the whole. Rather than focus on yourself, turn your attention to performing good spiritual engineering. Bring your gift and do your part to turn the mystical wheel that cooks the whole room.

If someone starts making sounds, noises, rhythms, or movements that are out of synch with others, an immediate adjustment is needed. In the Caribbean, where group ecstatic journeying is experienced as taking place on a spiritual ship, any kind of individual disturbance or interference is called "falling overboard." When you fall away from the collective vibe, the group "throws out a lifeline" to reel you back in. Someone might assist you by physically moving your hands, arms, and body to be in the right rhythmic time. Or folks might gather around to clap the rhythm and sing the song more passionately, implicitly encouraging you to grab hold of the song line and reboard the ship as a realigned participating member rather than as a disconnected drifter.

At other times a traveler may heat too quickly and require cooling down in order to reboard the ship. Whether you are too cold, too hot, or simply out of touch with the group, the conductor rallies the community to bring you back. When you are at home following a recorded travel track, make sure you are in synch with what you see and hear. Doing so will ensure you nurture the right interactional cooking habits that will serve you when it's time to spiritually cook live with others. It only takes one action that is too noticeably off and out of whack to sink a ship. Get on board and stay on board for the sake of your attunement and for the better resonance of all.

Emphasize Following, De-emphasize Leading

One dynamic we have noticed over many years of spiritual mentoring and teaching is the tendency among many spiritual seekers to quickly want to assume the role of leader, conductor, or shaman. For example, Brad took some people to the Kalahari to meet the Bushmen and attend their healing dance. Rather than participate as members of the community, more than a few of the visitors jumped into the dance and pretended that they, too, were like Bushman n/om-kxaosi. Afterward they returned home and claimed that they had learned how to doctor like the Bushmen. Upon witnessing this, the Bushman elders later had a good laugh as they further appreciated how easy it is for trickster to have its way with human beings.

We hypothesize that the overzealous desire to be a conductor is a bad habit perpetuated by widespread new age deceptive marketing that promises instant mastery of whatever the spiritual consumer wants. Whereas long-standing religious traditions, including indigenous shamanism, have built-in checks and balances for handling trickster ambition and self-deception, the "spiritual but not religious" new age landscape seems to feed and even celebrate people's desire to feel anointed, powerful, and magical. As we describe in our book, *Sacred Ecstatics*, when you embark on a spiritual path, you will at some point come to a crossroads where you face the choice to either crown yourself ruler of the kingdom of ego or take a vow to serve the kingdom of heaven. We refer to this as making the necessary part-whole adjustment through which you both recognize and congruently enact the truth of your life: you are a small part inside the greater divine whole. True joy, liberation, and spiritual magic are found when you hand your life over to the Higher Captain who will steer you on the journey and bring you safely through all.

It's not uncommon for people to spend years circling the intersection at the crossroads, split between a sincere desire to surrender their life to a higher divine will and the pull of trickster to "be somebody." Trickster will often trick you into thinking you can walk both roads at the same time, holding God in one hand and your ambition to be a big shamanic cheese in the other. When we see students in a hurry to teach, lead, or heal others, we immediately recognize that this personally inflated desire is what constantly puts out their holy fire. Their ego balloon constantly inflates and deflates based on whether they are feeling good about themselves or being recognized by others. This dynamic ultimately brings suffering and dissatisfaction, which may at some point lead to hitting an existential bottom. Such a defeat, however, is actually a gift when it inspires sincere surrender again and again until the small bottle is exited once and for all.

When you are caught in ego's cramped rising and falling elevator ride, it throws off your tone, rhythm, movement, and emotion. Your praying may feel mechanical, or during an intensive you may feel dissociated from the group, more caught up in what you're thinking or how you are looking to others rather than focusing on feeling sacred emotion. A lack of sacred emotion is a sure sign that you are not yet on sacred ground and are not holding on to a rope to God. Sacred emotion is the mark of true surrender to the divine. When it is present, even off-key singing sounds sweet and blends beautifully with other voices in the room. When sacred emotion is absent, even perfect singing, dancing, or drumming has the stink of showmanship and stands out like a sore thumb.

One of the most important tips for loosening trickster's grip is shifting your focus exclusively to gathering and blending the spiritual cooking ingredients, both at home and during a session or intensive. Don't fool around with other spiritual teachings when you haven't mastered good ecstatic spiritual engineering. Avoid being spiritually promiscuous by attending other spiritual workshops, reading best-selling self-help books, or working with spiritual advisors who lack the ecstatic know-how you are trying to master. Clear away everything that distracts your wholly devoted attention from learning to gather and blend the four ingredients of spiritual cooking. Whether it's past habits or new temptations, resist whatever puts out the ecstatic flames. By all means, reign in your drifting, free-associating mind and establish some ecstatic law and order. One rule should prevail: when thoughts trap you in a cold small room, stop and gather the cooking ingredients. This alone is the interrupt needed to move you along the spiritual highway. Your ecstatic learning cannot begin until such enacted commitment and disciplined focus is in full operation.

A good follower does not lead oneself astray. When you watch a video during a home workout, the main reason for your eyes and ears to be on the conductor is to help get you in line with the relevant rhythm, tone, movement, and emotion. Pay as much attention, and sometimes more attention, to the other people in the video who are skilled at following the conductor. Similarly, when you are at a Sacred Ecstatics group intensive, watch how the co-conductors follow one another. Also pay attention to those in the group who are following in an accompanying and uplifting manner. Stay focused on how to do the same — inspiring the conductor to build and spread spiritual conductance throughout the whole room.

When you observe a conductor, realize that they are actually an expert at following a higher conductor. To do this job effectively one must learn how to master the art of following. No one is prepared to receive an anointment to lead until they master and own the feeling for following. This is why those who want to lead from the onset seldom learn how to follow and therefore remain unqualified to lead. Aim to feel more woven inside the whole when you follow and learn how conductance better flows when the idea of being in the lead fades away along with all resistance to spiritual realignment.

Your goal is to be more resistant to trickster's desire for personal gain and more ready for divine flames. Have no goal other than to feel close to your creator. Willfully and skillfully do your part to make yourself ready for God's guidance. Aim for no target other than more communion and union with God. Profess no knowing other than knowing you must follow and be hollow in order to receive divine direction. Come without wanting anything except surrendering everything to God. Stay inside your gift, the most important of which is your longing to serve as an instrument in God's orchestra that inspires the world to sing and dance.

Help Strengthen the Conductor's Rope

When you participate in a group intensive or a private session, above all else make sure you uphold and support the conductor's rope to God. Help the conductor wake up and amplify their divine hookup so that the sacred vibration it brings down from above is pure and strong. In other words, sweep away the human debris of each of you and get the glee of your holy ropes into play. The more you help the ropes come to life, the stronger and more powerful the spiritual cooking will be for all involved.

On the simplest interpersonal level, encourage and motivate conductors to reach out and help, teach, and spiritually cook you. If you are cold, stiff, or just plain impolite, you cannot expect a conductor to readily share their gifts with you. The Bushman n/om-kxaosi always advise that doctors should never attempt to send the sacred vibration to anyone unless the recipient has an open heart. Be more lovable, teachable, and receptive so you increase the odds that you will be struck by spiritual lightning. When the conductors' ropes are held up and supported, they are more able to rise above the mundane and serve as sound spiritual instruments.

Assume that everything you do and say is seen, heard, and felt by the Creator. You should be sincerely calling on the divine to come near everyone and not pass anyone by, especially the conductors who are trying to get spiritually hot enough to be able to perform their anointed job of helping you get cooked. Exercise street smarts: the sacred vibration naturally resonates those who are spiritually soft, open hearted, and open minded, that is, ready to be touched and moved. Do whatever helps the sacred vibration be more easily transmitted to you.

Remember that group spiritual cooking is similar to musicians coming together to make music. The whole orchestra creates a more enriched sound and projects a more robust resonance than any instrument can generate alone, and for this to take place, a conductor is needed to help each instrumentalist's performance mix with the others to create a united and ignited whole ensemble. Come together, tune in, and fire up the conductors. When the leaders are on fire and all others in the room are feeding that fire, everyone cooks. Even the ancestors from the past wake up and get involved when spiritual cooking comes to life. This means that you are never alone — even at home — whenever the spiritual heat rises. When you are aligned with God, all who travel on the high road walk by your side.

Not Too Little, Not Too Much

This principle applies to everything you express in Sacred Ecstatics. Just as you need to initiate a bit of physical movement at the beginning of the seiki practice to get it going, you also need to appropriately join in whatever chant, rhythm, song, or dance is happening around you so that you can get on board the ship and feel something. Do so with appropriate measure, but don't exaggerate it. In other words, move just enough to help strike an ecstatic match, jumpstart a feeling, and hold others up, but don't try to take such a big step that you stumble and fall overboard.

When you step into the venue where spiritual cooking will take place, launch two prayers before things begin, one after the other. The first prayer should be spiritually serious, deeply sincere, and directly aimed at the Big Holy. It should convey your respect for entering into sacred space. You might ask, "Dear Lord, please take me and make me an instrument that serves you." Or more simply say, "Take me, Lord." Follow this with a second prayer that helps balance the previous prayer from being too heavy or serious. You don't want to become too pious and find yourself rigid, inflexible, and unable to allow divine play and experimentation. Remember that spiritual cooking requires both serious longing for God as well as humor and a childlike attitude of wonder and delight. Therefore, the second prayer should convey something like, "Let 'er rip!" or "Whatever, let's do it!" These prayers, internally spoken or whispered to yourself, help you bring the right mix of serious-ness and playfulness, reverence and irreverence to the situation.

Set yourself up so you are more easily moved. Be on the midpoint fulcrum between "too little" and "too much" and let this position rock you like a teeterboard so enough momentum is built up to throw you forward. Climbing the rope requires having just the right dose of ever-increasing emotion and movement that truly lifts rather than causes drift, rocking you between serious work and divine play.

Say Hello and Amen!

Old-school sanctified church leaders sometimes call out to their congregation, "Say Amen, somebody!' They are saying that if anyone feels the spirit, they should be outspoken and voice an acknowledgment. Among the Caribbean Shakers, whenever the holy spirit arrives, it is announced by shouting "Hello!" Expressing enthusiasm is a matter of basic spiritual engineering—emotion and movement are amplified when your vocal chords send acoustic vibrations of sound into the air while pulsing mechanical vibrations into your body. Anytime you are aware of the sacred, make a joyful sound. Demonstrate your joy when you feel or hear that the divine pulse is in you or someone else! Doing so can help spread the vibrational resonance, moving it from one person to another and circulating it inside your body as well.

Your spiritual temperature will not rise if you come to silently observe or be entertained as a passive audience member. Your body needs to ecstatically participate rather than idly cogitate, whether you're in a group intensive, a private session, or at home following an ecstatic travel track. Don't indulge in an internal discussion, critical review, or ongoing assessment of any kind. Doing so will keep you cold and unable to be caught by sacred emotion or motion, thereby distancing you from bringing on the sacred vibration. Sitting there like a stone when others are trying to get cooked doesn't hold up the conductor's rope or the vastness and heat of the room. Publicly acknowledge whenever you sense something sacred by clapping or shouting, "Yes!" or "Amen!" or "Hello!" If participants shout whenever the leader has struck a resonant chord, it helps guide the conductors to do more of what is working.

In general you should support, uphold, and celebrate someone else getting cooked every time you notice it. Divine resonance is contagious. The sacred vibration, the holy spirit, n/om, and seiki are socially transmittable to the extent that everyone feeds, celebrates, and encourages its presence in themselves and others. Experience someone else's attunement and the gifts that ensue as if they are your own.

You have most likely been taught to elevate stillness, subdue emotion, and seek the relaxation response. Now is the time to for you to experience the other side: amplify spontaneous movement and sacred emotion and elicit the sacred ecstatic response! This is the other half of life and it has been made taboo in favor of exaggerating the importance of self-control, obliterating your opportunity to experience a holy rock and roll inside the higher whole. There is a time to sit still and a time to move, a time for the cold and a time to heat up and cook. You've waited too long to step into the big room where mind becomes a servant of higher emotion and rest does not arrest ecstatic fervor but makes you ready to thunderously rumble. Say, "Hello, let's go" and start moving toward an intimate experience with the singing and dancing divine.

The Ecstatic Hand Clap

Clapping is a way you can contribute to empowering the rhythm set by a conductor. If you really want to cook, you must learn how to ecstatically clap. When something holy gets an ecstatic hold on you, it can make your hands spontaneously clap as they are pulled by a higher power. Sanctified church members refer to this experience as the "holy clap," an energized hand clapping that has so much spiritual power that clapping alone is enough to get you spiritually charged and cooked. This kind of clapping can change your life as you clap in accord with the sacred cord. Open your palms to the rhythmic groove clapped by higher hands. Grab hold of what circulates through a cooked community rather than force a clap that doesn't tap into the collective heat.

Clap for and with others, clap to set yourself and everyone free, and clap for and with God. In other words, don't pause, but applause all movement of the divine! When you clap with God, your clapping will not tire as it helps fan the sacred fire. The Bushman women who clap and sing know this secret. They receive as much n/om as those who dance and doctor. Clapping has provided the primary rhythm for the Kalahari healing dance for thousands of years. Clap your way up the rope to God. If you want to receive the divine zap, then learn to ecstatically clap.

A One-on-One Session Is a One-for-All Session

Sacred Ecstatics group intensives sometimes provide opportunities for a person to come forward and have a session with us in front of the group. You benefit most from such a moment when you regard this person as a kind of ambassador for everyone in the room. Whatever is communicated is a metaphor for a similar concern in your life. Likewise, however we respond is a response that is relevant and beneficial to you. If a mystical prescription is offered, consider it as one you should also enact. Experience each one-on-one session as a one-for-all session. Regard what happens to someone else as something happening to you. This builds up the higher mind, body, and heart wherein we each contribute to bringing one another into full ecstatic blossom.

Similarly, when you have a private session with us, equally consider yourself as someone chosen to bring a unique teaching into the world. Whatever takes place in a session will be something that has never happened before, and this includes the particular mystical prescription for action that is spontaneously created. Spiritual cooking in the big room recreates and reinvents your life each time. It does so by bringing together all sides of all things, including the resourceful side of defeat and the downside of victory. In the big room we find life's contradictions and oppositions ready to blend in order to mend, making a former dread a renewed thread of hope straight from the divine rope.

Be More Ready and Better Able to Receive the Sacred Vibration

When ecstatic conductors put their hands on you in a session or intensive, be receptive to their vibration so it can effectively resonate your body instrument. This may mean holding back or stilling your movement enough to allow your body to receive the current. Do your best to not interfere by trying to show that you also have a vibration or can ecstatically shake. Such posturing, even if it is sincerely naive, usually interrupts the required feedback loop between the transmitter and receiver. If you are jumping around wildly, a conductor's hands can't make enough contact to establish a mutually shared resonance. Be open, available, and receptive, something best accomplished by adopting more of a "thy will be done" attitude. Here, "thy will be done" applies to both the conductor's trembling hands and your body's reception of its vibration.

Also remember that the sacred vibration is not only transmitted through touch, but through enhanced rhythm, song, music, and the special shout of a cooked conductor who is on fire. If you wholeheartedly participate in a session or intensive through holding up the conductor's rope, empowering the ongoing rhythms, staying attuned to the music, and celebrating when you see someone else getting cooked, then you will become more open, available, ready, and receptive to catching and being spiritually charged by the sacred vibration. You can even experience the reception of the sacred vibration when another person receives it, feeling as if you were directly touched yourself. Allow the whole atmosphere to pulse the sacred vibration into you.

Never Forget the Primary Importance of Sacred Emotion

The sacred vibration is not possible without sufficient sacred emotion, especially the longing for a personal relationship with the divine. Without the continuous amplification of divinely inspired emotion, the sacred vibration cannot wake up and charge the room. All other somatic vibrations and emotions are different and should not be confused with those that arise when your heart is touched and pierced by God's love.

Getting cooked involves more than experiencing spiritual energy, electricity, magnetism, or power; it involves authentically *feeling* holiness. Do whatever helps you and others feel close to divinity — that's the rope to God. The more you feel an emotional relationship with the divine, the more you experience God's loving power radiate and resonate over everyone present as well as faraway friends and family. Remember that if God's love is felt strongly enough, it even enables you to love your enemies, which is the ultimate and most potent shamanic power and spiritual medicine.

What matters most to an ecstatic conductor is whether the emotional climate is spiritually cold or hot. In other words, are people feeling emotionally distant or close to their creator? You also should be both brutally honest and tenderly compassionate about the spiritual temperature of your life. If you rarely feel any emotion for the sacred, then accept this as a clear and trustworthy sign that you simply are not cooked and your rope to the divine is weak or broken. Whether you are a new age seeker who can't feel and value the heat in a gospel song or a card carrying Christian who can't feel the holy spirit in a Kalahari dance, you are more the same than different. You are still in the cold where trickster encourages the spiritual dictatorship of personal preference for solidified names, beliefs, and ritual. Go for a bigger, hotter, and more emotionally charged spiritual life that includes all that resides inside the Creator's infinite mansion of divine expansion.

Try this experiment before doing a workout, intensive, or session: assume you are cognitively clueless, ecstatically n/omless, and spiritually homeless. Such an "empty cup attitude" fosters the kind of humility that can help you get cooked. Emptiness is the receptiveness assuring that when divine rhythms, tones, music, and movement pour into your whole being, you become mended, blended, and remade. Without a doubt, you are no longer the same person as before. You will be surprised over and over again to find that God is waiting for you everywhere, inside all the forms, shapes, venues, and rooms where the changing of creation takes place. What remains unchanged is sacred emotion, the everlasting divine love that persists, even as Gods' trickster side assures that whatever you know about mystery shall forever remain mysterious.

Finally, always remember that the spiritual engineering of Sacred Ecstatics is designed to fill a room with extreme joy — the sacred emotion you feel when your heart and soul are set on fire. It's all about "the joy, joy, joy, joy down in my heart," as the old hymn goes, the kind of joy that can make you smile and weep at the same time. This inner joy is emitted by the sacred vibration and makes it impossible to resist trembling, dancing, singing, and shouting in praise. Extreme joy comes from feeling and celebrating your rope to God, an experience that is amplified when two or more people gather to do the same, whether in human time and space or God's mystical eternity and infinity.

The Spiritual Engineering of Surrender

Surrender involves more than simply waving a white flag and saying, "I give up." While this may be a good metaphor or even a meaningful ritual to perform when you feel like you have existentially hit bottom, surrender is not a one-time action, gesture, or ritual. Spiritual surrender entails constantly ceasing all resistance to communicate with God. More than surrendering to the idea of divinity, you surrender to a life that communes and seeks union with the divine. You submit your life to participate in ongoing creation, taking a vow to never stop calling and responding to God amidst the never-ending change of life.

The surrender of ecstatic spirituality is not the same as "giving up" or turning yourself over to an enemy, although trickster will attempt to interpret the end of its reign as an act of cowardice and defeat rather than acknowledge it as a bold and courageous feat. This kind of surrender is more a gift than a sacrifice—it conveys new life as it makes the static become ecstatic. Surrender to becoming a dedicated blender of the ingredients that render you willing, able, and forever ready to pray, sing, and dance with the divine. This is how you step into a long-lasting relationship where you and God never stop calling and responding to one another. Surrender then means, "Sir, render me into relationship with Thee."

It is inevitable that you will backslide and revert to former small room habits. Check your spiritual temperature and make sure that you don't mistake "feeling good about life" as an indication of spiritual heat or being on the right track. When things are going smoothly on the earthly plane, especially when material comfort flows and little suffering is felt, it is easy to think that you must be in good "alignment with your higher purpose," as the new thought/positive thinking new age chorus will tell you, and therefore will start to put less effort into your prayer because you feel less urgency. You fail to recognize that the bigger you feel, the smaller the room is. Minnows are only big fish in small puddles. It's more exhilarating when you surrender to being a molecule of God's vast ocean.

Surrender is required each time you fall out of the call and response to God. It is not enough to just talk about surrender, or even declare to yourself and others that you have surrendered. Talk is cheap and some of the people with the weakest ropes to God are very good at spinning all the right talk. Blend all the ingredients to form and turn the mystical prayer wheel. Stay in the divine call and response loop, because this circle is what must encircle you. As the old hymn sings, "I need thee every hour." You need to be calling and responding to God with each and every breath, making each moment an eternally sweet hour of prayer: "I need thee every hour, in joy or pain. Come quickly and abide, or life is in vain." In other words, when you are happy make sure you say, "Thank you, Lord! I need thee every hour. Help me, Lord." And when you are sad allow yourself to say, "Help me Lord! I need thee every hour. Thank you, Lord." Keep the call and response of the prayer wheel turning through every experience of your life, something not accomplished through the abstraction of thought but by the sanctification of ecstatically performed action.

Reverend Joseph Hart makes clear in his most popular hymn that it is not "fitness" — what you have accomplished or how good a person you are — that matters when it comes to communing with God. Instead it requires a special kind of emotion:

> Let not conscience make you linger,
> Nor of fitness fondly dream;
> All the fitness He requireth
> Is to feel your need of Him.[94]

Surrender to feeling the need of a close, personal relationship with God. Whatever helps you feel this need — whether it is adversity, diversity, or controversy — soak it in, feel it deeply, and then render your surrender to your creator. Doing so will set you free.

God's Unconditional Love Requires Unconditional Surrender

One of the key obstacles to receiving an ecstatic downpour of God's unconditional love is the trickster-fed belief that you are not required to do any spiritual work. It is naively assumed that you deserve all the love the universe holds because as a child of God you are entitled to an unlimited inheritance. Such a perspective is simply an excuse for avoiding the effort that helps make your inner vessel more ready, able, and willing to receive whatever God has in store for you.

Divine gifts are made abundant to those feeling and expressing an absolute need for divine intervention. Requesting a healing potion, guidance, teaching, or spiritual help of any kind requires a sincere emotional plea. Voicing a request without a deeply felt surrender to higher guidance blocks the message from being sent. Being clever with words does not catch God's attention, nor does showing off what you have achieved, conceived, or perceived. The more deserving you think you are, the more God will remain afar. You must turn the whole world upside down to open the spiritual valve so God's love can freely flow. Spiritually stand on your head so your heart is higher than your brain, elevating heightened emotion over trickster thought production. While God is ready to listen to every prayer, the divine telephone operator separates noise from pure signal. It takes ecstatic communication rather than trickster static for God's ears to hear that it is time to come near.

Making a sincere plea is what opens the line, activating the rope to God. The *felt need* to make such a desperate request arises from bankrupting any belief that perpetuates the myth that you can make it on your own. Until you feel ready to fall to your knees and admit that you need higher help all along the way, there can be no admittance of any request through the heavenly gate. It is feeling and expressing your state of being truly unfit, your never-ending errors and mistakes, your imagined or enacted debts, trespasses, sins, and crimes, and all else that is messed up about your trickster-guided living that matters. Drop the veil that covers your spiritual eyes and have a true look at what a wretch you are. Don't wallow in this clear perception and have a pity party, because that is no different than bragging about what a good person you are. Both perspectives make self-assessment more important than divine measure. To again quote Reverend Joseph Hart: "Your own goodness cannot save you, nor shall your wickedness damn you."[95] Surrender all self-assessment and instead develop good spiritual engineering habits. The greatest miracle of life is that the death of your self-centered world opens the door to more life in a divine-centered universe.

Keep in mind that those on fire with God's love are actually more at home with loss and defeat than earthly victory and material success. Suffering makes it easier to remember your true condition of being in need of perpetual realignment with the main pipeline. Those who feel the pain that is the side effect of human gain learn to prefer mingling with the suffering — the meek, weak, and poor whose need is more real than hunger for spiritual entertainment, shamanic entrainment, or self-fulfillment. The sacred vibration, seiki, or n/om of love is found more readily flowing in those whose channels have been opened and cleared of trivial pursuit. When the all-knowing self is found broken, lost, clinging to the end of the rope, and unable to flee, you are made ready to make your plea. To receive the big love requires feeling too broken to follow another token, symbol, or sign. Only then, in the ultimate, unconditional surrender found at the bottom of the cup, does the hard shell crack open and reveal the space where there's now room for the divine to come through.

Nothing is more misunderstood than the paradoxical requirement of earthly smallness and human brokenness to receive the bigness and wholeness of supreme holiness. Don't brush aside this thought as too negative and demeaning; the temperance of self-esteem and human pride are required in order to lift up one's spirit. There is a paradox that the more you believe in yourself, the further away you are from the highest spiritual elevation. Again, the world must be turned upside down to adjust your part-whole alignment and reveal why you must go down in order to rise up.

As many theologians and wisdom teachers have warned before, you have to be careful when you carelessly speak of the unconditional love of God and assume that it can be ordered by personal command or room service and received without the spiritual realignment that comes from turning your life around. Make the existential turn and go through the turnaround that feels the burn of God's love. Be careful with any overemphasis on unconditional love that ignores this preparatory condition because it might unknowingly indicate a narcissistic love of self that has the gloat of personal success and material excess rather than the humble glow that cares not to impress. To get ready for the holy zap, your heart must be made soft and tender for the pierce of divine arrows. Contrition makes ready your spiritual condition. Out of deep sorrow is born a new tomorrow. Once through the gate, never look back. Feel the remorse and then follow the course with eyes focused on the light ahead. Do this to have a courtship with heaven rather than give any importance to the courts of human judgment. When you turn away from all preoccupation with self, whether its inflation or deflation, there is less to interfere with reception of God's love.

God's love is unconditionally available and no one is excluded from it, including murderers, thieves, sex offenders, social oppressors, false friars, true liars, and scoundrels of every kind. But having enough room inside to hold big love is conditional on your making some effort. This especially includes recognizing and accepting that you are only a small part in the vastness of it all and that your spiritual innards need to be cleared so the bottom of the bowl can be hit and felt as truly in need of another kind of filling. Your trickster-ruling self will likely resist surrendering to such a get-on-your-knees preparatory condition. It may take many trials and tribulations to recognize how suffering is the supreme gift that helps the kingdom of self-glitter and litter crumble, clearing the table for an extraordinary love feast.

Keep in mind that when we speak of sacred emotion, it is more than the kind of emotion that is usually called "love." Sacred emotion is a mysterious experience that lies beyond all familiar names, descriptions, forms, ways, and means of delight. Even the words "bliss" and "ecstasy" cannot fully specify what true holiness feels like. Sacred emotion stirs the deepest longing for the divine while it simultaneously brings an oceanic sense of complete belonging to God. This emotion is so big that it is able to hold what before were contradictory and competing emotions, including the fury of protest and the peace of acceptance as well as the suffering and joy that now embrace rather than race to conquer the other. To receive God's *unconditional love*, offer *unconditional surrender*. God unconditionally gifts anyone whose contrition makes ripe the condition for spiritual ignition. Work hard to make yourself a good vessel, don't get too existentially or materially cozy, and actively engage all the ingredients so conditions are more favorable for God to deliver the mail and give you a nail.

It Takes More than Love to
Make the Spiritual World Go Round

One of the common spiritual pitfalls is assuming you can build sacred ground out of platitudes. One example is the conclusion that "it's all about the love" and that love alone makes everything right. It takes more than love to make the world go round. You also need a passionate, zealous, and ruthless no-bullshit mind whose sword has a sharp enough edge for making cleanly cut and clearly sorted distinctions. Otherwise, you will too easily become distanced from the effort and action needed to build sacred ground and expand the room, which includes both embracing and letting go, building up and tearing down, composing as well as editing. Reaching only for the feel-good spiritual truths is one way trickster avoids uncomfortable confrontations, including your confronting your own mistakes, partiality, and need for divine intervention. You also want to avoid an "anything goes" premise that permits anything and everything to have its place at the theological table. This results in a messy pile of disconnected metaphors, half-baked ideas, and a random collection of items that simply don't mix. You are left missing the guidance that clarifies and rarifies rather than obfuscates and makes it an unwise free-for-all.

Sometimes God sends something other than unconditional love down the sacred pipeline. This may include the sword of discernment and dissent that may upset others, making them feel uncomfortable. There are many forms of sacred emotion and inspired action that comprise the changing face of God. When Krishna revealed the many faces of divinity to Arjuna, as reported in chapter 11 of the *Bhagavad Gita*, the world was shown that there is a face, place, and time for creation and there is also a face, time, and place for destruction. The same holds true for all the other divine faces from absurd clown to critical frown, busy bee, sleepy pie, annoying fly, comforter, agitator, simplifier, complexifier, pacifier, electrifier, and deep fryer, to name a few.

At each degree of temperature and expansion, and for every moment in time, there is a face of God, a unique room, and a changing form whose arrival or purpose cannot be predicted beforehand. We must avoid reducing God to only either bringing love's sweet honey or the prophetic correction that has a sting. All the emotional faces of God comprise the whole body of divinity and this includes a demon or two thrown in for good measure. In fact, the changing faces are the changing forms of trickster itself, each image momentarily trying to have its time on the stage while begging to stay longer than it should. Face the whole of the changing God rather than freeze-frame any preferred trickster face. There is a time for love and a time for all the other sentiments, testaments, and heavenly sent embodiments.

Ecstatic spiritual engineering exists to help you from getting lost in either the syrupy platitudes or harsh moralism that keep you stuck in one trickster face, perhaps filled with all the right words and ideas, but lacking the spirited tone, rhythm, spontaneous presence, and sacred emotion that assure presence in a big room. How do you know whether you are psychologically faking or spiritually baking? For starters, you need other cooked people in your life to help you sort that out, because your own trickster mind is not a reliable consultant. Furthermore, an authentic spiritual path always requires ongoing unconditional surrender, which includes surrendering any habits of posturing to yourself what you spiritually understand and have experienced. Tall tales that boast and gloat never indicate a spiritual roast or journey on a sacred boat.

Do you resist any hallowed names, prayers, or songs? Do you resist being small and broken? Have you not mourned or do you not own a sword or a song? Are you afraid to ask any of these things in case you don't like the answer? Do you think there is no need to go further than whatever you think? Do you talk more about magical thinking than spiritual cooking? Are you more interested in your story than God's songs? Do you long to be held in the divine heart locket or would you rather place a god inside your pocket?

When you enter the big room, don't make any other prayer than "thy will be done," however this is articulated and requested. You may subsequently receive a bolt of joy, a jolt of love, a quieting balm, a burst of tears, or the emotion that sets in motion some social protest that may be regarded as politically, spiritually, and psychologically incorrect and incompatible with positive attitudes and touchy-feely platitudes. We had a student who claimed he didn't like saying "thy will be done" because it might activate the kind of heavenly tough action that he wasn't sure he'd be willing to face. He was right—God doesn't act to obey your desires to ease or please, but to meet your true needs. Make room for all of God's faces, emotions, and action, or else find yourself reducing mystery to trinkets worn around the wrist, a charm bracelet you believe has magical influence, when in truth you are under trickster arrest with handcuffs keeping you away from the big room.

The sacred emotion you feel in the big room includes all of God's many feelings. Let God choose whether to send a song or a sword, a feather or a hammer, sunshine or storm, or a positive, neutral, or negative outlook. All the faces are connected to every other face. Sometimes God will make your pain feel worse or leave you less at peace with the world. Yet all of these feelings will be held in a vaster blessed assurance that comforts and heals all lesser discomfort. When divine love comes, it will not make you shy or timid about holy trouble making and definitely will end all trivial placating. God's love arouses prophetic unrest and civil disobedience, not a desire to promote popularity, comfort, and mass appeal. The saints and holy ones were usually the most emotional, most radical, most revolutionary, and the least liked figures of their time. They were on a mission to build and expand sacred ground, overturn unjust laws, and embrace those with flaws by turning the wheel of prayers, songs, and dances of higher change.

God's unconditional love holds all the emotional faces of God and circulates the changing that keeps them all in play.

Reception of higher sacred emotion leaves you unsure how to describe it because words like "love," "power," and "glory" only hint at all the dynamics it stirs within. Try giving thanks with the action rather than only the talk of gratitude. If you truly feel it, then ask God, "How can I help and be of service?" Assume there is always work to do and that you won't know whether you need to apply the sword or sing the song unless you are feeling the sacred emotion and music inside you. God is always on the move, and there is always a revolving door whose circular motion keeps every face in motion, forever ready to enact its time and place.

Draw a happy face on one knee and a sad face on the other knee. Then draw a halo over each face to remind you that both joy and suffering belong to God's whole sacred emotion. When you get on your knees to pray, recognize that three faces are there to pray. Remember that when more than one face gathers, God listens in more ways. The divine then better hears your words, feels your longing for joy, and recognizes your suffering. More importantly, God notices that more parts of you have come to pray and this assures that more of God's many faces will be inspired to face and embrace you.

Spiritual engineering provides simple, cut-to-the-chase practical directions for getting cooked in the big room and strengthening your rope to God. While it is possible for a child to follow these practices and the overall recipe, adults are more likely to make all kinds of excuses to avoid changing their spiritually unresourceful habits, even when they clearly do not facilitate progression on the sacred highway. The term "spiritual engineering" shifts your emphasis to what you need to actually do in order to help build a big room and maintain ongoing presence, expansion, and heating within it. Its emphasis on specific action eschews emphasizing abstractions that are far away from real-time feeling and expression. Realize, accept, and utilize the fact that you communicate with more than words and thoughts. Let's assume you already have all the understanding you need. In order to walk your talk and keep trickster at bay you need to express what you feel for the divine in rhythm, tone, and movement that conveys the sacred emotion you feel. Bring all of the ingredients and all the changing faces of existence to your whole-bodied communication with divinity.

Leaving the Room

At the end of each round of spiritual cooking, whether it was a session, intensive, or home workout, be careful how you leave the room, whether you are heading for lunch, dinner, recreation, rest, or sleep. It is extremely important to learn how to sustain the sacred vibration, heated emotion, room expansion, and holy compass setting for as long as possible. Resist stepping back into the non-ecstatic grooves, entrainment rhythms, and dampened vibrations associated with small rooms of refrigerated interaction. Keep your resonator humming and your instrument tuned to remain a live wire for God, ready to act as called and pulled by the higher force you sustain within.

Post-cooking conversation and social interaction (whether face to face or online) arguably put you at most risk for spiritual de-tuning because this is trickster's playground. Aim for talk that maintains the vastness of the room and the integrity of sacred ground, which can include childlike humor and playful absurdity that resonate with creative life, sacred emotion, and inspiration. If you were cooked, the way you talk about your experience immediately afterward influences its sustainability. Some people have acquired spiritually impoverished habits of "gee whizzing" any possible presence of magic in their life from so-called synchronicity to dreams that presuppose magical or spiritual content. Or they just can't stop boasting about how many people they have helped or inspired. Be careful to not become addicted to the personal high that comes from posturing as a magical, spiritual, or cooked person. If you have this habit, then muffle it after a round of cooking and simply say, "Thank you, Lord!" Divine luminosity, ecstatic joy, and sincere humility should radiate from you and the way you speak.

Be wise in the hours that follow spiritual cooking. You need to work as hard to keep sacred ground intact when you leave the room as you did when you began. Don't retreat into a small room that leaves mystery behind. If you immediately walk out of the room and go straight into the social hour greased with beer and wine, you may unknowingly squash, dissipate, and eradicate the primary building blocks that were used to build up sacred ground. This is how trickster can tap into sacred energy and divert and convert it into social party energy. If you let that happen too often, your rope will shrivel and the gods will be less inclined to fill you up the next time.

After a dance the Bushman n/om-kxaosi continue singing and dancing in their minds and hearts and hope that this will help them have a visit to a spiritual classroom. One of the purposes of spiritual cooking is to tune and energize you for sleeping in a big room where further mystical possibilities are attainable. If you shrink afterward, you waste a precious opportunity for 'round the clock spiritual transformation. Keep one hand on the big rope and trust it will keep you in line even when you are silly and loose as a goose. We are definitely not saying that you need to be ridiculously pious, or pious to any degree. We are suggesting that you need to respect and honor what took place during spiritual cooking, and this can even be accomplished through absurd humor of the kind that you can imagine made the old-school saints and mystics chuckle in a wonderfully sweet way.

When spending time with others after an intensive, you should be recounting and sharing the moments that touched you during the event so you extend your cooking. Radiate the truth that is higher than any trickster encapsulation. Songs should be circulating in your veins—not taking part in bar talk, ice-cold digression, or trickster regression; scoring and comparing performances; critiquing human flaws rather than praising sacred thaws; gossiping about rather than uplifting others; displaying flirtatious behavior; and fanning the wrong fires; and all the rest of it.

In other words, when you leave the room after being touched by holiness, one question should rise above all else: *What are you going to do about it?* If you are going to piss it in the wind, it will come back to you as waste. If and only if you sustain this precious mystery and call for it to remain, can you develop a strong rope. Otherwise, you will become another trickster dope whose vice ropes are too easily pulled. Every time you are cooked a single degree in spiritual temperature, the temptations and tricks and distractions of trickster change their form. Keeping trickster at bay does not get easier the more cooked you are because every time you change, trickster changes and adapts as well.

After a workout, intensive, or session, imagine that the saints, mystics, and spiritual wonder workers are leaving the room with you. Act in a way that makes them want to continue hanging out. Divinity is a wonder working power that only resides within those who walk the straight and narrow ropeway with a fire within that sings with holy tones and shakes your dancing bones.

Dare to Share and Be For Giving

Cooling down after a round of spiritual cooking delivers a unique kind of spiritual rebirth. You find yourself more like the Kalahari Bushmen who value *sharing* as the highest human quality — being generous with whatever you own whether it's food, shelter, labor, medicine, wisdom, skills, talents, or other resources. You also realize that it is not wealth per se that makes it extremely difficult for the rich to pass through the proverbial eye of the needle, nor does poverty automatically grant your passage. Selfishness is what blocks the reception, activation, and circulation of the sacred vibration. The desire to hoard rather than get on board the spiritual train leaves you standing at the station with too much luggage in hand. Sharing is the remedy for clearing the holy track, unclogging the spiritual pipeline, opening the closed mystical door, and moving toward the big room. The natural desire to share is reborn in the big room fire and brought back to the everyday.

In the Kalahari, those who are successful hunters and gatherers are teased and lampooned upon return to help bring any ballooned egos back down to size so that felt equality will inspire sharing. A successful hunter may be hilariously accused of singing courtship songs or overtly flirting with a kudu. Such a tease is voiced with open tenderness rather than masked jealousy, ensuring both respect for the hunter's skill and a caring concern that the Kalahari archer does not become too oversized and made easy prey for trickster to hunt. Similarly, when you come back from the high ground of spiritual cooking, don't gloat because that will easily sink your boat and dilute whatever was learned when you burned.

In the big room, the meat of a hunt and the song of a dream are shared with everyone. Here the voice of a singer belongs to the community as does the hunter's bow and arrow. Life in a non-Kalahari small room is always selfish because there is no room for others at the inn. Neither capitalism nor socialism can help get you to the big room—both political orientations too easily lead to shrinkage of goods and goodness. Only spiritual expansion and heat can convert you to dare to care enough to sincerely share.

After spiritual cooking, you exit with the desire to relate to others as you most deeply wish they would relate to you. If you only focus on how good you feel and aren't hearing the calls of those needing what you can share, then you weren't really cooked. Go back to the fire and become inspired to share the meat, roots, and songs as you spread the warmth. That's the point—the point of the n/om arrow and the point of ecstatic spiritual teaching—to get cooked so you are a more shared part of the whole.

Sharing involves taking a stand *for giving*. Forgiveness is the ultimate gift because it asks you to share what can't be taken— your sincere forgiveness of someone else's debt, trespass, and wrongdoing. Here we come to another spiritual fork in the road: on one side is found the road to so-called justice. But justice is typically "just ice," human judgment fueled by an "eye for an eye" mentality that only makes room for punishment. On the other side is the road to God's forgiveness. It offers the choice to be in a big enough room where the spiritual heat expands your heart to be *for giving* all you can give. The most radical political orientation, social ethics, and activism are offered by membership in the Big Room Party. There you praise and raise the bar high enough for everyone to be equally human as warm and generous sharing brings a spiritual melt shared by everyone.

Human beings cannot will themselves to be a good, just, or ethical person while they remain in a small room. The primary choice is not between choosing to be bad or good. The bigger choice is to enter the big room's equal inclusion rather than perpetuate inhumane division. When standing on vast sacred ground, you automatically do the right thing even if it seems out of step with human law and order. The spiritual path is not walking on the king or queen's highway. God's higher way leads to caring, sharing, giving, and forgiving. When you have an irritation with someone, the holy option is for the whole community to cook together. Courtroom trials, lawsuits, corporal punishment, and imprisonment make the world a colder place that locks up everyone — from criminal to judge and citizens — in a prison of trickster. Let's usher in a world that spiritually cooks rather than secularly judges and reaches for a spiritual thaw rather than the hammer of law.

Take another look at the three-step recipe of Sacred Ecstatics — building a big room, getting spiritually cooked within it, and then exiting with a heart that is for giving and a mind that aims to include everyone. There is no greater revolution than bringing on the spiritual heat. It alone enables you to rise above whatever drags you down. Walk away from war-faring combat and become a minstrel of mystery who fears no danger. Give enough praise to raise the dead and cook holy bread. Dare to share and care enough to give all you have to offer. And above all else, be for giving. This is what it means to return to the everyday after you have been cooked by God's fire. Be the ember that remembers there is a more ecstatically tender way to live with one another.

VISIONARY TEACHINGS ABOUT THE SPIRITUAL ENGINEERING OF EFFECTIVE LEARNING

After the basic principles and practices of spiritual engineering were developed, Brad had a dream:

> Hillary and I were at a gathering held inside the country church where I grew up. Several of my former teachers were there and they came up front to face the group. Sam Gurnoe, a traditional Ojibwa medicine man, friend, and former spiritual teacher of mine came first and said he wanted to offer some words about how to be a good student and foster the best learning experience. There was no admonishment in his voice. He simply wanted to share some practical advice to those who sincerely wanted to learn. Sam began by sharing his memory of what kind of student I had been with him: "More than anything else, Brad was sincere and respectful. He followed my instructions without complaint, always honoring me as a teacher."
>
> The other teachers also testified and as they spoke, I recalled that when I was a student I had such a passion for spiritual learning that I did not want anything to interfere with a teacher's motivation to teach me. I also recalled the stories I had heard about Hillary being a dedicated academic student. She was even more dedicated and disciplined than I had been at school. She made clear with every fiber of her being that she was there to learn and it showed. We simply had a strong and overflowing desire to give learning our very best and this included our uplifting those who bore the burden to teach.

We didn't naively exalt our teachers, especially our spiritual teachers, as infallible beings. Nor did we concern ourselves with their human shortcomings. We primarily related to their high and divine rope, doing so with beginner's mind, heart, body, and soul. We wanted their rope to be stronger so our ropes would get stronger. In this mutual strengthening of both the ropes of teacher and student, we would each be tuned and altered by higher hands.

The following night Brad dreamed that we heard a master teacher tell the same group that learning spiritual engineering itself requires using effective engineering to learn. Generally speaking, this means showing sincere respect that helps good teaching and learning take place. Big room education cannot take place with small room habits, just as spiritual cooking cannot take place through actions that refrigerate.

Real learning always involves having your ego and its conceptual frames and habitual behavior shaken and perturbed. The bigger the change a teaching can deliver, the more that personal discomfort may knock on your door. But if you persevere, you will be able to get past being jerked around by your own ego's inflation and deflation and become more ready for the nourishment that spiritual wisdom teaching provides. Learning begins when you welcome and celebrate correcting, editing, and having someone point out how things can be done differently. As any good teacher will tell you, living a spiritual life requires continually surrendering all forms of "knowing-it-all" and allowing God to work on you. If you can't follow instruction or receive constructive feedback from a teacher without having a crisis, it will be difficult for you to later sustain the kind of higher surrender required to stay on the vertical rope.

Effective engineering for learning begins by taking responsibility for how your actions contribute to the pedagogical environment and shape what you learn or don't learn. Some people have never really been good students, whether it was in grade school or as an adult. Instead they coasted along and did the least, managing to learn or change very little. Some students respond to every instruction by first analyzing whether they like it or dislike it, picking and choosing which part of teaching to follow based on their preferences. When students spend more time analyzing and assessing rather than acting and absorbing, the door to learning never fully opens. However, when students choose to throw themselves wholeheartedly into learning and doing all they can, it builds a big schoolhouse room that inspires the highest teaching and learning to take place.

Always remember that what you say and how you say it will either motivate a teacher to give you more or communicate that you don't want further teaching. If you want a baker to give you the freshest, tastiest loaf of bread, you should make clear how hungry and appreciative you are for the baker's work. Come to school empty and hungry to learn, and do your best to sincerely motivate your teachers to provide all they are able to teach. We personally have always done our best to follow ordained instruction with delight because despite our own human shortcomings and those of any teacher, we are there to learn and spiritually burn. If a teacher could help cook us, we cared not whether they spoke of the moon or a loon.

Some people develop the bad habit of contradicting themselves at school — showing up as a student but then acting like a teacher. Such posturing is something that we have experienced over the years both in academia and in our spiritual teaching. We always are amazed that some people would bother to commit their time and resources to learn, only to spend most of the time trying to prove to the teacher and other students how much they already know. When a student tries to show off being spiritually cool, an opportunity for learning how to cook is chilled. Come to school less motivated to debate belief, posture infallibility, or be lauded and applauded; be more interested in exploring and experimenting with how to get spiritually cooked.

Following Instruction

In the dreamtime Brad also recalled the time he was flown on a seaplane to an island in Canada where he attended a shaking tent ceremony. His friend told him on the flight, "Our community is related like a closely knit family and how you conduct yourself with our medicine man affects us all. If you ask him for help, make sure you do what he suggests. Otherwise, you will harm the community. Don't ask for help unless you intend to accept the help offered and follow through with what is suggested."

Those words have forever rung in Brad's ears, especially when someone comes to us for help or mentoring and after we advise some action, we notice that there will be no follow through or that they will only half-heartedly go through the motions. Such a student or client weakens the ropes of all involved, especially when divinely inspired instruction is not respected and followed. Be careful what you spiritually ask for because if you reject what is given, there is a systemic consequence that affects the lives of others and this ultimately comes back to you.

Bumping into your resistance to follow instruction inside an anointed spiritual teacher's schoolhouse is likely a sign that such action is the very bitter medicine needed to remedy any artificial fake sweetness. Do it as an experiment to see if altered action leads to *altared* experience. Do it for the whole community. Do it for no reason other than to honor the rope above a spiritual teacher's head and to strengthen the rope above yours.

Participating in Ceremony

In a subsequent dream that also took place in the same country church, Brad told the group how he had learned to participate in diverse spiritual ceremonies over the years:

> If I had to make prayer ties at a Lakota family's house, my mind did not ponder whether it was really necessary to do such a thing to please the Creator. I knew that my host believed in this kind of offering and I wanted to do everything to boost his bond with the Great Spirit because this

brought a blessing to everyone. Similarly, I didn't show any discomfort when hearing Hindu priests pray over me in Bali even though the tone was unfamiliar. In the black church, I never winced when I heard a preacher's sermon go outside my intellectual comfort zone.

I arrived with practical street smarts that didn't voice displeasure or irritation with whatever it was that personally linked the teacher, preacher, medicine person, or spiritual elder to their higher power, no matter the form of prayer, song, or visionary teaching. I also respectfully used the leader's preferred name for the divine to pray when I was in their ceremony, doing so to honor their rope and help empower their traditional way of making the holy connection. I also didn't say "Aho" at a church service or "Amen" at a Micmac ceremony. I changed my conduct to be respectful of the teacher's lineage. To receive good teaching, healing, or spiritual experience requires doing everything to help the leader open and strengthen their relationship to the holy source that sends the holy force, making it more likely that you will receive blessings from a divine pipeline that is in full working operation.

Along the way I learned a practical method to keep my spirit high no matter where I was in the spiritual universe. If I was in a Kalahari Bushman dance and didn't feel the spirit, I sometimes secretly sang another song inside myself that I was able to more readily feel. I might sing "Amazing Grace" internally while a Bushman song was going on around me. I did the same when I was at a sanctified church and didn't feel the spirit there. I would sing a Bushman song inside myself to help light the match. I learned there were many ways to *change myself* in order to make an emotional adjustment to the immediate spiritual situation, rather than fuss about changing what was going on around me. I found that once the spiritual fire started, I could then easily transition to feeling whatever music, movement, and emotion were being offered.

I recalled meeting a very powerful healer in Bali who had cured all kinds of incurable diseases. He told me that he had been taught and ordained by a leach in a rice field. Years ago while gathering rice, a leach spoke to him and began teaching. It was his link to the divine and enabled his healing ability. I neither questioned nor disqualified that leach as being anything less than any other being that might have been chosen as a divine teacher. In the big room, there is enough room for stones, pebbles, insects, butterfly wings, and falling stars to teach side by side the holy ones of every stripe, color, size, and shape. When you are spiritually cooked you are made able to even reach for a leach that can serve as a link in the chain that connects you to the Big Holy.

Do your best to assure that you do not interfere with a conductor's divine hookup. If a teacher, healer, or spiritual leader said that she communicates with Jesus, Buddha, Krishna, mice, lice, or an oak tree, suspend assessment of what that means to you and only focus on the rope overhead, accepting that the mystery of divinity has many forms and names. Spiritual engineering reminds you to pay less attention to the names that are spoken and instead notice how somebody blends tone, rhythm, and movement with sacred emotion. Turn the same engineering assessment on yourself when you are in any ceremony: Are you acting to make the room bigger, gathering and blending the ingredients, and helping the conductor turn the mystical prayer wheel? Follow the sacred recipe if you want to be in ceremonial relationship to the rope above everyone's head.

Brad once dreamed and later learned about an old medicine man who conducted the Inipi ceremony without any stones and without having to set a physical fire. His prayers alone were enough to heat the lodge. He embodied good spiritual engineering and knew how to spiritually cook his prayer into a song and then into a fire of holiness so everyone perspired as they were inspired by the presence of spirit. You are the stone, match, fire, pipe, drum, horn, piano, and any instrument the Creator wants you to be. To be a more active part of creation — the ongoing changing — requires that you be open and willing to change. This includes changing how you participate in learning someone else's spiritual way. Over the years we have found that the more we sincerely participated in diverse spiritual traditions and religions, the more we experienced the truth of each as more similar than different. We find no real difference between a sweat lodge prayer meeting and a Wednesday night prayer meeting in church. When people pray with all their hearts, songs spontaneously burst forth and set a fire that spiritually heats both wigwam and church. The underlying spiritual engineering is the same even when the names, symbols, clothing, and interior decorating are different.

Always Uphold the Rope

In the next dream, Brad was taken to his grandfather's church:

> I sat in his chair and recalled how both my grandfather and father had to constantly endure the challenge of church "know-it-alls" who claimed to know what God wanted for the church more than the pastor. Or they postured to others that they better understood the interpretation of scripture, who should be given special church roles, how lessons should be taught, what social functions should be included, how much tithing

should be required, whether a building should be built, what hymns should be included, how long a service should last, and all the rest of it. The challenges of ministry make most other professions seem like a cakewalk.

At the same time, I remembered feeling then as I do now, a warm gratitude for those loyal and dedicated-to-the-rope folks that could be counted on to steadfastly hold up the conductors, leaders, teachers, and preachers, enabling them to get through any troubling or confusing social times. Every spiritual school, church, tribe, or community needs a core of dedicated elders who assure that the big room can weather any human storms that inevitably are a part of it all. Ever since I was a child, I learned to spot and admire the elders of a sacred community, the true supporters who made it possible for a leader to fulfill a calling. Though often invisible to others, they were actually the truest and highest leaders, leading others by how they graciously followed.

As an adolescent, I overheard other ministers pour their hearts out in our living room parsonage as they spoke of how mean spirited and outright cruel their parishioners could be, always done while posturing as do-gooders or God-led, God-loving people. My inside view of ministry did little to attract me to the profession or to the institution that welcomed such cold politics. I too often heard senior ministers privately say, "The church is the devil's playground." By the time I went to college I was definitely a "born again *not-*Christian." I loved what my grandparents and parents spiritually taught and I accepted the infinite wisdom and equally immeasurable love of Jesus, but distanced myself as far as possible from those who called themselves Christians.

They too often had a spiritual stink and an unpleasant incongruity between their actions and the teachings of Jesus — both inside and outside the church.

As an adult I became the confidant of many holy elders, spiritual teachers, shamans, and healers from all over the world. I heard them lament what I had heard before as a child and adolescent — reports about the suffering they endured from being the target of others whose wolf-natured jealousy, insatiable selfishness, and addictive lust for power were almost always cloaked in sheep's attire. I had no trouble taking a stand for my teacher or preacher, but I did not want to be in their shoes or wear their robes. Fortunately, there seem to never be more than one or two rotten apples in a community at any given time. I later wondered in my academic career whether every social system always has one of these stinkers show up from time to time, just like a family occasionally has a symptom bearer whose problematic experience arrives to bring the whole family into a new kind of alignment.

Ultimately the spiritual engineering of teaching and learning are the same: both teachers and students must attend to the rope to God more than the mood swings, mind games, and other psychological garbage that resides below the rope. We must focus on whether our actions and interactions help everyone enter the big room and get spiritually cooked. All precepts, ethics, and wisdom are situational, and therefore we can't indulge in rigidly applying a few simple rules to all situations. Thankfully the spiritual engineering of ecstatic cooking provides us with the pragmatic exit from whatever stumbles, conflicts, confusions, or detours we encounter together: gather and blend the ingredients, turn the mystical prayer wheel, and head to the big room fire. Only when we are constantly seasoned, tenderized, and cooked in God's vibratory love can we continue being good stewards of all the ropes of relationship.

Teaching and Learning Are Nothing without N/om

After the above dreams in Brad's father's and grandfather's churches were completed, he was sent to another visionary classroom:

> It was a big room filled with all kinds of musical keyboards. Most of them looked like deconstructed pianos that had been incorrectly reassembled. They looked structurally weird, functionally off, and aesthetically ugly. Behind each instrument was a different anthropologist I recognized as someone who had previously studied the Kalahari Bushmen. As they took turns trying to explain the mixed up instrument in front of them and what its operation entailed, I grew increasingly irritated and frustrated. I finally couldn't take the nonsense any longer and shouted, "It means nothing unless you have n/om!" My piano, a beautiful Steinway concert grand, suddenly appeared in front of me and I proceeded to play it.
>
> In the moment of the dream when I could not tolerate listening anymore to the arrogantly voiced ignorance of those whose tone, rhythm, movement, and emotion were out of whack, I was powerfully struck by the truth of how n/om is absolutely essential. Whether it is called holy spirit, wonder working power, seiki, wakan, manitou, sacred vibration, or whatever name is used to indicate the supreme mystery that is ultimately nameless—its ecstatic fire must be burning inside you in order for anything truly spiritual or profoundly healing to take place.

Mother Samuel from St. Vincent knew and felt this mystery deeply in her bones. I shall never forget how emphatically she would remind me that a person is not capable of talking responsibly or truthfully about God unless the spirit trembles within. Don't just know and say you are close to God; feel close enough to God to tremble with so much joy and love that others feel it. The "something within" [w] that matters is a sacred vibration that resonates throughout the room. Until you own it and others confirm its presence, you are in need of further softening, preparation, shaking, and baking.

Many folks who talk a lot about God, spirit, love, or higher consciousness don't emit a sacred vibe. There is something obviously different, however, about those who belong to the lineages of ecstatic spirituality held inside the big room. Their talk exudes the warmth of the fire whose flames rise above the paper, ink, and trickster stink of those who think they know it all. Spirituality isn't about claiming to know God but aiming to be a target of God's archery, pierced and made an instrument that resonates with the sacred vibration after you have been struck by an arrow of divine song.

Spiritually cooked teachers can tell whether your instrument looks off, sounds wrong, feels mixed up, or is not prepared to host divine resonance. They can smell, taste, feel, hear, and see whether you have the special and rare vibration within or whether you are deluding and misleading yourself and others. Some folks are disappointed when they don't receive the grade

---

w This phrase comes from Baptist hymn writer Lucie E. Campbell (1885–1963) who wrote the gospel song, "Something Within." According to the Baptist Women in Ministry blog, it was published in 1928. See "Great Women of History: Lucie Campbell-Williams by Courtney Lyons," Baptist Women in Ministry (blog), May 18, 2010, accessed May 1, 2016, http://bwim.info/great-women-in-history/great-women-of-history-lucie-campbellwilliams-by-courtney-lyons/.

or the results they had hoped for when they enrolled at school. A temptation may then arise to discount other students, the teacher, the teaching, the school, or the whole educational system. Doing so only makes you spiritually colder, darker, and more distant from the divine. The alternative is to receive all constructive feedback as that which contributes to your spiritual learning.

Don't deny that you may be suffering from jealousy of others who have received spiritual gifts you have yet to own. If someone was given a nail of n/om, don't act like Antonio Salieri who thought he was more deserving of receiving God's music than Wolfgang Amadeus Mozart. After all, Salieri had worked harder than Mozart, who was more of an undeserving rascal. Know that God works in mysterious ways that are beyond human ability to comprehend. The divine plan is more aligned with Mother Nature's ecological wisdom where a gift for one is a gift for everyone. When someone else gets a nail of n/om, accept that this was required as part of the process for you to later receive it. Perhaps what happened to others and not yet to you will help make you softer and more broken, better prepared for the deepest reception of the sacred vibration. Everything works together in the ecology of the greater whole and community.

We will now speak to the part of trickster in all of us who at times becomes a restless and rebellious student who thinks it knows it all:

> "Think you're ready to graduate? Go ahead and take the final exam. It involves ascertaining what happens with your rhythm, tone, movement, and emotion when you step into a sacred context. Dare you ask a cooked teacher to take your spiritual temperature? Dare you ask if you have successfully gathered all the required ingredients for spiritual cooking, or do you prefer only pretending that you have made the holy blending? Do you think you have all that you

need, including no need for external evaluation and confirmation from a teacher, preacher, or pointer who might tell you otherwise? Do you want to face the possibility that doing it your way is only getting you more lost and distant from holy ecstasy, or would you rather maintain the fake bliss of ignorance?"

What do you want? Do you want to be spiritually cooked? Do you want to receive an installation of the sacred vibration? Do you want to stand underneath the heavenly sunshine? Do you long for a strong rope to God? Do you aim to come closer to the divine? Do you want the utmost joy of sacred ecstasy? Do you want to be an instrument that serves and performs rather than observes and informs? Do you want to fulfill your highest destiny? Do you want to learn Sacred Ecstatics? Do you want God's will to be done in your life? Do you want all of these things? Do you know that if you want any of these things, you actually are asking for them all?

There is more to the universe than questions and answers. The road that leads beyond knowing what to ask and what to answer is the ecstatic highway that takes you to the big room where spirit cooks. Here you do not hesitate or pause to ponder any cause. Instead, you immediately gather what you need to bring to the big room. Follow the sacred instructions and take the necessary action to learn what is taught, receive what is given, and enact what is prescribed. Do it to spiritually cook more than yourself and others — do it to help cook God.

PART FOUR

THE VISIONARY DREAMS
BEHIND SPIRITUAL ENGINEERING

Spiritual engineering was inspired and informed by a series of visionary dreams that started in May 2017 and continued for nearly six months. Every time we received a vision we wrote down its teaching. It all began with dreaming our admission to a mystical university where we were going to study the technical work of Charles Henry, an early pioneer of sensory physiology. Other dreams followed nightly that specified the basic concepts and practices that constitute what has become our treatise on spiritual engineering. In addition, we dreamed about technical diagrams for the construction and setup of technological equipment that primarily came from Charles Henry and secondarily from Nikola Tesla.

Several times when we doubted the source or the technical implementation of the visionary material, we would the next day find previously unknown documentation showing that the experimental setup actually had been carried out by Charles Henry in his laboratory at the Sorbonne University in Paris. When Tesla's engineering ideas came to Brad in a dream, Hillary had a related dream experience that same night. This unexpected dream series led us to the edge of mystical wonderment as it deified logical explanation. Some of the visionary material has been mentioned in the previous sections.

Here we offer additional visionary reports to provide a better glimpse of the mystical context related to the origination of this work. These accounts and any accompanying thoughts were written the morning after each visionary dream.

ADMISSION TO THE MYSTICAL STUDY
OF CHARLES HENRY

Here is Brad's report of the first vision that inspired our study of spiritual engineering:

> I was sent in dream to a special university, the same place in which I previously saw the ropes with wings hanging from the ceiling and the large rope to God hanging in the chapel.[96] This time I was greeted by a group of administrators and professors. My parents and Hillary were with me and everyone was celebrating our admission as new students.
>
> At the end of the tour, the head person announced that he wanted us to meet the faculty's most distinguished professor. An old man walked forward and as he shook my hand, I asked him what his scholarly subject was. He replied, "I am the foremost authority on Charles Henry." I was so shocked to hear that he knew about one of the most influential thinkers in my life that I immediately burst into tears. Upon seeing that I knew of Charles Henry and was so moved by this news, the old professor also burst into tears. We wept uncontrollably with surprise, delight, and gratitude until I was shaking with ecstatic fervor. I woke up and came back to myself, excited about the forthcoming studies as a student of mystery. I immediately knew that a whole new series of spiritual teachings were on the way.

MORE ABOUT CHARLES HENRY

Charles Henry first came into Brad's life many years ago via a mystical encounter with one of Henry's books from the 1890s. We tell the story in our book, *Climbing the Rope to God*. Here is the excerpt:

A few years after my first mystical illumination at age 19, I was browsing in the Arizona State University Library and a book literally flew off the rack and nearly struck me on the head. I picked it up and found that it was a handmade book placed there by an anonymous donor: a translation of a treatise by a nineteenth century eccentric scholar from Paris named Charles Henry. Initially a librarian and later a director of a laboratory at the Sorbonne in Paris, Henry proposed that what he called "vibratory energy" is the creative force behind artistic expression and that an artist can use specific know-how about vibrations to evoke "dynamically expansive" experiences. When art is appropriately attuned to the rhythms of life, it becomes an effective medium for spreading joy.

Extending this perspective to mysticism, Henry regarded the latter as the "deployment of biopsychic energy according to cosmic laws" and that mystical experience could be activated by a "therapy" capable of reestablishing "autoregulation to the biopsychic resonator." [97] He dreamed of a future form of transformative experience (articulated in his *Essai de Generalization de la Théorie de Raynonnement*) that would go past art as we know it and be a new kind of therapy or multisensory "bath," where the participant would experience a "total harmonic keyboard for the human body" based on the principles of contrast, rhythm, and measure.

This "therapy" would aim to "provoke the equivalent of an excitation of the complete nervous field, analogous to the sensation of the physiological white . . . [and] would appear to define that which literature and current language understand by the word 'love.'" Henry added, "the excitation of music and the appropriate locomotion, combined with that of a young perseverant, determines the nervous exaltation well known by the dervishes."[98]

Henry concluded that "there is fundamentally only one therapy,"[99] and it requires a plunge into mystical light and love. Reading Henry's words deeply resonated with what I had experienced that first night in the chapel. His vision became a recurring dream for me, as I would often envision creating a special room where people could be immersed in that same luminous spiritual energy that had transformed my life. For decades I called this dreamt place "the room" and later named it the "Life Force Theatre." Hillary and I now call this mystical space "the big room" to connote a context vast enough to host the ultimate transformative experience. Sacred Ecstatics was created to foster "big room therapy" with its sacred vibration, whole body awakening, and reception of immeasurable love.

Charles Henry stumbled on important truths about the multisensory, vibrational nature of mystical experience but fell short of realizing that exciting and uniting all the senses into the mystical light of love requires a source of inspiration beyond the human sphere. Any attempt to achieve the highest mystical experience will fail without an authentic hookup to divinity — a rope to God. There is simply no way to find your way to a full immersion in the mystical light without cultivating a personal, intimate relationship with the divine creator, the ultimate source of the vibration that resonates love and sets your whole life on fire.

THE MYSTICAL PUMP AND
THE RHYTHM IN THE EARTH

Less than two weeks after dreaming his admittance to the university to study Charles Henry, Brad dreamed that we arrived at a small country farm in the Midwest. A group of elder teachers met us and provided a special tour of the property. It had a narrow road that wound around various hills.

I was stunned at the beauty of the place with all its trees and varied landscape. The old house, a classic 1930s farmhouse design, was painted white. The whole place appeared frozen in time. Though I did not know where we were, it all felt strangely familiar and I wondered what we were doing there. The elders were very serious about what was taking place and seemed to be performing an important duty. This was the first lesson in the Charles Henry series of spiritual classroom teachings.

We were finally led toward the barn. Nearby there was a square slab of concrete on the ground that looked like the base of something that had once been mounted to it. I walked over and stood on this concrete foundation and suddenly heard the sound of a loud, rhythmic pounding coming up from deep below the earth. It sounded like a pump buried directly below my feet. When I stepped off the concrete, I could no longer hear the sound. The elders then circled around us and I noticed my mother was with them. It then dawned on me that we were being offered this house and land. Someone said, "It's yours if you want it." I could tell my mother was quite interested to see what decision Hillary and I would make.

Though we were impressed and humbled by the offer of such a beautiful home, I could not stop thinking about the sound beneath the earth. I again stood on the patch of concrete and heard the rhythmic pumping from below. As I looked around the perimeter I remembered that I had seen this view before as a child. I suddenly recognized where we were—it was the country farm and home of the woman who originally taught me how to read music and play the piano. Mrs. Bea Sanders of Smithville, Missouri, was the organist in my father's church, and when I was a second grader, she gave me my first music lessons.

When I realized where I was, I went inside the house and saw that the old upright piano was still in the same place it had been when I was a child. More importantly, I remembered that the mysterious concrete area outside was where the old windmill had stood that pumped water up from the earth. I was instantly flooded with emotion and overcome with gratitude for having learned music at this place. Suddenly the pumping sound from beneath the ground became louder and louder until I could feel its pounding rhythm both within the earth and inside myself as it lifted and moved a pulsing current of pure life force.

In the visionary dream, a mystical farm was offered to us that had been the home of a childhood teacher who taught me to count the beat, make rhythm, and play music. Over the years this know-how was deeply instilled inside my body and now expresses itself automatically. In addition to being a musician, I have also become the embodiment of the windmill that pumps and lifts the sacred vibration from deep inside the earth and carries it to others. When I stood on that mysterious spot on the farm, I was shown where I am meant to stand—the place where the holy wind above and the sacred fire below are in dynamic alignment with one another. Only when I stand on this spot will the rhythmic pumping of spiritual current come forth.

I woke up weeping with wonder at the connection between the beat, rhythm, music, sacred vibration, n/om, ecstatic pump, holy water, sacred wind, pipeline, rope to God, turning wheel, and all the changing forms of mystery. All of these are inseparable from the vertical line that goes deep down into the earth and high into the sky where the wind moves the wheel that pumps and circulates the numinous liquid fire, turning the farm into a blazing soulful body of praise.

The sacred vibration or n/om is found below the earth and it takes a spiritually cooked human being (SCHB) or n/om-kxao to stomp and pump to bring it up. Moved by the holy wind from high in the sky, the SCHB is the wheel that turns, the pump that pulls, and the pipeline that delivers this powerful and mysterious vibration. Let us listen for, celebrate, and uphold the heartbeat that gives life to sacred experience—the n/om-pump-drum of Mother Earth.

Sacred Ecstatics emphasizes what many religions have either never experienced or have lost familiarity with—the ecstatic rhythmic body pump that lifts the sacred vibration from the earth. Without such a pump, the pulse of spirituality never arrives, the spiritual temperature never gets very hot, and spiritual cooking never gets started. Although some traditions may discuss "spiritual energy," if a human body does not activate this internal ecstatic pump, there is no engine for syncopated transportation, soulful transformation, and musically driven heavenly ascent.

In St. Vincent and Trinidad, among other places in the African diaspora, this ecstatic pump underlies the experience of 'doption. The latter is a rhythm-making automatism that spontaneously comes on the human body and makes you feel like you have been *adopted* by the holy spirit to be used as a percussion instrument. Its pulse and sound are believed to arise from a mysterious sacred energy located deep in the earth. This energy is arguably the same as what is called n/om in the Kalahari, also believed to arise from the earth and enter the feet and legs of the ecstatic dancer to bring forth trembling and shaking throughout the body.

True soul is earthy. It grabs hold of your flesh and turns you into a rhythm machine. This rhythm activates the pump that pulls up the sacred vibration that wakes you up in an extraordinary way. This vibration is never subtle or still; it never can be held in a frozen posture, can never be experienced without extraordinary emotion, and belongs to music rather than thoughts, words, or silence. The sacred vibration makes a joyful noise and brings the clang of a cymbal rather than the insight of a symbol. It is ecstatically sweaty rather than spiritually pretty. Without it, dare we have the courage to say, your spirituality is simply dead on arrival.

It is time to welcome back the shaking, stomping, pumping n/om-kxaosi whose alignment with earth and sky gets the n/om circulating, making it available to all who get out of the way and allow its shaking medicine to doctor, its holy bread to feed, and its ecstatic fire to ignite your soul. N/om has arrived for modern times and is now also called the sacred vibration of Sacred Ecstatics.

There is a vastly larger and hotter spiritual universe waiting for you. But only when you stand on sacred ground can its rhythms and music be felt and heard. When you are aligned with the rope to God that runs high into the sky and deep into the earth, you will be pulsed, drummed, shaken, and sung— made ready to receive the sacred vibration of n/om and to be adopted by the utmost holy mystery. You will be given exactly the amount of n/om that you need, whether it is a splash on the surface of your face, a sip, a cupful, or a full immersion.

This experience is what you have been hunting all your life. At the First Creation farm is found the changing of dead beats into live beats. The pump is waiting to fill you with Bushman n/om, Caribbean 'doption, a rhythm machine, and jukebox, as well as all other yet-to-be-known forms of embodied mystery. After this happens to you, there is no turning your back on the ecstatic and going back to the static.

MORE DREAMS OF CHARLES HENRY
AND NIKOLA TESLA

Once the Charles Henry mystical teaching started, the dreams continued one night after the other. However, all the teachings sat on the foundation of the first lesson—there must be a spiritually cooked person who can pump the sacred vibration in order for heightened mystical experience to take place.

We were surprised to find that many of the dreams were technologically oriented. Brad was shown schematic diagrams of electronic instruments, experimental setups for enhancing the conduction and transduction of the sacred vibration, and additional teaching about the technical specifics of spiritual engineering. We were both excited and puzzled by the shift in emphasis this dream series brought. Previously we had only received more metaphorical, allegorical, philosophical, theological, mystical, musical, and lyrical teachings, but now we were being downloaded with technological engineering information.

We sometimes laughed at the thought of trying to explain this to anyone. Brad, a former university student at MIT, a winner of the International Science Fair, and a pioneer of applying cybernetics to therapeutic change, was at first cautious and appropriately skeptical. He began checking whether the information he received in dream had any relationship to current technological development. To our surprise, two ideas he had dreamed required a technology we did not know existed, but we found that patents had been filed within the last year for their invention. We were particularly shocked to find that some of the technical information included a particular schematic drawing that had originally been drawn by Nikola Tesla himself.

Just when we thought it couldn't get any stranger, Brad started having dreams of being in a laboratory and conducting numerous experiments with various kinds of instrumentation and pathways for connecting them. He was shown what worked and what didn't work about each experimental trial. We later discovered that Tesla had similar dreams where he performed some of his experiments in dreamtime rather than in a physical laboratory. However, the majority of Brad's dreams were related to the work of Charles Henry. These dreams were most responsible for inspiring what today we call spiritual engineering.

Before sharing any of this dreamed information with anyone else, we prayed for confirmation that this work was important and relevant. That night Brad had a dream of an experimental setup for transducing acoustic information into electricity that was related to Charles Henry. He woke up and entered some keywords into a Google search and found an archival photograph of Charles Henry's setup, essentially the same arrangement Brad had dreamed. We thought we had exhausted the search for any and all information about or photographs of Charles Henry over the years, but we missed this one — the most relevant to our work. This surprise finding was the last straw and we no longer doubted that we must pursue this course no matter where it led.

One of Brad's most important visions during this episode was the longest dream he remembers ever having. In it he was shown what seemed to be every imaginable configuration of transmitting the sacred vibration with the assistance of

Translation of Musical Vibrations into Electrical Ones for Therapeutical Purposes is
Suggested by a French Inventor Here Shown.

technological instrumentation. Specifically, however, he learned
how each method was incomplete. Then he was taken to a
different laboratory and told that he would be shown the ultimate setup for enhancing the sacred vibration with technology.
This arrangement would implicitly embody all the helps understand its basic nature as well as advance its practice. In addition,
Brad was told that the technology could actually be built and
implemented in the world. What he saw in that laboratory shook
him to the core. He was completely startled by the arrangement
because it involved following premises that were contradictory
to many of our primary assumptions about science, engineering,
spirituality, mysticism, healing, and transformation. He stood
and wept as he beheld the mysterious array.

Dreams continued to teach and inspire our experimentation with enhancing the transmission and reception of the sacred vibration. In this pursuit we never overlooked the fact that sacred emotion must always be present and highlighted. No mechanical, electronic, or acoustic machine alone can give you healing, transformation, or mystical experience without appropriately elevated sacred emotion on your part. When we include technology in the loop of our work with others, it only serves improving whatever already takes place without it. We have no doubt that technology can enhance what takes place in Sacred Ecstatics. For example, an exceptional high-fidelity sound system enhances the experience of music more than a public address system that distorts sound. A well-tuned Steinway grand piano is a more effective resonator of sound than an out-of-tune upright piano. A masterfully crafted acoustic gong from China resonates the air better than an audio recording of its sound. A well-designed body piano placed on the client's body and played by an SCHB can also amplify the vibrational experience of body tuning. All of this is an enhancement rather than a replacement of the natural process that only requires the equipment already present in the human body.

The spiritual engineering of Sacred Ecstatics aims to further advance and enhance the body keyboard and its performance in order to better facilitate spiritual attunement, healing, and mystical experience. We are presently experimenting with the design and construction of instrumentation that further elucidates and operationalizes this approach. For example, we have designed a different kind of array of tactile transducers that are aligned with the frequency distribution of auditory tones found in an acoustic keyboard. When applied to the body, transducers enable external sound to be converted and transmitted as mechanical vibration. The vibrating keyboard is attached to the body and activated and performed by external music that is either played live on a separate musical keyboard or played from previously recorded music. Whether its form is percussive, vocal, instrumental, or ensemble performance, the acoustic performance is mechanically pulsed into the body, facilitating vibrational transmission to its biopsychic resonator. Our work brings a new dimension to the use of vibration in healing and spiritual development, in part because it takes place inside a radically different kind of transformative session that utilizes all the ingredients of ecstatic experience.

We also dreamed an imagined future for Sacred Ecstatics that entails the vibratory algorithms of an SCHB in interaction with a human client—a hypothetical n/om-kxao avatar. But a simulation of an SCHB must still host the equivalent of internal sacred emotion and be able to utilize its relationship with external body movement to bring on gradual amplification with all its gear shifts and entrainment disruption, all done inside an interaction with another human being whose emotion and motion are sympathetically coupled with that of the avatar. Finally, the fantasized avatar must have a rope to God whose divine resonance is felt guiding the performance. The more we fantasize about an avatar or any kind of machine replication, however, the more we will likely find ourselves needing to return to the Kalahari sand. There we can hear the songs whose rhythms and tones inspire us to be emotionally moved, sung, swung, and danced by God.

GRADUATION

Several months after the spiritual engineering visions began, Brad dreamed that he was back at the liberal arts college with the hanging ropes. In the vision we co-presented to the faculty what we had learned from our various experiments with facilitating and enhancing the reception of the sacred vibration. It was like a final presentation of our graduate research and implied that we would soon be graduating. After our talk to a distinguished group of scholars we were led to a large performance hall where Brad performed a concert on a most unusual piano. It was the double keyboard we described in Part Two, the one with a horizontal and vertical set of keys. Not long after dreaming of this final exam, Brad had another vision.

I dreamed that Hillary and I were at an airport terminal getting ready to take off on a trip. We recognized several people who had come to give us a good sendoff. Someone asked where we were going and I replied, "We just graduated and we are taking a short trip to celebrate the completion of our education. We now have two more master's degrees and a doctorate. There are no more science courses remaining for us to take. We are heading to celebrate our graduation."

Another person encouraged Hillary and I to quickly get to the gate so we wouldn't miss the plane. In a relaxed manner, I sat a small suitcase on the floor and said, "All is fine. I already have the tickets." I then bent over, opened the suitcase, and pulled out a beautiful, long, white piece of clothing that looked somewhat like a robe, but it was more like an artist's smock. The body of the shirt was silk while the collar was more formal and perhaps starched. I put it on and then added a necktie with black and white stripes that were arranged at a 45-degree angle. Finally, I slipped on a charcoal sports coat and said, "Let's go."

I woke up wondering whether the Charles Henry mystical teachings were now complete. We had faithfully written up many dreams related to what we called the "spiritual engineering" of Sacred Ecstatics. I was both happy and a bit sad because we were thoroughly enjoying all that we were learning about the induction of mystical experience in an unprecedented manner. I eventually fell asleep and woke up later with a song on my heart, an old hymn that I learned as a child. Then a thought came into my mind that brought me pleasure: after you graduate from the university, there is then no end to *postgraduate* study.

MYSTICAL MAPS AND FOLLOWING TRACKS

The day after the dream of our graduation, Brad prayed intensely for guidance, this time doing so with different words than he had used before: *"Dear Lord, tell us what you want and where you want us to go. Guide us and show us the way. Tell Hillary tonight, Lord. Or tell me if you want. Tell both of us, but I especially ask that you guide Hillary and lead us in this work we are doing for you. Please, Lord, tell Hillary tonight for we are in immediate need of being led."* Brad later had a dream and could not remember the details, other than he witnessed more about how to teach students the spiritual engineering behind sacred ecstasy.

> In this postgraduate visionary classroom I was shown how to "put the engineering pieces together" for prayer so it comes alive for others. I woke up doing what I was shown in the dream—praying in a newly engineered way. As I tried out this alternative way of praying, I felt wildly exhilarated, as if we had found the ultimate way to make prayer come alive. It involved a means of combining fascinating rhythm, spontaneous seiki movement, and the body's alignment to tone. I felt excited to begin experimenting with this new way of praying in our mentorship program.

Sometime later just before dawn Hillary woke up to say that she had a big dream:

> I dreamed that Brad and I were on a long road trip, traveling by car with people from the mentorship program. Brad sat in the passenger's seat and I sat directly behind him. Different people took turns driving as Brad and I navigated the way. At one point my late father was behind the steering wheel. I felt the presence of everyone we have ever mentored riding along with us,

though in real life it would be impossible for us all to fit in a four-door sedan!

It was nighttime and I knew that we had been up all night driving and still had a long journey ahead. The trip felt important, and we all carried a sense of urgency and certainty about it, though the exact destination was never named. I was holding a "map" comprised of many pages of printed sheets stapled together in the corner. We had compiled this map before leaving home. Some pages had directions in words; other pages only contained a picture.

We were discussing which way to turn next, turning up and down different streets. At one point we passed a woman who was lost, driving in the wrong direction into oncoming traffic. Then I looked up and saw in the distance a train on a long, high bridge that crossed over the river and the rest of the city. It was a beautiful sight to behold! The highway ran alongside the train tracks over the bridge. I looked down at my map and saw a picture of that same train on the bridge and said, as I pointed, "That way — we need to be on that track." Suddenly I realized that my map didn't go further than that page and I was worried I had forgotten to print the rest of the map. I looked up, however, and saw that Brad was holding the other half of the map, which began where my map ended. Then dawn broke and someone remarked how strange it was because it was only two-thirty in the morning. We drove onto the bridge and proceeded on our way.

Along the journey we had been stopping at various churches. With the car running I would run into the church lobby and collect materials and print more pages for the map. This time we pulled up to a church that I knew was some type of charismatic church whose congregation was both black and white. A woman greeted me in the lobby and pointed me to a kiosk that held prayer books and other pamphlets about the church. I looked down and saw two black leather-bound books. The first one was a collection of prayers, entitled *The Pinnacle Prayer Book*. Underneath the title it had an embossed picture of a child praying. I couldn't wait to tell Brad about this prayer book because I knew he would be very excited. The next book was titled *Instructions on How to Reach the Pinnacle Spiritual Experience*. I picked up these books to take with us as I waited for the printer in the lobby to print out more pages for our maps.

As the pages were printing I looked out the front windows of the church and saw everyone in the car was waiting patiently for me to return, their gaze turned toward the church doors. I noticed that one of our mentorship students, Lance, was now in the driver's seat. He looked fully attentive and focused on his task. I felt comforted and supported at the sight of him ably serving his turn as a driver on this important mission.

Upon returning to the car I woke up from the dream, filled with amazement, hope, and new inspiration. I was flooded with the realization that this is not a trip we can make alone — it requires us to share the burden of driving and navigation, helping each other stay awake and alert all night and into the wee hours of the morning. Though this journey toward the pinnacle spiritual experience and pinnacle prayer is long and it is easy to get lost, I knew that we were being guided by the wisdom of other travelers who left maps, directions, and anointed instruction manuals along the way. All I could do was celebrate: Let us head together straight for those tracks over yonder! That train is bound for glory!

After hearing Hillary's dream, Brad was filled with tears because his prayers were answered. She had received guidance and we both had been given pieces of the map that would take us to our next destination on this beautiful journey without end. I was struck by the fact that she discovered the manual about the pinnacle prayer while I was dreaming it and woke up trying this new way of praying. All we could say to one another was, "God is good. Thank you!" We made a commitment to write the book on spiritual engineering that shows the means of creating the pinnacle prayer that readies you to receive the pinnacle spiritual experience.

ABOVE ALL ELSE, BUILD SACRED GROUND

Brad dreamed we were in an old-fashioned one-room school-house. Poet, novelist, and farmer Wendell Berry was at the blackboard writing away with a stick of chalk.

> His first lines were written in Hebrew and then he changed to Greek. Inside these sentences I noticed several words written in English but they were too faded to clearly distinguish. As he wrote and talked, he looked like he did when I first met him over thirty years ago. I have always valued his special way of teaching us how to live the truth that we are small and inseparable from it all.
>
> Wendell Berry honors divine mystery and the complexity of systems that can never be reduced to simple methods and interventions without risk of fractionating and harming the whole ecology. This is as true for agriculture as it is for spirituality and human relationships. I spent my whole career in psychotherapy advancing an ecosystemic approach to working with human suffering, only

to see this vital wisdom get laid to waste by every so-called helping profession, including the family therapists who once claimed to be its guardians. Wendell Berry has experienced equal frustration challenging the profit-driven insanity of Big Ag as Hillary and I have had challenging the profit-driven ignorance of psychotherapy and Big Pharma:

> I think there really is something like a national insanity, this fiction we have that we are living in a service and knowledge economy is insane—just horribly misleading and dangerous. Because of course we live in, and from, the land economy. . . . There are hard-headed realists now who think you're a sentimentalist for talking this way—a bucolic idiot. But of course you're not, as I have to keep reminding myself. . . . It's been clear for a long time that the powers that be were not going to hear this argument—that they were not going to be reachable by the mere sanity of saying that we live from the land economy. Still, one is called upon to keep saying it. But maybe it's instructive to be thrown back repeatedly on the need to make an act of faith, and one shouldn't complain.[100]

These are the words of a man who lives on sacred ground. We are not referring to his Kentucky farm, but the foundation he has built through finding value in being reminded of his smallness and the need to act on faith. Berry once proposed that if we take our spiritual life seriously, then we must face "an entirely humbling question: How must we live and work so as to not be estranged from God's presence?"[101] In case that question stymies you, Berry answers:

It may be that when we no longer know what to do
we have come to our real work,
And that when we no longer know which way
to go
we have come to our real journey.
The mind that is not baffled is not employed.
The impeded stream is the one that sings. [102]

Not a man to placate or be wishy-washy, Berry wisely recognized that, "You can best serve civilization by being against what usually passes for it."[103] He taught us in the dream that whether you are teaching, healing, spiritually ministering, or running a farm, don't be so eager to create a "big business," for such a perspective carries the pompous arrogance of oversimplification that invalidates whatever truth and vitality were originally present in one's endeavor. We later read that when the agricultural powers told Berry and his fellow small farmers to "get big or get out," they countered with the axiom "get small and stay in."[x]

In general we live in a time that exalts bigness in the form of excess wealth, military power, box stores, and social media popularity. Even large, "perfect" fruits and vegetables are favored in the grocery aisle. Arguably more problematic is the insidious exaltation of a big self in charge of making its own destiny, taking on the world one selfie and "personal branding" opportunity at a time. When the primary frame of reference is the individual self-improving it, understanding it, reflecting on it, "embracing" it, and so on, the ground of our life is shrunken and impoverished. What else then must we aim for in life? Berry responds in *Hannah Coulter*:

You mustn't wish for another life. You mustn't want to be somebody else. What you must do is

---

[x] This advice was given to Berry from his friend and fellow farmer and author, Gene Logsdon. http://livablefutureblog.com/2016/12/wendell-berry-wants-us-to-get-small-and-stay-in.

this: "Rejoice evermore. Pray without ceasing. In everything give thanks." I am not all the way capable of so much, but those are the right instructions.[104]

Wendell Berry has always been a praying man and he brings us a wisdom that is contrary to the naïve and oversimplified "positive thinking" and "prosperity" obsession of our time that somehow assumes life is about having your desires fulfilled. God's will is not necessarily your will. Reflecting on The Lord's Prayer, he wrote in *Jayber Crow*:

> This, I thought, is what is meant by "thy will be done" in the Lord's Prayer, which I had prayed time and again without thinking about it. It means that your will and God's will may not be the same. It means there's a good possibility that you won't get what you pray for. It means that in spite of your prayers you are going to suffer.[105]

Hard work, discipline, civility, contrariness, joy, suffering, tears, and song are all required in a life lived on sacred ground and close to God. In the dream, Brad thought he noticed some of Berry's other key words and themes that appeared and disappeared amidst the chalk: "company," "home," "laughter," and "land." He even saw William Blake's phrase, "Divine Analogy," though we are not sure Berry ever wrote about that notion, though he was fond of Blake and has even been compared to him.

Wendell Berry does not mine and exploit the earth, or its creatures or its spirits, to serve his lowest desires and unwise ambitions. He has always emphasized interdependence and smallness in relationship to God and all of creation. Quoting St. Paul, Berry said, "We are members of one another."[106] In this wholeness, interrelatedness, and ecological interactivity, we find the dynamic behind all creation: constant movement and change. Berry's sacred ground-building poem-prayer says it more tenderly:

Thrush song, stream song, holy love
That flows through earthly forms and folds,
The song of Heaven's Sabbath fleshed
In throat and ear, in stream and stone,
A grace living here as we live,
Move my mind now to that which holds
Things as they change.[107]

Above all else, we pray that Sacred Ecstatics will help bring people to sacred ground. Our Charles Henry visionary teaching began with a return to the farm Brad cherished in his childhood. As we neared the end of our exposition on spiritual engineering we returned to the foundation of prayer that, when spun on the mystical wheel, becomes poem, song, and dance, all changing as the windmill pumps the source of life up from the earth and into our bodies, hearts, and souls.

ORATIO MUSICA

One night Brad decided to pray only with a singing voice. He heartily sang all his prayers internally to God. Later, at four in the morning, he heard a voice say in dream, "Sing in order to ring a prayer."

> It woke me up and I was pleased and tickled that I had dreamed words that were a response to how I had prayed. I then internally sang my prayers again, this time with even more variation of tone and rhythm. I included a sung prayer request for Hillary and I to be led to wherever the next episode of our journey with Sacred Ecstatics would be housed.
>
> I fell back to sleep and was sent to a spiritual classroom. In the dream, Hillary and I were shown a physical place to house our work. What was most striking were the floors — they were so

beautiful that we couldn't take our eyes off them. They were refinished old wood floors and their splendor powerfully mesmerized us. In fact, the floors were so incredibly gorgeous that we didn't even look at the rest of the house. As we stood on the wooden planks, someone handed me a beautiful piece of amber that was shaped as a small train locomotive about ten inches in length and five inches wide. Inside the amber were around four or five different kinds of seeds, perfectly preserved from the past. I realize now that this object indicates the spiritual train, the ecstatic means of transportation that is created by blending the four ingredients—seeds from long ago lineages of ecstatic wisdom.

Hillary and I then said to each other at the same time, "We must live here because the floor is so beautiful." The wood looked like it had been installed in the 1880s or 1890s, the historical time when Charles Henry conducted his work. We started to laugh because we had no clue as to our geographical whereabouts in city, nation, or continent. The dazzling floors were all we needed to make the decision to live there. At the moment of decision, a large piece of paper, like a screen from above, dropped in front of our eyes and these words were written and heard spoken: *ORATIO MUSICA*.

Oratio is Latin for making a prayer and *musica* of course refers to music. We found the manor we were looking for by praying in a musical manner. Sacred music, the sound of cooked hallowed prayer words, establishes sacred ground for your life no matter where in the geographical world you are located. If the spiritual ground on which you live is holy and beautiful, this is all that matters. From a sacred musical foundation, prayer-songs soar as rhythm leaps across every trickster schism dividing heaven and earth, as well as each person from everyone and everything else.

We invite you to pray with ecstatic musicality rather than cling to any static semantic understanding of spirituality. Sung prayers carry the divine resonance found in all instruments of creation from ringing rocks to clinking stones and even grand piano tones. Build the sacred ground that can host a heavenly song. When you sing your prayers you, too, become the ground, the sky, and the instrument of creation through which divine music can ring and wing you all the way home.

6958: DIVINE RESPIRATION

Brad dreamed that he faced a scroll that dropped in front of him to show a sequence of numbers shining and burning on its surface: *6958*. He woke up and immediately wrote the numbers down with no idea what they meant. The next morning we found that this number referenced a scientific paper, entitled "'Il Flauto Magico' Still Works: Mozart's Secret of Ventilation," that was published in *Multidisciplinary Respiratory Medicine*.[108] It describes research conducted by professors at the Medical University of Vienna and the University of Music and Performing Arts in Vienna.

Their study empirically confirmed what accomplished musicians have long assumed — that music is enhanced when a musician's breathing patterns are in synch with the rhythmic structure of musical composition. Two forms of breathing are involved — one active and one passive, in which the musician's breath is either in synch with the composition as they play or is responsive to the playing of another instrument in the ensemble (i.e., the soloist). This dual breathing allows the coupling of musical and physiological oscillation or vibration. In other words, the experience of music and its exhilarating emotion is interwoven with the most basic movement of the body, which is breath. As the article notes, the physical movement of respiration itself drives musical creation, performance, and experience as musical structure also drives respiration.

Here we find that while the so-called Mozart effect remains mysterious and controversial, "Mozart's impact on respiration's movement is incontestable."[109] To receive more of what music has to ecstatically offer you, your body has to move in a way that is aligned to its inherent movement, a fundamental tenet of the spiritual engineering of Sacred Ecstatics. You must not only dance to better hear the music, your respiration must be in synch with both the downbeats and the off beats, enabling soul to be awakened and taken on a soaring ride to the heavens from whence the music came.

MARRIED TO RHYTHM

Earlier in the book we shared the vision Brad received of his former teachers addressing our students inside his father's church in which he grew up. Shortly after that Brad dreamed again that we were back at the church. This time it was not the original building, but a newer church building that had been built when he was in high school.

> Many people were there because a celebration was taking place. Hillary and I were told that we were getting married — not to each other, but to an African lineage. I introduced my mother to our new in-laws, an African couple who were formally dressed and looked like royalty.
>
> Our new father-in-law was also accompanied by an elder man who served as his helper. They invited us to take a walk with them. Together we walked from the church to my former high school, which was located just one block away at the top of the hill. We arrived at the school and entered the gymnasium. The elder man took off his shirt and I noticed that his skin had many scars from being beaten and cut. Our father-in-law said, "He was a former slave." I then realized that I was facing an ancestor from long ago and that I was in

a spiritual classroom. His lineage required a matrimonial ceremony before admittance to learning was permitted.

The African elder started to march and go into a form of 'doption I had not experienced before. He made rhythmic movements that looked like he was using a shovel and sometimes a hoe to till the soil. Other times his movements appeared as if he was swinging an axe to break up rock or chop wood. As he moved he voiced a combination of rhythmic and melodic sounds that changed as he sang. "Boom, de boom, boom, boom, ditty, ditty, ditty, ditty." There were times when he was fierce and times when he became gentle. Sometimes his physical appearance would change into an animal-like creature and then back into a man again. The performance was extremely powerful, but the rhythm and melody somehow also carried the sweetness of a children's song.

I came back to myself, and Hillary later told me that she had been awakened in the night by my singing so she knew something was happening. I told her I dreamed that we were now married to an African lineage and that we now own a new song and dance.

That night we returned to African soil, the fertile and originating source of all lineages of ecstatic spirituality. There we were reminded that our marriage to divinity is expressed through rhythm, song, and dance. Whether it is the farm of my musical childhood, the sacred agricultural practice of Wendell Berry, the divine perspiration and respiration of Mozart's composition, we end where we all began—ultimately standing on the ancestral ground of Africa. There the soil must be tilled, the divine rope uncoiled, the sacred song sung, and the body moved and breathed in accord with the next ascent up the highest cord.

A FIRST CREATION FLOWER

Several days after receiving the vision of 'doption, Hillary woke up in the middle of the night feeling despair. She had been reading in the news earlier that afternoon about the refugee crisis in Europe. For many reasons it is a polarizing and complex issue, but she was struck by how easily human beings succumb to the temptation to demonize whole groups of people based on the actions of a few, thereby breeding the very same hatred and bigotry they claim to denounce in others. She had also read that same day about the alarming drop in certain insect populations in Europe and North America. Her mind raced, oscillating between feeling anger at the ignorance of xenophobia and human prejudice, as well as dread about the environment. She prayed strongly and then fell asleep and had the following dream.

> Brad and I were standing in a vast expanse without walls, surrounded by a colored mist that was part turquoise and part golden yellow and white. It looked like we were standing inside a watercolor painting and the colors glowed softly like the sky at dawn. Brad spoke, lamenting, "The world is losing touch with First Creation."
>
> Suddenly to our right a plant appeared. Its stem and leaves were a bright turquoise green. I looked more closely and noticed that on the plant was a most unusual insect, perched as if pausing from its climb. The insect was shaped exactly like a flower — its head surrounded by a halo of pink petals. Its hands were like leaves and its limbs were shaped like plant stems. The flower-insect also looked a little like a monkey climbing a tree. As we gazed at it we were struck with the certainty that wherever this special insect is found, it is a sure sign that the changing of First Creation is still alive. It was clear that this insect

was some kind of "familiar spirit" found only in First Creation — a sign of First Creation's presence and an integral part of its ongoing changing, mirroring how plants, insects, and animals cooperate to help an ecosystem thrive. This flower-insect-monkey was itself an embodiment of First Creation — a blend of living things whose form shape shifts at the very moment when you think you see clearly what it is. I woke up to sketch what we had seen in the dream.

In these times it does often seem as if we are losing touch with the mystery, vitality, and changing of First Creation. The more we try to control and manipulate our environment, the more we distance ourselves from the wisdom of nature's wildness. It is then more difficult for the insects, plants, and other creatures to survive our intrusion and all the confusion we impose. Likewise, the more we try to sort the world and its people into categories of good and bad, us and them, or here and there, the more we lose touch with the unclassifiable changing — the dynamic that underlies health, harmony, well-being, and creation itself.

We are ultimately as fragile and vulnerable as the tiniest insects, so it's no wonder that change often feels more life-threatening than life-giving. Insects are capable of destroying entire crops, and human beings' capacity for hatred and violence against one another is very real. Out of fear, we entrench ourselves inside the fabricated walls of Second Creation, a freeze-framed world built by trickster mind where we presume all lines can be neatly drawn, all enemies clearly marked, our own bigotry rationally justified, and whatever threatens or is a nuisance can be thrown out, banned, or squashed. But the cost of trying to make everything line up or be arranged in the order we prefer is destroying the very ecological complexity, natural messiness, and contradictory juxtapositions that constitute the fabric, weave, and processes that make it all work, even when things appear not to operate in the way we think they should.

In the dream, we were both filled with hope, awe, and delight at the sight of this extraordinary insect perched on a plant whose stem and leaves were like a vine climbing all the way to the heavens. In the expanse of never-ending dawn, First Creation is alive and well and ready to turn you into anything from dust to an otter, whale, bread-and-butter-fly, tiger-leaf, acorn-horse, or a singing, falling star. Let's not forget to regularly sing the songs and clap the rhythms that lead us back to our true home. When we pray with our whole bodies and with all our means of expression, we work the divine soil and participate in the continuance of First Creation. We are most alive inside the ecstatic flux and inspirational pulse of God's creative power. Let us toil the soil so an insect may flower and a monkey may climb the holy stem, with holy water painting us anew in the many colors, splendors, and wonders of life. Let us rejoice in this garden where God is odd and even odder is Eden.

ZORA NEALE HURSTON AND THE SPIRITUAL ENGINEERING OF SANCTIFICATION

Brad dreamed that he was reading the pages of an old manuscript. It surprisingly contained the same terms and ideas we had developed regarding spiritual engineering. These are the words Brad read in the dreamed text:

"A sanctified voice requires a fascinating rhythm and the right tone aligned with a moving body. A sanctified song brings sacred emotion to the mix. To be sanctified, you must gather the sanctified ingredients, blend, and improvise. This is the basic spiritual engineering of sanctification. "

I looked to see who sent the manuscript and found this handwritten note and signature at the end of the manuscript:

Sanctification requires good spiritual engineering!
    Zora Neale Hurston

I woke up remembering that in addition to being the most prolific African American woman writer of her day (during the 1920s and 1930s), Hurston had done early fieldwork on black folklore for anthropologist Franz Boas. She interviewed members of the sanctified black church and later wrote a book based on this information that was entitled *The Sanctified Church*.[110]

Zora Neale Hurston is known for both her extraordinary prose and independent spirit. Her biographer Robert E. Hemenway wrote that "she constantly stressed a need for a 'natural' art that did not emulate a bourgeois world, that was true to one's instincts of the moment, and she seldom hesitated to follow a whim."[111] Journalist Jacquel Trescott described her as follows:

With equal aplomb, her head wrapped in African cloth or a spangled tam pulled over her eyes, Hurston would dance on a table for Sinclair Lewis, throw herself on the floor to make a point, or close her bedroom door on her guests and write through the night. She felt comfortable experiencing a voodoo initiation, "woofing" with lumberjacks, writing for the American Legion Magazine, bringing gospel singers into the Park Avenue living room of a white patron or knocking out some joker who made a pass in the elevator.[112]

While most fans of Hurston's work are aware of her Vodou initiations in New Orleans and Haiti, she also had early involvement with the sanctified church. Hurston's father, Reverend John Hurston, was a traveling Baptist preacher and her mother, Lucy Potts Hurston, was a teacher and the superintendent of the church's Sunday School. She knew from early age that a preacher like her father had to be called by visionary experience. She herself reported numerous visions as a child that marked her for spiritual work. Hurston wrote of her own visionary roots: "I do not know when the visions began. Certainly I was not more than seven years old, but I remember the first coming very distinctly."[113] Like many preachers, she initially resisted the "call" her visions brought:

> I was weighed down with a power I did not want. I had knowledge before its time. . . . Oh, how I cried to be just as everybody else! But the voice said No. I must go where I was sent.[114]

While Hurston never became a preacher, she ultimately answered her own visionary calling by doing her spiritual work through literary rather than liturgical means. Her writing contained the elements of a preacher's performance. In particular, her book, *Dust Tracks on a Road*, is regarded as holding "the same characteristics as the folk sermon," a progression of rhythmic cadence: "Beginning in prose, it gradually progresses to chant and an emotional climax which frequently culminates in song, then recedes to a calm summary of message, testimonial, or extension of fellowship."[115]

Hurston's early experiences in the church made her qualified to later pronounce that the folk preacher was Afro-America's "only true poet."[116] Weaving a "preacherly voice" into her written work,[117] she tapped into the spiritual engineering that underlies the evocative power of the sanctified preacher's expression, which includes the blending of rhythm, tone, and sacred emotion. Consider the following report in Hurston's early field notes, written while attending a sanctified church in Beaufort, South Carolina:

> It's keynote is rhythm . . . [prayer is] liquefied by intermittent chanting so the words are partly submerged in the rising and falling of chant. The form of prayer is like the limbs of a tree, glimpsed now and then through the smothered leaves. It is a thing of wondrous beauty, drenched in harmony and rhythm.[118]

After studying her style of prose, Harriss suggests that "literary scholars should find studies of liturgy, homiletics, and other disciplines among the 'ministerial arts' invaluable for articulating new modes of literary discourse that contribute to a broader understanding of vernacular literatures."[119]

Follow Zora Neale Hurston's advice: *sanctification requires good spiritual engineering!* Like Hurston, you too are receiving a call to come nearer the source of creative inspiration and divine excitation. You are being asked to both love and fight, that is, to yield a song and a sword. The trickster side of God brings the sword of language — use it wisely to cut holier distinctions and build sacred ground. The steadfast love of God brings the song of sacred emotion that instills the sacred vibration — the pulse of a spiritual life that walks the old dust road leading to those who walked before — on their way to God's praise house. Bring the sword and the pulse together in all you do. Be as bold as Zora Neale Hurston, ready to sanctify the art of everyday living that uniquely improvises your life. This path requires a rope to guide every divine whim and take you near the songs and dances that keep creation on the move: "Oh to be a pear tree — any tree in bloom! With kissing bees singing of the beginning of the world!"[120]

"YOU AND THE NIGHT AND THE MUSIC": REVISITING THE LIGHT IN THE CHAPEL AND THE SAINT IN THE JAZZ CLUB

During one of our daily walks in Vérmező Park in Budapest, our discussion turned to Brad's first full-blown ecstatic experience when he was just nineteen years old. He reflected on what had been going on in his life at the time, and we ruminated on the particular conditions that may have contributed to his mystical experience. That night he woke up with these visionary thoughts.

> I woke up, as if still in a dream, imagining the chapel where I had my most important mystical experience as an undergraduate university student. An inner voice said, "Revisit this chapel and the jazz club where Saint Erroll played" (referring to jazz pianist Erroll Garner). As I remembered what happened to me many years ago, I looked at it now through the eyes of spiritual engineering.
>
> At age nineteen I decided to experiment with learning how to improvise music with my own pedagogical method: while sitting at the piano and before touching the keys, I built up energized emotion as I imagined hearing the music internally. I then waited for it to be impossible to hold back physical contact with the piano, wanting the music inside me to spontaneously launch into an actual keyboard performance. Something like this had accidentally happened to me before, so I wanted to figure out how to do it when desired. The feeling that triggered this way of playing was not like everyday emotion. It was an extreme excitement and joy that came straight from the music, combined with an intense desire to be able to play it—all this made my fingers

want to respond. This emotionally felt and musically inspired force didn't happen on its own. It revved up whenever internally heard music was so clearly and loudly heard that it became alive like an actual live performance.

I had previously learned to read notes when I was in second grade, taught by Bea Sanders, the church organist whose farm we described in an earlier dream report. On my own I figured out how to read sheet music and embellish it through trial-and-error experimentation. When I played the piano at church services, I made it come alive with endless runs of arpeggios, turns, grace notes, and other ornamentation familiar to both the old-time revival pianists and the early café pianists of the 1930s. As a child, the adults in my community described my playing with the phrase, "He plays with feeling." This not only meant that my music evoked emotion in others, but implied that my emotion, more than memorization and schooled technique, was responsible for what came forth. There are two kinds of musicians—those who play with feeling and those who play mechanically like a machine. I learned early on that what mattered most was the "feeling," not technical mastery alone. Later in my adolescence, when I discovered the world of jazz, this same discernment was said differently—musicians either had soul or they didn't. With enough soul, a wrong note could sound right. Without soul, all the right notes sounded wrong. To make music sound right, you had to "feel it."

I discovered that I had to personally capture the feeling of music in order to play it in a manner that evoked emotion in others. With the vague notion of "playing by feeling," I attempted to explore improvisation by emotional means. The required feeling preceded technical execution and the latter naturally came together with a bit of trial and error under the right emotional conditions. This approach to improvising music was further motivated by what I learned about the musician whose music I enjoyed the most — the jazz pianist Erroll Garner. I discovered that he couldn't read music and had no formal training. When asked whether it was true that he couldn't read music, he replied with his famous line, "No one can hear you read." I decided that if I wanted to make music the way he did, I should go at it in the same manner — without the restrictions imposed by too much conscious knowing. The musician had to play with deeper chops and more unconscious roots, tapping into a vast mystery mind, holy muse, and sacred repertoire.

Reading the notes of scored music was the extent of my musical education and, for the most part, I was and still am musically ignorant. I don't know the different chords, but I learned how to play them with tacit knowing — when my fingers automatically play them, my mind's lack of knowledge does not interfere. When I went to college, I was ready to more seriously pursue the mystery of music and improvisation. During my freshmen year, it was a part-time pursuit. By my sophomore year, I was dedicated to the musical quest on a full-time basis. During that time and afterward, I knew I risked missing something by bypassing formal music education, but I feared more would be lost if I didn't solely follow the strictly heart-and-soul path.

With over a year of tinkering with emotion as the driver of improvised music, I "accidentally" turned on an inner switch that brought a new dimension to my playing. When filled with enough emotion, I found I could internally see musical notes on a luminous score inside my mind. This enabled me to compose music if I quickly wrote down what I saw and heard. I also learned how improvisation is composition in real time—it flows without pause. Both traditional composition and improvisation are awakened and moved by an internal emotional performance that can, with sufficient emotional energy and inner-to-outer body alignment, overlap with external enactment. It's as if there are two musicians: one internal and the other external. The goal is to activate the feelings of the inner musician while internally playing and hearing the music, and then align what is felt and heard internally with the expression of the external musician. When the two musicians are perfectly in synch, the body and soul of music merge into one integrated and whole musical being.

Using this method, I also found that embellishment of a melodic line as well as harmonic coloration and variation happen automatically as long as emotion is sufficiently intensified and synchronization between the inner and outer musical bodies is appropriately regulated. Within a month following this development, I was composing and improvising music by emotionally charging and releasing what I heard and saw scored in my mind. In addition, I found that music was now constantly playing inside me day and night. I both heard it in my ears and internally sang piano notes. The more the latter took place, the less prominent the visualization of notes became. What was sung on the inside jumped to the outside and expressed itself via my fingers on the keyboard. My internal singing and external playing became fully in synch, a seamless circular call and response between the two.

I wondered whether my experiments had rewired some neuronal connections inside my brain that enabled music to be heard and seen when empowered by raw musical excitement and performance desire. I was experiencing a kind of synesthetic music that sometimes could even be tasted or smelled. When the rhythmic pulse was strong or the vibe of a melodic line was intense, my body naturally responded and moved along with it. Music for me became as somatic as it was chromatic and romantic. One day I was surprised to experience the keyboard as if it were a 3-D geographical landscape with mountains (the higher black keys) and plains (the lower white keys). Since each key can be in an up or down position, each chord could be reimagined as a unique cluster like a geographical landform. I began physically grabbing clustered shapes rather than relating to abstract chords. The more these variant ways of experiencing music and musical performance emerged, the more I thought of other ways to experiment.

Without knowing it, I was developing spiritual engineering skills. All this musical experimentation took place in the daytime when I had access to the music department's upright practice pianos or could find an available grand piano in a residence hall. However, there was more going on in my life than musical experimentation. In the evening I read contemporary liberation theologians and spiritual writers whose religious life inspired social activism. This interest stemmed from my background growing up in a country church as well as the turbulent political times going on at the time, between 1969 and 1971.

I studied and admired Dietrich Bonhoeffer, Harvey Cox, Rosemary Radford Ruether, James Cone, and Mahatma Gandhi, among others. They filled my heart with sacred emotion — the desire to feel close to God, something that awakened a passion to help others be liberated from any oppression and suppression.

During this period, and before later studying at MIT, I briefly attended a small Christian college in Missouri. I wrote an underground newspaper called *For Christ's Sake* that angered other students so much they asked the dean for my expulsion. I experienced firsthand how supposedly religious folks could be masked agents of evil, and this insanity brought vicious and duplicitous cruelty. The perversion and inversion of religion often accompanied inequality, racism, misogyny, ecological destruction, trivial education, iatrogenic medicine, censuring and shortchanging the arts, individual and corporate greed, and especially the big profit-making business of war.

Even today I find it impossible to believe that someone can be spiritually cooked if their political thinking has gone haywire. It is unimaginable to have the discernment that true spiritual transformation brings and still vote for a leader or belong to a political party that is primarily motivated by excessively hoarding personal resources. Furthermore, to claim a personal relationship with Jesus or any other embodiment of spiritual love, forgiveness, and stewardship, while at the same time turning one's back on his radical situational ethics is a heresy and mockery that only demonic thinking can inspire. Such spiritual contortionists and distortionists lie to themselves and others when claiming to be spiritual while behaving in an opposite way, empowered by cold and idiotic interpretations of scripture that only corrupt, rot, and destroy its wisdom.

Spiritual cooking breeds a radically different kind of social and political outlook that aligns itself with the meek, weak, and poor. For instance, the Bushmen, above all else, value sharing and "insulting the meat"[y] rather than selfishly collecting treasure and boasting about achievement. The latter values, too often associated with patriotism, tribalism, and nationalism, are antithetical to spiritual values, as practically every prophet and holy person has previously declared.

Sacred emotion, the most important ingredient of spiritual cooking, is complex — it is far from syrupy goo with artificial sweetness. It can be sour as a lemon and sweet as honey, along with many other seasonings and flavors that make it spiritually rich. Sacred emotion includes the same extreme feelings that inspire radical political ideas, absurd insults to authority figures, and open geophysical, mind, and heart boundaries as those advocated by wisdom holders who were most spiritually cooked. They did not placate or bow to any president, king, or queen who claimed that God served one nation's or one political party's will and purpose. Plain and simple, the latter pledge of allegiance is a trickster lie that enlists you up for a dead-end death march. Sacred emotion brings extreme love, the kind that upsets our certainties and perturbs

---

[y] "Insulting the meat" refers to bringing people down to size whenever there is a risk of self-inflation. For example, a hunter may be teased by absurdly suggesting that his hunting success is due to his flirting with and seducing the animal. This social practice is similar to the medieval "feast of fools" when religious leaders were lampooned and rendered absurd. See Harvey Cox, *The Feast of Fools: A Theological Essay on Festivity and Fantasy* (Cambridge: Harvard University Press, 1969).

the status quo as it heals, reveals, and throws us into intimacy with all of creation.

In summary, it was in the midst of my musical experimentation and embrace of spiritual and social revolution that I received my first electrified spiritual awakening. It took place following an afternoon trip to a record store. Afterward, I walked into a nearby university chapel and had a full-blown mystical experience that I have never recovered from to this day. The sacred ecstatic fire awakened and arose within me, the sacred vibration was installed, and my rope to God was connected and forever strengthened. More than anything, this experience was born out of sacred emotion with its deep cuts of radical discernment and protest, as well as the equally powerful healing balm of big love that poured from songs of grace. I went into the chapel with a song in my heart and a sword in my hand and came out with an anointment to own each for the rest of my life.

The emotional fire I experienced in that chapel was without question a love bigger than any love I had felt before. It was all-inclusive yet it had no room for pretense or artificial sentiment. I later found that the mystical "something within" could automatically discern what was truly divine from what was falsely concocted. I was spiritually cooked all the way through and remade into something new that immediately knew what was spiritually real.

Today I am able to say that I had unknowingly gathered the ecstatic ingredients and blended them into a mystical wheel that transported me to the big room. Then and there I experienced the alchemical chain reaction that is brought on by music that is deeply steeped with sacred emotion, providing an aural bridge from humanity to divinity. These sanctified musical notes scale up and down the highest mountain, a climb that forever changes everything in your life. For nearly half a century, I continued to climb, each time a different experience of the same mountain. At its peak is always found the hottest divine flames of the strongest emotion, an infinitely vast ball of fire. Inside it, mystical senses awaken as the body is shaken and trembled by the ever-changing and everlasting universality of God.

A year later I entered a different kind of holy place — a jazz club where I sat near the musician who helped inspire my experiments with music that led to spontaneous combustion of the ecstatic kind. I went to a jazz club in Boston called Paul's Mall and sat at a table right next to Erroll Garner and his bassist, drummer, and conga percussionist. I still remember the songs he played that night. I wept through every measure as the emotional power and aesthetic beauty of the music evoked a similar extreme joy to the one I had earlier encountered in the chapel.

Being almost within reach of his body (there was no stage for the piano and the musicians were on the main floor), I could hear and feel the percussive sound he made when he played — the famous grunt that can be heard on every one of his recordings. It was like a pump that brought down the music from its divine source. Maestro Garner was truly an instrument of God. I thereafter called him Saint Erroll and considered him the greatest teacher of how to read and express music with your heart and soul. He knew he owned a spiritual gift and simply explained his music this way: "The good Lord gave it to me and I'm trying to develop it." By the time he was an adolescent, "Garner's natural ability was recognized by his high school band teacher, who encouraged him not to take lessons for fear it would corrupt his extraordinary talents."[121] Mary Lou Williams later said the same when she thought she'd try to teach him how to read music, but then recognized he knew more than any musician already and did not want to risk interfering with whatever musical mystery was taking place. Left uncontaminated by conventional teaching, Garner developed a radically different approach to musical performance that I dedicated myself to exploring.

Erroll Garner's whole teaching required few words to define: "Playing is like life. Either you feel it or you don't."[122] The feeling he is talking about is emotion so heightened that it makes your body automatically express rhythm, sound, and movement. Many years later, I would find the same grunting among the Bushman n/om-kxaosi and the Caribbean Shakers. Erroll helped me see what was going on, noticing and highlighting what anthropologists had essentially missed. The Bushmen, in turn, helped me realize how important Erroll's grunt was in the creation of his embellished melodies, rhythmic changes, and emotional flights. The Bushmen recognize such a rhythmic grunt as a spiritual pump that shoots n/om into your body and spreads it throughout your surroundings. Suffice it to say that Erroll Garner was the first n/om-kxao or ecstatic shaker I ever encountered. His pump was the key to his music and the magical emotion that touched others. Without the grunt, there would be no life force in the performance. The grunt was his musical pump, just as it is for all spiritually cooked human beings. It is no wonder that when I was introduced in vision to the pump underneath the earth, Hillary and I were taken to my first piano teacher's home. Wherever soulful music is being made, the mystical pump is nearby.

In a 1975 letter to renowned music critic Ralph Gleason, Martha Glaser (Erroll's manager) proposed that Erroll's grunting was a form of conducting: "The reason EG grunts louder than he used to (my theory) is that when he grunts—he is conducting—and stomping and hollering his group into time."[123] He was conducting more than his musicians; he was conducting every body in the room to get aligned with his divine musical alignment. He conducted a mysterious, electrical-like, pulsing force, something inseparable from a cooked ecstatic's spiritual energy, and shot it all around him like a living Tesla coil. He lit up a room with more than jazz; he did it with an ecstatic body pump. Erroll's grunt empowered the complex beats that made his music feel incredibly alive and full of ecstatic joy, the latter a description bestowed by practically all music critics of his work. Marshall Winslow Stearns described his special rhythmic production and its effect on others:

> Erroll Garner is justly famous for what jazzmen call "fooling around with the beat," because he doesn't seem to let his left hand know what his right hand is doing. In general, his left hand plays a steady 4/4/ march rhythm, quite opposite to the modern trend, but his right hand is playing the melody in a variety of changing tempos: first he drags behind and then he more than catches up in constantly carrying fractions of the beat. The effect is schizophrenic, like rubbing your stomach in one direction and the top of your head in another. A good example of this is at the beginning of the second chorus of "What Is This Thing Called Love?" by Garner (Roost 606).
> Here is a quality that gives jazz its appeal. Psychologically, Garner's left hand creates and

fulfills the expectancy of a continuous rhythm. His lag-along right hand, however, sets up a contrasting tension which is released when, by means of more unexpected accents, he catches up. It's like a sprinter who saves himself from falling on his face by an extra burst of speed. It's also a kind of rhythmic game. The effect on the listener varies: he may mean to sing, dance, shout, or even hit somebody. Somehow he wants to express himself.[124]

What Stearns is pointing to is the power of Erroll's "call" as part of an ecstatic call and response — his call prompts our bodies to respond. It touches us with emotion and stirs all kinds of commotion. This is the mark of an ecstatic conductor, and aided by his inner pump Erroll could circulate the energy throughout a nightclub or concert hall. Everyone could feel it pull on the heartstrings, body springs, and spiritual cords.

One of his record album titles made clear what was essential about Erroll Garner's music: *Perpetual Emotion (Garnerology)*. Paul Conley wrote, "There exists in Erroll Garner's playing an emotional infectiousness from which no one with the slightest affinity for music is immune."[125] Pianist George Shearing said, "Every time he played piano, you could hear the smile in his touch, you could hear the smile in his rhythmic approach."[126] Woody Allen characterized Garner's playing as "imbued with a feeling of emotional uplift."[127] Steve Allen described his impact on an audience: "There was always a rare kind of excitement when Erroll Garner played . . . the audience first of all could be observed to be smiling . . . there would be this happy look on the audience's faces." Record producer George Avakian referred to Erroll's mojo as a "Garner Rock" that he applied to each song so the "way he played it . . . man, you were dancing in your seat before you could even get up to dance!" Jazz pianist Billy Taylor claimed Garner's "audience was the fourth member of his trio. He reached out to them and that was his barometer."[128] We would add that the audience was also his spiritual thermometer, helping him know when to raise or lower the heat.

Dizzy Gillespie summarized Garner best: he was "the most sanctified pianist that we had."[129] Garner was such a pure channel of music that his albums were typically first takes. In a single recording session he could sit down and record two or three albums. He was regarded as a major influence by leading jazz pianists — George Shearing, Keith Jarrett, Bud Powell, Bill Evans, and Ahmad Jamal, among others. There will never ever be another Erroll Garner. All attempts to impersonate him usually fail because something vital is missing — the grunting pump, the mystery music box within, and the rope above that plugs into pure creative joy.

Erroll was inspired by all of life: "I always play what I feel. I always feel like me, but I'm a different me every day. I get ideas from everything. A big color, the sound of water and wind, or a flash of something cool."[130] His personal life was as improvised as his music. In a *New York Times* profile of Garner in 1959 by John S. Wilson, it was "observed that the musician refused to make any kind of plan until the very last minute; he cooked elaborate dishes without the aid of a recipe book by simply throwing different ingredients together and tasting."[131]

Erroll Garner also had a great sense of humor and play. A regular patron of the famous Russian Tea Room in New York City, he was approached one night by the maître d', Anatole, who said that a lady standing up front was a big fan of his and wanted to meet him. Erroll noticed an older woman with white hair and a cane at the entrance so he climbed down from the bar and went up to introduce himself. He extended his hand and said, "Hello, I'm Erroll Garner." After looking him over, the woman did not shake his hand and announced, "You're not Erroll Garner! He's much taller than you." (Garner was around 5 feet 2 inches.) Erroll was stunned and could not think of how to respond. He then had an idea and walked away to the men's room. When he came out, she had been seated at a table. He walked up to her and stood on his "tippity-toes," saying, "I'm Erroll Garner." Delighted, she responded, "Yes! Of course you are. *You're* Erroll Garner."[132] Erroll Garner's life, including cooking at home and social dining, enacted the wisdom directive formerly given by George Gershwin in 1929: "Life is a lot like jazz—it's best when you improvise."[133]

Sacred Ecstatics finds music in God and God in music. It also finds both in Erroll Garner, the man with the ecstatic, cooking, musical pump. His life was jazz, improvised rather than organized by a memorized script. Every once in a while an original talent comes to earth whose soul is not inhibited in any way to bring down the magical tones and sprightly rhythms of music. Like Mozart, Bach, Liszt, and Beethoven, Erroll Garner was an ambassador of ecstatic joy via pure musical conductance and conveyance without resistance or interference.

To be more aligned with the divine, you, too, must learn how to be more aligned with God-given music. Spiritual engineering offers a practical means of helping you get rid of whatever blocks anointed music from being able to pierce your body and install its rhythmic and tonal vibes. You need to be spiritually cracked open, unwrapping the ecstatic dreams that are held inside your deepest acoustic soul chambers. Rather than add music to your life, uncover the already present music so it passes through the epidermal boundary and leaps across the somatic divide to resonate with the holy vibe. Dig down deep to find the music machine, beat box, and grunting pump within.

Zora Neale Hurtson described the human situation as follows:

> When God had made The Man, he made him out of stuff that sung all the time and glittered all over. Then after that some angels got jealous and chopped him into millions of pieces, but still he glittered and hummed. So they beat him down to nothing but sparks but each little spark had a shine and a song. So they covered each one with mud. And the lonesomeness in the sparks make them hunt for one another, but the mud is deaf and dumb. Like all the other tumbling mud-balls, Janie had tried to show her shine. [134]

When the mud is wiped away, you hear the divine and this alone makes you shine. Erroll Garner was mud repellent—he shone the light and was sung by God. Ask a saint who experienced the same:

> Love once said to me, "I know a song,
> would you like to hear it?"
>
> And laughter came from every brick in the street
> and from every pore
> in the sky.
>
> After a night of prayer, He
> changed my life when
> He sang,
> "Enjoy Me."[135]

This same song was later sung with altered lyrics on the Broadway stage, in a tune composed by Arthur Schwartz and Howard Dietz:

> You and the night and the music
> Fill me with flaming desire
> Setting me completely on fire

Rather than add more mud to your life, learn how to remove it—unlearn whatever makes you unable to experience the joy, desire, and fire of music. To spiritually undo and then redo your life, recognize that every spark inside of you has a song and that you must surrender to fully enjoy it. Sweep away, wash away, and burn away the mud, the goo, and the trickster slime that clogs your ears, immobilizes your body, represses your emotion, and hides your ecstatic joy. Past the sludge is the rhythm budge that readies you to be musical and mystical again. Your life needs a house call from the singing doctor whose name is music—this *muse* heals the *sick*. The journey from mud to music is a transition from dark to spark. It requires a musical flight, a born again song and dance life.

Be less mindful and more musical. There is nothing more profound than a melodic line, a beautiful tone and harmony, or a rhythmic surprise that invites your body to dance even before you stand. As Marv and Nancy Hiles write: "We will never 'solve' life, crack its ultimate code, or frame it with consistency. It is forever enigmatic and resists control by words or concepts. What is left to us is the rise and fall of a songline and the vision of a Great White Rose."[136] Erroll Garner's pragmatic wisdom can't be taught enough: "Either you feel it or you don't." Spiritual engineering helps you feel spirit as well as rise and fall on the divine song lines and their numinous rose vines. Don't be afraid to make a mistake because in jazz there are only mystical takes or "mystakes" — each error is simply a call for an altered musical carol. Let us *garner* the ecstatic ingredients and blend them to *err* and *roll* in joy, singing our way to heaven, merrily stumbling and tripping toward the light fantastic.

THE DANCE BEGINS

Brad dreamed that he went to a high spiritual classroom where both the mystical saints and the saints of music were assembled. A teacher's voice spoke in the dream: "If your rhythm is pure, the right tone arrives. If your tone is pure, the right emotion comes. If your movement is pure, be assured that God is near. The music starts, the dance begins."

As wonderful as human-made musical instruments are to hear, they are not needed for you to get spiritually cooked. You were born with the only sound- and movement-making equipment that is required to send you up the rope to God: your body. We are not speaking of how you publically sound or professionally appear to others, but to something within you that can produce a private command performance for the divine. Make this a vital life focus: imagine a jukebox, live band, orchestra, ensemble, or chorus residing inside your heart. It is unplugged and the musicians are sleeping. Your initial mission in life is to plug in the power cord and wake up the music. Once this is done, all else will follow. Music's emotion sets your body in motion. Without music, the dance cannot begin. Everything you do, all of your action, moves in accord with the ongoing musical flow. This is the highest secret of living — something beyond understanding, standing still, or going under the influence of any mind-altering substance. You must dance to the inner music that God provides. Inside of you is the sacred music — this is your true soul. It moves you to act on the world stage, one graceful step after another. This is the dancing body choreographed by God.

Not only march to the beat of a different drum, hum to awaken the dance that sacred music inspires. "The way you look tonight" should come from a song within. The way you move tonight should fill the world with light. The songs are found everywhere, from the decaying juke joints of Mississippi to the shiny Broadway and London musical stages, as well as the churches, temples, mosques, ashrams, ceremonial grounds, and dreams of those who long for immortal love. There are songs of silence as well as the long tonal song of Om and the immortal Song of Songs that courts the divine. Listen carefully, for there are also songs in the changing tones of a solitary ancient drum as well as postmodern tunes performed by the urban percussion ensemble of a city that includes honking horns, barking dogs, squeaky breaks, clanging hammers, shrilly pitched drills, oscillating sirens, the soft purring and loud growling of cars, trucks, and buses, and the clickety-clack of a tram on a track. The hills are alive with a sonic landscape, the woods are alive with daybreak and twilight symphonies, and the sea is alive with its own call and response with rhythm, tone, and movement aligned with the moon, human mood, bloodstreams, tributary rivers and streams, and all the dreams that sing and dance the universe into creation.

Who are you? You are a lyric in search of its music:

> I'm a little lamb who's lost in a wood
> I know I could always be good

To one who'll watch over me.

Listen as sanctified gospel singers respond to Broadway's call for someone to watch over you:

> Be not dismayed whate'er betide,
> God will take care of you;
> Beneath His wings of love abide,
> God will take care of you.
>
> God will take care of you,
> Through every day,
> O'er all the way;
> He will take care of you,
> God will take care of you.

A faraway Hindu priest, heard as if nearby, joins the First Creation Kali Garden chorus with a Rig Veda hymn:

> Sing the song of celestial love, O singer!
> May the divine fountain of eternal grace and joy
> Enter your soul.
> May Brahmin, (the Divine One),
> Pluck the strings of your inner soul
> With His celestial fingers,
> And feel His own presence within.
> Bless us with a divine voice
> That we may tune the harp-strings of life
> To sing songs of Love to you.

Be more like King David, Orpheus, Erato, and Pythagoras whose musical lyres could bring a song that chased away any troubling spirit to make you feel refreshed. Remember how the holy medicine people of the Lakota, Ojibwa, Micmac, Cheyenne, Dine, Cree, among others, realized that a better world can only come into existence through praying, singing, and dancing. The Aboriginal people of Australia sing the natural world into their lives and the Kalahari Bushmen sing the songs that awaken the creative force of creation to bring its change to every sacred dance.

Follow the romantic saints who surrendered the whole of their being to have a close relationship with the hallowed wholeness of divinity. In First Creation, you can sing the dance from *My Fair Lady* and dance with God:

> I could have danced all night
> I could have danced all night
> And still have begged for more
> I could have spread my wings
> And done a thousand things
> I've never done before
> I'll never know
> What made it so exciting
> Why all at once
> My heart took flight
> I only know when he
> Began to dance with me
> I could have dance, danced, danced all night

You must do the same—sing and dance yourself to heaven, bringing its holiness back with your return so that the notes, beats, and steps of divine creation can be heard and felt in all your actions. Pray to sing, dance, commune with God, and be made more immune to anything less. Return all over again as you seek being even more in union with the divinity held inside the dance of Shiva, Jesus, the Holy Mother, the Holy Father, Kali, the Great Spirit, the giraffe, the bumblebee, the sacred tree, and all the divine forms, gods, and heavens that are ready to musically leap down to earth.

The lesson from our mystical dreams is very clear: the secret to life is adding a soundtrack. Follow that track and it will take you to the big room. We recognize that it will be impossible for your mind to easily believe and accept this. You are likely as habituated to your philosophizing and contemplating as

Socrates. He had a repeating dream that came in different forms throughout his life, but with the same message. A voice would always tell him, "Socrates, make music and work at it." He thought this instruction was a metaphor for what he was doing and regarded "philosophy as the greatest kind of music." After he was sentenced to die, Socrates realized that he had been mistaken. The dream was a literal prescription for action: "The repeated dream really meant to tell me to make this which is ordinarily called music, I ought to do so and not to disobey." He then composed a song for a god.[137]

One more time: Who are you? You are a lyric searching for its music. Find the better half and make yourself complete, the highest feat of living. Don't ponder what this means. Hum, drum, sing, and dance your soul into the sweet fire that will ecstatically cook your life!

PERMEATING DIVINITY, PENETRATING JOY

Recently, Brad dreamed of being sent to a spiritual library where important books and manuscripts are held.

> I sat down in the library and read a page from a book that highlighted a particular number: 2305. Staring at this number, I knew that it must be remembered so I immediately woke up and wrote it down on a piece of paper. When I researched the number the next day, I was led to the book I had been reading in the dream. It was published in 1890 and was originally called *The Exhaustive Concordance of the Bible*, authored by Dr. James Strong, an American professor of theology. Later called *Strong's Concordance with Greek and Hebrew Lexicon*, it is a special index that cross-references every English word in the Bible with the original Greek or Hebrew word that was translated.

Each original word is assigned an entry number and listed at the end of the concordance. This is known as "Strong's Number." Whereas the main concordance lists each English word of the KJV Bible in alphabetical order and specifies every Bible verse in which it appears, Strong's Number appears on the right of the reference. The number enables the concordance user to check the meaning of the word in the original language found at the end of the reference book, where there are 8,674 Hebrew words and 5,624 Greek words presented in two separate lists.

I found that 2305 is the Strong number for the Greek word θειότης, ητος, ή, or *theiotes*. It is a feminine noun derived from *theious*, meaning "divine," which is derived from *theos*, meaning "God." Strong's Concordance defines it as "*deity manifested*, i.e. the *revelation* of God (His *attributes*) which *reveals* Himself for people to know." The word is used only once in the Bible, usually translated into English as "Godhead": "For the invisible things of him from the creation of the world are clearly seen, being understood by the things that are made, even his eternal power and Godhead [theiotes]; so that they are without excuse." (Romans 1: 20 KJV)

In other words, there is no excuse for your feeling distant from divinity because the properties of God permeate and radiate throughout the world. You were made to feel the energizing vibration, the inspiring sound, the illumining mystery, and the exciting emotion of God. Many early scholars and translators like Thayer incorrectly defined theiotes as referring to the Godhead, but the specific Greek word for the latter is *theotes*. Theotes refers more to substance (deity), whereas theiotes refers to its attributes or properties (divinity) manifested through what God creates. As W.E. Vine concludes in his *Expository Dictionary of New Testament Words*: "*Theotes* indicates the Divine essence of Godhood, the Personality of God; *theiotes*, the attributes of God, His Divine nature and properties." [138] Rather than quibble over the possibility of perceiving the matter and substance of God, remove the obstacles that block you from *feeling divinity*, the properties of God that are revealed through all of creation.

The same Strong number, 2305, is also found in the Hebrew lexicon where it indicates the Hebrew word חדוה, or *chedvah*. Defined as joy, it is a particular kind of joy that is not contrived, but spontaneously received when one is adjoined with Yahweh. According to *Strong's Concordance* chedvah is only used once in the scripture: "And the children of Israel, the priests, and the Levites, and the rest of the children of the captivity, kept the dedication of this house of God with joy" (Ezra 6:16). Chedvah comes from the root, *chad,* which means "sharp," describing "the initial 'point' of joy, which as a laser beam pierces through one's hitherto unrelated state of consciousness."[139] Being pierced by chedvah signifies directly felt contact with the divine.

The Paleo-Hebrew pictograph of chedvah is shown as a fence or wall with a door. As Harold Smith explains: "this [door] not only represents 'a way in,' but it is also considered a way into covenant with someone."[140] Smith proposes that the joy of God "is the gladness of providing a door in the fence [for you] to enter into covenant with Him— a path for coming into His Presence!" In other words, God is waiting eagerly to greet you at the door and once you enter, you will be spontaneously struck by a joy that can escalate into utmost ecstasy.

Chedvah is the first entry of sacred joy known to saints speared by God and Bushman n/om-kxaosi shot by God's arrows and nails of n/om. This sharpened joy crosses the somatic border, installing the sacred elation vibration in your body and setting a fire in your bones. Chedvah is the "joy on the inside that wells up so strong we can't keep still."ᶻ This joy-fire is a special kind of sacred emotion that makes the body sing and dance, the point of entry into full divine union.

The two words derived from a single Strong number— "theiotes" and "chedvah" —summarize what is most essential about Sacred Ecstatics—seeking and experiencing *sacred* divinity as *ecstatic*, heart-piercing, spontaneous joy.

God has your number and once you make your way to the threshold, you are made ready to receive God's number, the strongest number in the universe. It is the combination that unlocks the door in the fence that stands between you and the divine. These elements combined—permeating divinity and penetrating joy–are the ultimate dance partners and co-conspirators of spiritual ecstasy. In order to be pierced by sacred joy you need to fully meet, greet, and welcome the divinity that radiates everywhere. Likewise, when struck by God's joy-arrow, you will feel, rather than just know, that all is one and divine in nature, without exception. It is time for you, every part of you, to be in complete concordance with holiness as it is revealed in all things, and thus to be penetrated by the truest, sharpest joy that is the emotion of God.

As the old gospel hymn celebrates this entry into sacred ecstasy: "What a fellowship, what a joy supreme, leaning on the everlasting arms."[141] Get on board the ship of ecstatic fellowship and prepare for an adventurous pilgrimage to the big room. There are no more excuses for you to delay making your way to the always available and never-ending manifestation, aspect, attribute, quality, or gift of God that was made for everyone. Mine eyes have seen the glory! Mine ears have heard the songs! I'm marching and dancing to Zion! Gather the ecstatic ingredients, blend them to form a prayer wheel that turns, and God will pierce you with the joy that sweetly burns.

ᶻ From the quote, "There is a joy on the inside and it wells up so strong that we can't keep still. It is fire in the bones." Clifton H. Johnson, ed., *God Struck Me Dead: Religious Conversion Experiences and Autobiographies of Ex-Slaves* (Philadelphia, PA: Pilgrim Press, 1969), 74.

THE SPINNING WHEEL

I dreamed that Hillary and I were in India where we met an old teacher who wore round eyeglasses. His face looked familiar, but in the dream I could not remember his name. He spoke to me, but I was hesitant to really engage in a conversation with him because of my general distrust of spiritual teachers I haven't experienced spiritually cook. He then went to Hillary and gently touched her. Soon Hillary had a heart opening and began to ecstatically tremble. I hugged her, too, and the three of us cooked together.

Afterward, I turned to the old man and said: "Now I can tell you what needs to be reported. I must tell you how all this began." I started to give the testimony of my early formative mystical experience in the university chapel. Before I could continue, he said, "Yes, this must be heard. But this time in your recounting you must remember everything and tell me exactly what happened. If you leave anything out or do not precisely indicate what happened, then its truth will perish. Tell me everything so its whole truth can sing forever more."

In that moment, I dug deep into my heart and mind to find every detail of what had happened when I was nineteen years old. Rather than discuss the events that led up to my mystical awakening, I started with the actual experience. As I described that momentous time, I re-experienced it, this time with a deeper understanding provided by spiritual engineering knowledge. I began by telling him, "My heart exploded." Then I paused and corrected myself to make the description as accurate as possible.

"Actually," I said, "I felt my heart expand and a big love was released inside it that was unlike anything I had felt before. To be more precise, it was not so much that I felt this love solely in my heart, but rather I felt my whole body as inseparable from an infinite field of love that spread to every corner of the universe. I could feel its far-reaching intensity. This immersion experience took place after a ball of compressed energy in my belly had spontaneously heated and turned into a liquefied fire that crept up my spine. As it climbed, the expanse of love reached farther outward. By the time it arrived at the physical area of my heart, the fire had become pure love that was pouring into all directions."

I kept changing the description over and over again as I spoke to the old teacher in order to get it even more accurate than before. I discussed how my inner body was filled with energy that changed to love and then light and how this inner body seemed to become bigger than my physical body. Its size did not pertain to the material occupation of space, but to the degree of radiance. Whereas before my inner body was small and unnoticed, it was now expanding and becoming an obvious radiant field that rendered my physical body secondary. The descriptions became even more intricate and detailed, revealing changes and changes of changes that took place at every imaginable level of process. As I spoke to the old teacher it was no longer my mind describing what took place because I am not able to indicate such complexity. It was the big mind I remembered experiencing that memorable night.

I went on to say, "As this new kind of sacred love expanded, so did a different kind of knowing and understanding. I had no doubt that any question could be asked of me and that a response would automatically occur, in either the form of a spoken reply, a musical sound, or a vibratory means of transformative touch." The tiny seed of heaven within had expanded into an outwardly infinite heaven. I understood how the reversal of inner and outer bodies was the same as the part-whole adjustment required for building sacred ground.

As I continued to describe the experience to the teacher, I learned more about the nature of the pinnacle ecstatic experience. The power of life force did not just transform into love and then later transcend into higher knowing and mystical luminosity. Each of these experiential dimensions was simultaneously expanding and radiating with all the others. Being all loving, all energizing, all knowing, and all illuminating were both distinguishable phenomena as well as blended unity. As I spoke I recognized that different orders of phenomena require different means of expression, whether for indication or evocation. It became apparent to me that the ego self disappears not by destruction but through the natural dissolve into divine expansion. Similarly, divinity is inseparable from spiritual heat, and the latter involves full body attention that extinguishes any contemplative dissociation. The senses, heart, and mind I experienced that night in the chapel were essentially that of "the room" or the radiating field itself, which was becoming more whole and holier by the moment.

When power, love, and knowing—words that ultimately fall short of what I felt at the time—converged as a mystical light and came out of the crown of my head, I faced an egg-shaped body of light the size of another human being. I now realized as I recounted the story that I was seeing my inner spiritual body in its rightful place—the primary conductor of the external physical body. As the difference between inner and outer bodies soon dissolved in another luminous wash of tumultuous emotion, I experienced the light in front of me change its form from one spiritual icon to another. It began as Jesus and shifted to other incarnations of holiness from around the spiritual and geographical world, not as distinct jumps from one entity to another, but in a stream of shifting forms that came from the same source and force of creation. The egg-shaped luminosity began and ended as Jesus, who I deeply felt as a vast and radiating presence that encompassed all the holy ones.

As I finished my report I suddenly recognized that the teacher in my present dream was a luminous spiritual elder from my early vision whom I had forgotten after all these years. It was Mahatma Gandhi in his white robe and familiar spectacles. He shone with a deep wisdom that matched a godly love that cared for all. In an instant, I recalled how his life story, *An Autobiography or The Story of My Experiments with Truth*, was one of the books I read before my spiritual awakening. I was inspired by how he dared to both stand like a prophet and sit like a student, erasing all prejudice in favor of embracing every religion that seeks nearness to God. As I remembered this, Gandhi stepped forward and said, "I pray with a spinning wheel. It is my prayer rope, my rosary. Each thread I spin is filled with God."

I realized that it had taken me nearly fifty years to fully learn and appreciate that the mystical prayer wheel is what spins, weaves, and creates the world of God — the sacred ground of the big room. When such a space is built and entered, all else takes places spontaneously. Inside this vastness, you are spiritually cooked and made ready for higher action that responds to every divine call. Only on sacred ground in the big room are divine communion and union made possible. In divine fire you truly desire taking care of your neighbor and this includes forgiving debts, trespasses, and sins. In the highest heat the dichotomous knots are untied, the borders dissolved, and all prejudice and hatred are overcome by familial love. We become shamans of a mojo love who doctor whatever stands in the way of us all entering the big room together.

The miracle of Gandhi is that both his heart and his wheel resided both on earth and in heaven at the same time. He spun the spiritual ropes that could be climbed to the heavenly light and the material threads that could clothe those in need. He did not separate mysticism from worldly service. Rather than retreat to a cave or forest, he spun wool and fought a revolution against material addiction in favor of spiritual conviction that alone cures selfish affliction. In actual practice, how Gandhi prayed and how he served took place on the same wheel.

The next morning after Brad's vision we found that Gandhi said this about his spinning wheel:

If I am strong enough to turn the wheel, and I have to make a choice between counting beads or turning the wheel, I would certainly decide in favor of the wheel, making it my rosary, so long as I found poverty and starvation stalking the land. I do look forward to a time when even repeating the name of Rama will become a hindrance. When I have realized that Rama transcends even speech, I shall have no need to repeat the name. The spinning wheel, the rosary and the Ramanama are all the same to me. They serve the same end, they teach me the religion of service.[142]

Gandhi also said, "I see God in every thread that I draw on the spinning-wheel."[143] Furthermore, "the music of the wheel will be as balm to your soul. I believe that the yarn we spin is capable of mending the broken warp and woof of our life."[144] Gandhi's personal mystical aspiration was described as wanting to "see God face to face."[145] He wrote:

What I want to achieve — what I have been striving and pining to achieve these thirty years — is self-realization, to see God face to face, to attain Moksha. I live and move and have my being in pursuit of this goal. All that I do by way of speaking and writing, and all my ventures in the political field, are directed to this same end.[146]

He further clarified: "I am striving for the Kingdom of heaven which is Moksha."[147] While scholars will always debate their preferred definitions of "moksha," its Sanskrit roots mean being set free like a horse released from its harness. For mystics, moksha involves an experience of oneness with Brahman, something that delivers the emotional bliss of sacred ecstasy.

When you encounter words like "moksha," "satori," or "salvation," among other religious terms for high spiritual realization and transformation, it is easy to get sidetracked into intellectual discussion and forget that it is accompanied by an actual physical and emotional experience. More than anything else, divine union features sacred emotion rather than inspires another bout of philosophical or scriptural speculation. The Bushmen of the Kalahari were among the first ecstatic cultures Brad met after his experience in the chapel. He discovered that they never forgot to emphasize the pragmatic engineering required for being spiritually cooked and how easily trickster can hijack the mind. Rather than chasing textual interpretation and never-ending exegesis, the Bushmen, like other ecstatic lineages, hunt the raw experience of God.

I also learned in the Kalahari that the pinnacle ecstatic experience isn't a one-time event that leaves you permanently in a state of "enlightenment," but rather an inner fire that must be lit again and again. There is only one effective way of striking the match and building a holy temple and infinite cosmos within—constantly spinning the mystical prayer wheel. It takes more than one affirmation, one prayer, or a single round of turning the wheel to keep the space vast and the fire lit. You must constantly spin the wheel to such an extent that when you leave it to do something else, you are still spinning the wheel inside, keeping it bigger and more prominent than what is taking place on the outside. Remember that whatever you spin will grow and bring you inside it. If you spin prayers, your life and relationships will be wrapped in holy cloth made of threads filled with God.

If what you spin only concerns your personal growth, development, and attainment of anything from material to professional and even spiritual outcomes, then you are not spinning the right wheel. The Bushman n/om-kxaosi teach that a voyage to God's sky village makes you ready, willing, and able to go back to earth and help others get on the high road. The purpose of spiritual journeying is not to indulge in spiritual candy, get stoned on inflated fantasy, or to become a spiritual somebody. You mingle and tingle with the gods to receive the most advanced preparation for subsequent service. You are purified, energized, and outfitted to administer intervention of the highest kind. Heaven must embrace earth, and the way you dance and sing with God must mirror how you dance and sing with other human beings, and vice versa. A true saint of any religion meets God when room is made not only for the trees and forests but also for all of human nature. There isn't enough room for God until there is enough room to include every human being.

Gandhi's spinning wheel helped others feel they were inside a big room. He spun his wheel while praying for those who were poorer, weaker, meeker, sicker, and more in need than him. He liberated himself by helping liberate others. True healers heal others and find themselves healed. A true teacher teaches others and finds learning. A truly cooked person does whatever is required to help cook others and becomes cooked as well. A big room never stops making more room for the fire to sustain its flames that aim and shoot music and dance into all hearts praying for the heavenly ray. The absence of exclusion means total inclusion, and this includes every part of you. We invite you to gather the ingredients and blend them into a wheel that never stops turning and spinning the holiest weave that reaches and shelters all of God's creation.

WELCOME TO THE BIG ROOM: EXPERIENCING EARTH AS IT IS IN HEAVEN

Every spiritual classroom is a changed form of the big room and every sacred vision brings a changed version of the teaching about how to spiritually cook. Any truly cooked visionary teaching is designed and meant for anyone who can feel its inherent sacred emotion. Even a barely felt trace, echo, tingle, drop, or molecule of such emotion is all that is needed to qualify for admission to the teaching. Be assured that there is no need to be a dreamer to receive the teachings of the spiritual classrooms. The original recipient of a visionary teaching is simply a mail carrier who delivers the news, carries the messages, and delivers the prescriptions to others. To get on the mystical mailing list, sincerely have your heart promise to be involved in receiving the report so your mind won't get bossy or cross when it is at a loss to understand any unfamiliar or unexpected teaching that goes outside your logical or theological box.

Our first major book in what has become an ongoing series, *Sacred Ecstatics: The Recipe for Setting Your Soul on Fire,* was our way of building a big room for teaching ecstatic spirituality. Its creation began with dreams that provided the primary meta-phors and basic ideas, starting with the notion of a "spiritual thermometer." Soon after came the three-part "recipe" for getting spiritually cooked, a means of prescribing the way ecstatic experience naturally and universally unfolds. We were then better equipped to more effectively teach how to interact with divinity in order to bring forth sacred ecstasy. Completion of our foundational text allowed us to move to a different room and world with a new dictionary that could articulate the importance of sacred expansion and spiritual heat.

To our surprise, the Sacred Ecstatics big room kept our mystical fire blazing in a nearly non-stop manner. We started visioning almost every night and it continued for years and is ongoing. More teaching came down the rope, bringing material we shared with our mentorship students. It also directed what we did with clients seeking help. These collected visions led to our second book in the series, *Climbing the Rope to God: Mystical Testimony and Teaching*. It powerfully demonstrates that there is no end to the teachings of the big room and its ongoing visionary offerings keep us all amidst the changing of First Creation.

We, as well as our students, had to learn that you should not remain stuck in any particular classroom form or lesson, for this risks freezing its content and the learner as well. Beginner's open and empty mind (rather than know-it-all closed and filled mind) is needed before going to sleep at night as well as waking up and entering the day, always ready for whatever God has in store. A syncretic spiritual blend or crazy quilt provides a wider weave for holding all of God's religious forms and their decorated rooms. Once you get a taste for spiritual heat you are eager to go wherever the fire is burning, just as ready and excited to dance with the Kalahari Bushmen as you are to go worship in a sanctified church, ecstatically pray in the hollow of a tree, or walk, dance, climb, journey, and explore the mystical sea. When preference for a particular name or form is stronger than the longing for spiritual expansion and heat, it indicates a return to frigid and static rigidity rather than presence in hot and ecstatic fluidity. Sacred Ecstatics regards all frozen true believers, from

New Age fundamentalists to evangelical Christians and science thumping secularists as essentially the same: in need of an ecstatic thaw and spiritual deep fry. Spiritual cooking invites you to be hooked in the heart and moved by the spirit rather than memorized and mesmerized by any dry doctrine, including an antidoctrine. To be spiritually cooked, you must be danced by big room changing rather than fixed by the lesser forms that transfix the mind.

As it became clearer that Sacred Ecstatics is a never-ending odyssey rather than the establishment of a concrete building, we found that higher guidance means allowing God to change whatever is in need of alteration, whether it be the music, the dance, the destination, or the means of getting here and there. We had no clue that "spiritual engineering" was coming down the pike, and yet last May, in between our mentorship intensives, Brad dreamed we were back in the visionary university to which we had traveled in vision before, this time being admitted to study the work of Charles Henry. This turn came as a complete surprise, another unexpected visionary launch and unanticipated developmental course. Further visions about spiritual engineering provided instruction for how to mentor others in the practical nuts and bolts of ecstatic performance — the "how to" of Sacred Ecstatics. This enabled access to sacred ecstasy in a new way that has never before been available. Its unique specific practices help others learn how to expand and heat a room wherein they feel more ecstatically alive and vibrantly well.

The term "engineering" is itself a rich metaphor because it reminds you that a train bound for glory needs both an engineer and a well-engineered vehicle of transportation. Behind all successful locomotion, commotion, and motion is found reliable and durable engineering that assures that the wheels will turn and that the right fuel will effectively empower forward advancement. In particular, spiritual engineering adds and highlights a particular vital ingredient that has gone missing or been diminished in most spiritual practices — elevated sacred emotion. Above all else, sacred ecstasy is the utmost emotion and pinnacle spiritual experience. To reach the highest spiritual destination, some degree of an emotional relationship with God or the felt need for God is needed from the onset. You can master gathering and blending all the other ecstatic ingredients and practices, but without a sincere desire for God (however that is named), there will never be a true ecstatic fire. Those finding themselves absent of such emotion need not despair, for feeling the lack of sacred emotion can valuably lead to longing for what is missing. After trying to do it on your own time and time again, and still not feeling what others over the ages have been ecstatically blessed to receive, you are more able to face the fact that something important really is missing. With this confession of spiritual impoverishment, surrender to knowing that now is the perfect time to long for what lies beyond the boundaries of you, something found amidst the greater mystery of divinity. Persist and do not resist this reach. Over time your longing will shift and become a pulling on your heart from a higher source that brings you closer to the heightened emotion of spiritual belonging. This is the climb up the rope to God.

Go ahead and close your eyes and imagine you are entering the big room. Hear its sounds, see its sights, smell its fragrances, taste its nourishment, and most of all, feel its sacred vibration. Its particular location can change at any moment because this place is vast enough to include every kind of sacred site. From the Notre Dame Cathedral of Paris to a Kalahari dance fire, a Caribbean praise house, a Mississippi sanctified church, a Congo Square drum circle, or a Japanese seiki jutsu room, the big room is home to the spiritual classrooms of the divine. Anything can happen in the big room because it hosts the constantly reborn creation of First Creation. This is earth as it was, is, and shall be in heaven.

It is now time to turn the wheel of prayer. Begin by inviting the holy ones who are most inspiring to come join you. Feel the presence of Jesus, Mary, and Joseph of Nazareth, Krishna of India, Black Elk of the Great Plains, Osumi Sensei of Japan, Abraham of Mesopotamia, Buddha of Lumbini, Saint Teresa of Avila, Mother Ralph of St. Vincent, Ti'!ae of Tsumwke, Joseph

Hart of London, Saint Catherine of Siena, Grandmother Doe of St. Joseph, and any other legendary fire tender who can help you get cooked. If you have previously had ecstatic visitations to the spiritual classrooms, make sure you notice all your teachers nearby. Fill the big room with all the important spiritual teachers, preachers, mystics, saints, shamans, and healers that empower your rope to God. Let go of the lesser trickster forms and only go for the big holy ambassadors, messengers, and incarnations.

When you pray at night, never pray alone; make sure you and your spiritual company reside in the big room. The next morning when you wake up, make sure you are still inside this sacred space. Your felt awareness of the big room and its inhabitants is the most important experience of your daily and nightly life. Make the heavenly realm and its participants as real as your earthly surroundings and those living around you. Know that you are free to adopt any spiritual parents and grandparents, including the Holy Father and Holy Mother. Your spiritual family consists of all those your soul feels pulled to pray, shout, sing, and dance with. In the big room the divine light shines when earthly eyes are closed so spiritual eyes can open. Concentrate on feeling a longing for the holy ones, especially those who have passed on. Observe them now as they arrive and bow to the ancestors who previously built sacred roads and steadfastly led the way to the big room's spiritual fire. Pay the most attention to their divine ropes. Act toward them with celebrative consideration, enacted respect, felt affection, and expressed adoration. Experiencing this shift to the higher plane helps you better meet and greet those who are physically present around you. Personal involvement with the occupants of heaven is what sanctifies earthly relations. Your rope must pull down heaven so it is able to embrace all that is below.

When we heal another person, we dance with the saints. When we teach a class, we sing with the mystics of old. When we preach, we shout with the heavenly hosts and the holy ghost. When we vision in the spiritual classrooms, we are on a mission to come nearer to God, made ready to bring back the mail and the holy nails for others. In this communion with divinity we embrace all forms of prayer, creating a timeless, infinite, energetic, creative matrix that is spiritually on fire. We surrender to the interaction with holiness, for this forms the mystical wheel of sacred circularity, expanding the room and cooking the soul.

Open your heart and make room for the Kalahari, the praise house, the temple, the wigwam, the ceremonial ground, the Life Force Theatre, the Sacred Ecstatics intensive, and any other certified, sanctified, and deep fried spiritual cooking place. This is the longed for home of your inner body — your true spiritual nature that was originally made in God's image. As your inner spiritual body awakens from its slumber your earthly self becomes smaller, occupying less existential space. Your outer worldly nature will continuously dissolve as your inner spiritual nature comes to life and progressively grows, preparing you for the ultimate life-changing breakthrough. Your whole inner spiritual reality will expand until it touches and then merges with the vast field of heaven. When this process commences, your inner spiritual body is felt passing through the boundary of your skin and is surprisingly, even shockingly, experienced as a pierce coming from the outside. The highest crossing occurs in both directions at the same time — your inner spiritual nature crosses the divide to meet and host God as divinity steps inside to live with you forever. This is what it means to receive an arrow of n/om, to be speared by God, to be filled with seiki, to be baptized by spiritual fire, and to have the sacred vibration installed.

Making earth as it is in heaven requires an ecstatic pierce and an emotionally explosive breakthrough. The sacred vibration physically settles within as you reenter the earth spiritually reborn and prepared to fulfill your mission in the everyday world. Rather than attempt to achieve enlightenment, turn the prayer wheel to expand and heat the inner big room. Amplify the sacred tones, rhythms, movements, and emotion until divine mystery is able to burst forth into the world. This is the ultimate alchemical, metaphysical revolution: bringing heaven into earth. Welcome to heavenly earth, the kingdom of unlimited creative freedom where big love inspires true forgiveness, where utmost joy reigns supreme, and where song and dance bring the sunshine and rain that grow a blessed life.

APPENDIX

THE SACRED ECSTATICS LEXICON

Anointment
That which has been divinely blessed, consecrated, ordained, and authenticated. A gift, tool, skill, knowledge, or role "anointed by the holy spirit" is something offered directly from God. It is usually experienced in a spiritually cooked sacred vision rather than coolly dreamed at night, imagined in a daydream, personally chosen, or ritually administered by another person. Anointment divinely certifies and sanctifies a spiritual role, whether it is the work of ecstatic conducting, teaching, preaching, healing, ministering music, singing, drumming, drawing, dancing, and so forth. Physical signs of anointment also occur during the experience of being spiritually cooked. These include the way one's vocal sounds, body movements, rhythms, and expressed emotion are incredibly soulful, full of joy, and saturated in divine passion.

Big room
The big room is a metaphor for the vast and expanding sacred space that embraces all of creation—the most encompassing whole of life. It is synonymous with what the Kalahari Bushmen call First Creation, a place of pure process or "the changing"— the dynamic underlying God's never-ending creation. Anything

can happen in the big room including spontaneous healing, whole life transformation, radical learning, extraordinary spiritual growth, installation and empowerment of the sacred vibration, strengthening of the rope to God, spiritual traveling, or the reception of a sacred song, spiritual gift, mystical tool, holy instrument, or any other anointment. For all practical purposes, the big room is the ultimate sacred ground and heavenly residence of God.

Body instrument
The human body is analogous to a resonating musical instrument that receives and transmits both mechanical and acoustic vibration. The body instrument can shift its form of expression from a singing voice to a percussive drum, a humming saxophone, a blasting horn, a growling trombone, a whistling piccolo, or a whole grand piano, among other sounds. Like a musical instrument, mechanical vibration can initiate acoustic vibration of the body instrument and shape the quality of its tone. In addition to producing and conducting an acoustic or mechanical vibration (and the transduction from one to the another), the body also can further resonate and amplify both, fostering the increasing intensity that leads to sacred ecstasy.

Body piano
The body piano, functionally similar to a musical piano, is the most complex body instrument form that enables the broadest performance and the maximal excitation of vibration. This is the keyboard envisioned by Charles Henry who proposed it could produce the ultimate experience of mystical light and its extreme love.

Body tuning
The body instrument must be frequently tuned and regulated to maintain its readiness for optimal performance. It requires the equivalent of adjusting a piano's strings, a trumpet's valves, a drum skin's tension, and the like. Body tuning begins

with clearing the immediate vibrational field of rhythmic entrainment to impoverished movement habits and then resetting the instrument to be more responsive to a fascinating rhythm. This rhythmic alignment is only part of the process that tunes the body. Next comes tonal alignment where the body is calibrated to move in synch with varying tones. When both rhythms and tones are aligned with body movement the whole body is tuned, making it better able to (1) mechanically pulse with changing rhythms; (2) acoustically resonate with musical tones; and (3) convert mechanical and acoustic vibrations from one to the other in order to catch and absorb the emotion held in song and dance.

Building sacred ground

This is the first step of the Sacred Ecstatics recipe for setting the soul on fire. It begins with the initial preparation of gathering the required ecstatic ingredients. Once they are gathered and blended, the construction of vaster sacred ground continues as the mystical prayer wheel is turned. Also referred to as spiritual stonemasonry, the purpose of this step of the recipe is to resituate your life as a small part inside the divine whole, making the existential space big enough to facilitate communion with the divine and make the conditions favorable for ecstatic union.

Call and response

The circular interaction involving a call for something to respond, followed by the anticipated response that, in turn, functions as the next call, and so on. The call and response, whether it's between a conductor and a congregation or one's own voiced prayer and body movement, creates a virtuous cycle that amplifies and intensifies the ecstatic ingredients. The ultimate call and response of an ecstatic spiritual life involves an ongoing call to the divine as well as an ongoing response to the divine's call. This circular interaction between humanity and divinity makes the room vast and heated for spiritual cooking.

Catching (or owning) the feeling

An expression for experiencing the particular emotion that is conveyed in virtually any form of expression including music, dance, visual art, a sermon, a song, or a healing session. You can even catch the feeling of the movement or expression of an animal or plant. Catching or owning the feeling of a song, dance, or ecstatic expression is regarded as more important than technical skill alone. Here "ownership" strictly pertains to owning the feeling for something rather than materially owning it. This notion, traceable to the Kalahari Bushmen, also radically changes human pursuit to be one that aims to own feelings rather than things. Here ownership is a metaphor for an emotionally felt relationship rather than possession. For example, owning a song is owning the emotion that inspired its composition rather than legally owning its copyright, and owning God is owning the emotion of loving God rather than claiming to possess the right definition or belief.

Conductor

An anointed person called to lead Sacred Ecstatics intensives, sessions, and the composition of workouts and ecstatic travel tracks. Similar to electrical conducting material, a Sacred Ecstatics conductor has high conductance of spiritual electricity. Also similar to a train conductor, this spiritual appointee helps guide others when a group mystically travels together in the big room. In addition, like an orchestra conductor, the Sacred Ecstatics leader selects the songs and makes sure everyone is in synch with the ecstatic beats, tones, and movements.

Cornerstone

The primary metaphor, concept, or theme that serves as the first building block in the construction of sacred ground. A person's perspective and phenomenological world are built around such a cornerstone. It indicates the most important basic tenet or founding principle from which all other associated notions and secondary building blocks are derived.

The first step of the Sacred Ecstatics recipe aims to construct sacred ground, a vast space built around a hallowed cornerstone. In the Lord's Prayer, the first line, "Our Father which art in heaven, hallowed be thy name," is such a cornerstone. Upon this primary building block the successive lines of the prayer are built, each a natural extension of the previous ones. The next line immediately calls for the big room to be constructed upon the divine cornerstone: "Thy kingdom come, thy will be done, in earth as it is in heaven." The beginning lines enact step one of the Sacred Ecstatics recipe for the big room of heaven that now frames earth. Inside this sacred place, the rest of the prayer is ready for the spiritual cooking and partaking of holy bread, the interpersonal forgiveness that arises, and the major holy outcomes that then pervade the everyday — presence in the vast kingdom, revitalization by vibratory power, and ecstatically felt glory.

The cornerstone is equivalent to what our method for analyzing communication, Recursive Frame Analysis, calls the "primary distinction," a metaphor or theme that when sufficiently re-emphasized or re-indicated becomes the main frame that houses an experiential reality. A cornerstone may also be conceived as a "compass setting" that orients the life path you tread. In general, a cornerstone either points toward a small room that shrinks life or a room that expands the possibilities, potentialities, and actualities of living. A cornerstone cannot stand by itself; further indications, re-indications, elaborations, extended associations, interconnections, and weaves must be made with no drifting away from its original orientation. Otherwise, another cornerstone, primary distinction, and compass setting may take over — usually a formerly habituated one that promotes small room containment.

Crossroads

The Sacred Ecstatics crossroads is the point at which you face the ultimate choice of the existential room that houses your life. Here the choice is between a small, self-serving room that promises earthly delights or a vast place that ecstatically praises and wholeheartedly serves the divine. The choice cannot be made while standing in a small room. Only when the self is broken and its walls have crumbled is it possible to truly arrive at the crossroads. There you either head to another kind of small room or you change course and follow the holy resonance that leads to big room residence.

Cutouts

The mind acts like a pair of scissors or a sword that cuts, slices, and extracts pieces from the whole fabric of reality. The latter's wholeness is undifferentiated until mind arrives to chop it up. "Causality" is then proposed by linking selected pairings of cutouts so that one part is claimed to cause another part, obscuring the fact that they are actually inseparable and only appear causal after the act of cutting and linking them by association. Even scientific confirmation and legal evidence are constructed by a group of people who follow the same way of making and connecting cutouts. When R.D. Laing suggested that "data" should more accurately be called "capta," he was saying that what we presume to be objective data is actually an arbitrary cutout that captures a fragment of experience.

The cutting operation of mind is inevitable and can either help or hinder, either highlighting primary cutouts that are hallowed cornerstones which guide the construction of a big room or emphasizing less important distinctions that only lead to a muddled mishmash in a small room. A sharpened mind is required to make clearly distinguished sacred cornerstones, whereas a dull mind cannot ably distinguish small from big, humanity from divinity, or trivial from profound. A sharpened mind is also capable of making the finer cuts that eschew naïve dualisms and allow for complexity and contradiction as it discerns and changes with the shifting relationship between the whole and its cutout parts.

Divine

The divine is the *mysterium tremendum et fascinans,* the numinous, luminous original source of all that is holy, from the most profound extreme love, sacred vibration, and wonder-working power to all creation, groundbreaking change, and pinnacle ecstasy. We have taken a vow to never precisely define the divine, for if we ever thought we knew enough to reveal its light through opaque words and encapsulated meaning, we would risk becoming more distanced from its felt living presence as a holy embodied mystery that resides on the altar of our hearts, singing and bringing all of heaven into every grain and brain of earth. In other words, it's better for wit to keep you lit than define and confine what lies beyond the mind. The same may be said and unsaid of God, the Lord, Brahma, Jehovah, and the Big Holy, all names for the divine.

Divine resonance

The original vibratory force behind the creative action of God, whose supreme reverberation generates all subsequent vibrations found in life. When the holy vibe is felt, it inspires a person's anointed coparticipation with the divine in the continuing action of ongoing creation. The body instrument must be finely tuned and regulated to sympathetically catch divine resonance and host it as a sacred vibration in the body.

'Doption

This term comes from the Shakers (today known as the Spiritual Baptists) of St. Vincent and refers to the ecstatic experience of being "adopted by the spirit," something that can only occur in a big room where the spiritual temperature soars. One of the hottest forms of spiritual cooking, it is typically expressed through rhythmic movement, stomping, and vocalized drumlike sounds but may also include other musical instrument tones. This experience is most familiar throughout the African diaspora, especially among the Caribbean ecstatic traditions.

Ecstasy

Ecstasy is the strongest and highest emotion, a blissful joy so powerful that its recipient is unable to remain still and quiet. True ecstasy always leaves you trembling, quaking, shaking, dancing, shouting, and singing with utmost passion. The original meaning of "ecstasy" is sometimes corrupted to indicate an unemotional, hypnotic-like trance state. As a result, profound sacred ecstasy is virtually absent among textually focused and emotionally repressed spiritual traditions. Sacred Ecstatics brings back original ecstasy, the most excitable sacred emotion whose divine flames pierce hearts and open spiritual doors.

Ecstatic body pump

With sufficient spiritual heat, sacred vibration, and the singing of holy songs, the body may experience the spontaneous activation of a pumping motion in the belly. It gives rise to 'doption as well as the pulling of sickness and the transmission of the sacred vibration. The ecstatic body pump is an involuntary body automatism and an anointed spiritual gift that cannot be voluntarily activated nor acquired independent of divine administration.

Ecstatic prelude

This simple and quick practice helps keep you simmering on sacred ground throughout the day. It starts by taking a few seconds to gather and blend the four primary ecstatic ingredients before each micro-event and macro-event of everyday life. Then toss a few words of prayer on the mystical wheel and give it a spin. No more than thirty seconds to a minute or two is needed to conduct the ecstatic prelude. Never cease interspersing the prelude throughout each day to remain inside the power of a cooked prayer—this is the key to sustaining sacred expansion and spiritual heat and strengthening your rope to God.

Entrainment busting

This is a method of clearing away rhythmic entrainment and attachment to lifeless, soulless, and divineless rhythms. In the context of spiritual cooking it refers to interrupting repetitive movement and monotonous rhythms with spontaneous shifts in both movement and beat. Here we also find the spiritual engineering associated with liberation from unnecessary vicious cycles of living in which people get caught in repeating rhythms that maintain impoverished experience. These include rhythms of the body, thought patterns, daily habits, and patterns of interaction with others. When change is sought, it is not the content of mind or any particular behavior that should be highlighted. What must be disrupted is the unchanging rhythmic pattern that binds experience together to constantly recycle a vicious circle that brings more of the same.

Monotonous rhythms keep you trapped in the monotonous action and monotonous experience of a monotonous life. Disrupt the rhythm and the content it holds will naturally separate and fall apart, making you ready for the reception of a more life-inspiring, fascinating rhythm. Spiritual awakening and rebirth are inseparable from detrainment from monotonous rhythms and the subsequent boarding of a more soulful rhythm train. Bust the rhythms that entrain redundant performance and set the body free to be more spontaneously and creatively moved.

Fascinating rhythm

A surprising rhythm that interrupts any redundant, non-ecstatic beat. Here, soulful syncopation and polyrhythms overthrow the tick-tock lifeless beats that encapsulate habituation rather than liberate creative invention. Monotonous rhythm is not fascinating and too easily induces perceptual inattention, behavioral incapacitation, cognitive dissociation, somatic fragmentation, and emotional stupefaction. On the other hand, fascinating rhythms awaken mystical perception and ecstatic expression as they expand the room, turn up the spiritual heat, stir the sacred vibration, and precipitate divine celebration.

Fire

The amplified emotion, heightened somatic excitation, and supercharged sacred vibration that are inspired by holiness are so spiritually hot that the experience is referred to as a *fire*. Divinity itself is sometimes manifested as a pillar of fire, burning bush, or other form of flammable phenomenon that transfuses its holy heat, light, and power to human beings who are ready to receive it. Without the fire of sacred ecstasy there is no experience of being near the divine. This fire must be ignited, stoked, and spread by gathering and blending all the ingredients and following the ecstatic recipe that has been handed down through the ages.

First Creation
The Ju/'hoan Bushman term (*G≠ain-g≠aing≠ani*) for what Sacred Ecstatics calls "the big room." It is described as the original birthplace of all life that hosts "the changing," the primary force behind creation. In First Creation nothing remains the same long enough to be named, conceptually fixed, and ontologically solidified. Significant life change, from healing to spiritual rebirth, requires a voyage to First Creation, the big room, or heaven. There "the changing" is experienced as a sacred vibration activated by blending the ecstatic ingredients into a mystical wheel whose momentum amplifies the whole ecstatic process and sustains presence in First Creation.

Flipper
"Friend of sea." A Sacred Ecstatics term (inspired by a vintage television show) that indicates the "porpoise" of the first step of the Sacred Ecstatics recipe—the spiritual turn, part-whole reversal, room shift, and *ecstatic flip* required for admission to the vast sea where holiness is afloat.

Four directions of ecstatic living
The four directions of ecstatic spirituality refer to the main experiential orientations of ecstatic living: (1) absurdity that can expand and warm a room when things start to shrink and cool down; (2) creative work that taps into what was received in the spiritual heat, metabolizing it to be aesthetically transformed and made shareable with the world; (3) climbing the ladder for another spiritual recharge in the big room fire; and (4) stone-masonry of thought and word that builds, rebuilds, patches,

repairs, and extends sacred ground. An ecstatically vibrant life keeps revolving around these four directions.

God

All you need to know about God is what a child can understand: *God is love.* If you thirst for a lengthier definition, then pause to regard these three letters as a special set of initials that provide further instruction for your insatiable knowledge quest. The letters, G, O, and D stand for the unspoken spiritual prescription: *Get Over Definitions* that try to cognitively pin down the ultimate source and force of creation. Be aware that too much mental meaning and too little hearty emotion can turn this name and the person saying it into its opposite spelling: *dog,* referring to Pavlov's classically trained dog that salivates when the word is associated with a trickster treat. This initialed message cannot be understood in any ecstatically meaningful way outside the big room. It can only be felt in the vast heat where the infinity of divinity subsumes the whole of you rather than offers another con, that is, another reduced *con*cept to mentally *con*sume and presume you know what can never be known.

Healing

Making whatever is broken whole and holy again through the spiritual cooking that is only possible in a big room. Suffering and disease always have the same diagnosis—the fractionation of whole life into a partialness bound by small room containment. Healing requires a healer skilled and anointed to expand and heat the room, accomplished by uninterrupted interaction with the divine. This interaction charges the atmosphere with holiness and guides others to enter the big room where whatever needs to be done may be accomplished by a transfusion and infusion of higher power. Note that healing is not necessarily limited to symptom alleviation, problem evaporation, the banishment of suffering, or the naïve idolization of solutions. It is the placement of everything—from pain and pleasure to suffering and joy—inside the big room. While there are many kinds of help that include sitting quietly with a person in need of company, healing is an art form that requires spiritual engineering know-how.

Holy spirit

A hallowed name for n/om, seiki, or what we call the sacred vibration. All these names of the highest vital force refer to concentrated, undiluted, non-subtle, extremely powerful spiritual energy that always makes the body tremble, shake, and quake. Although the term "holy spirit" (which is typically capitalized) carries many different connotations among Christians, from an ecstatic perspective the holy spirit is spiritually hot and is felt as a somatic vibration, and when it enters the room or one's body, it triggers ecstasy. Also called "holy ghost power," the holy spirit is the "wonder working power" that makes you sing, shout, and dance rather than get entrenched in an ideological stance.

Holy water

Holy water is one of the many forms in which spirit is delivered and experienced. This water can be drunk from a cup, used to baptize, or wash and cleanse. It is the golden elixir and the Holy Grail sought in legendary odysseys and pilgrimages. Other changing forms of holiness include holy wind (*spiritus*), holy fire, and holy bread (or any flesh, meat, or material of earth). Earth, wind, water, and fire are the four divine forms of holiness that we may access through sensory experience.

Ingredients for spiritual cooking

The experiential elements required for spiritual cooking: fascinating rhythm, seiki movement, tonal alignment, and sacred emotion. While the ecstatic maximization of any ingredient can activate all the others, it is more effective to blend them all together to create a call and response between each ingredient in a mutually amplifying manner. This call and response blending initiates the formation and turning of a mystical wheel that is ready to be infused with the hallowed words of prayer.

Inner body

The inner body is essentially a homunculus of the external body, conceptualized as a spiritual form not encumbered by the habitual constraints acquired by physical form. This notion offers a practical technique for learning how to "catch the feeling" of others' ecstatic expression, from vocalization to body movement, rhythm, tone, music, dance, and other forms. This is accomplished by imagining that your inner spiritual body can perfectly imitate and be in synch with whatever is spiritually enacted in the external world. Rather than prematurely attempt any external conduct that is assimilated, distorted, or short-circuited by formerly acquired habits, the inner body first perfectly conducts the Sacred Ecstatics workout in your imagination. This practice is done while your physical body is restrained, allowing you to build up enough emotion and commotion inside until it can no longer be held back, finally resulting in the spontaneous breakthrough of congruent outer body expression.

This practical engineering learning tool is based on the experimental finding that "catching the feeling" of ecstatic performance is a prerequisite for successfully bringing it forth externally. Spiritual engineering also specifies how to work with the ingredients and turn the prayer wheel using your inner body, so you may experience inner ecstatic commotion even as your external body is still and silent. Using the inner body further enables you to produce sounds, movements, and tones that you are not able to produce with your physical body, including superhuman tones, impossibly prodigious singing, and dancing that defies the laws of physics.

Jesus

The name of a man, son of man, God, son of God, divine incarnation, healer, teacher, rabbi, prophet, messiah, pacifist, revolutionary, wanderer, mystic, shaman, carpenter, n/om-kxao nail man, parable maker, law breaker, water walker, sacred conductor, or any combination of these, whose spiritual and material essence, history, ancestry, purpose, role, mission, heavenly and earthly impact, and every other form of definition, ontology, epistemology, eschatology, theology, and philosophy are always disputed and impossible for everyone to agree on. Yet inside big sacred space and hot spiritual temperature, this name can evoke a personally felt realization of earth as it is in heaven, an experience of being touched, moved, and changed by divine mystery. Past any ink on papyrus or quibbling over whether he raised dead Lazarus, the name of Jesus points to a kingdom whose tones, rhythms, and movements promote alignment of humanity with divinity. In the upper last supper room, Jesus may be met as a sacramental wine maker, holy bread maker, a wonder-working power, a supreme mystical light, and a pinnacle sacred vibration that sings and dances with all creation.

Life Force Theatre
Another name we use for a Sacred Ecstatics intensive where people gather to spiritually cook. Use of the term "theatre" emphasizes dynamic live performance over static post hoc conceptualization. Theatre also invites all expressive forms of the performing arts to the sacred stage, providing more creative fuel for the ecstatic fire. The Life Force Theatre creates a performance space for the big room of First Creation, bringing the greatest show and holiest glow on earth as it is in heaven, held underneath the big top sacred canopy. Here we find that constantly shifting the name from the big room to sacred ground, heaven, First Creation, Life Force Theatre, Sacred Ecstatics Intensive, Burning Bush Festival, and the like helps free us from static naming so we can better step into the holy changing.

Mystical prayer wheel
The circular dynamic that creates (1) sacred expansion of existential space, (2) spiritual heat for cooking, and (3) a means of mystical transportation. The mystical wheel is built with the four basic ecstatic ingredients (fascinating rhythm, spontaneous body movement, tonal alignment, and sacred emotion) that are

blended together through a call and response pattern that form the wheel's spokes. When all the ingredients mutually call and respond to one another, a wheel forms and starts to turn. This is when words of a prayer are added to the wheel's motion. Prayer itself changes form as the wheel continues to turn and amplify all the ingredients. As prayer moves from chant to song, dance, 'doption, pulling, and all the rest of the forms of communion with the divine, the wheel also changes its function, moving from a tool for the expansion of sacred ground to spiritual cooking, mystical traveling, and the ultimate ecstasy of divine union.

Mystical prescription

An assigned task that helps sustain and extend the vastness, heat, and changes brought forth through spiritual cooking. Prescribed at the end of a Sacred Ecstatics session, it highlights the newborn experiential reality that has been constructed and will now be put into action in the everyday world. Mystical prescriptions are like "action koans" meant to trip and flip you into more spontaneous, improvisational, Taoistical, and co-participatory involvement with the sacred force of creation.

Mystical traveling

The highest, purest, and most important form of spiritually oriented traveling occurs inside a big room. Such traveling is not contrived but takes place spontaneously when the spiritual temperature is high. Mystical traveling can happen while awake or sleep. As with everything associated with spiritual cooking, it requires a gathering of ecstatic ingredients and their blending into a mystical prayer wheel that, when hot enough, becomes a means of spiritual transportation. Mystical traveling takes you to the spiritual classrooms where the highest gift is the reception of a sacred song. Ecstatic mystical traveling does not involve guided imagery or fantasized visualization, but emphasizes the actual embodiment of the rhythms, tones, physical movements, sacred emotion, songs, dances, and expressive forms of spiritual cooking from ecstatic lineages found throughout the world.

Mystical travel to the Kalahari, for instance, refers to the enactment of Bushman ecstatic expression that "takes" your whole body there. The emphasis is on emotion, music, and movement rather than image, symbol, and post hoc interpretation. The ultimate spiritual classroom journey is going straight up the rope to God's heavenly village in First Creation. All other cooked ecstatic adventures traverse the tributaries of the central rope's mainstream and require guidance from the divine.

Mysticism
Mysticism refers to the experiences found inside the big room where divine mystery resides. The schism between small rooms and the big room must be leapt across, enabling entry to the holy mist, steam, and fire it inspires. All other definitions of mystery point to less mystery. An encounter with mystery leaves you filled with extreme emotion while shaking in your boots. You are more inclined to whoop, holler, and sing rather than brag about having another fling with magic that ignores how tragic it is to return without a holy mystery fire in your bones.

N/om
The Ju/'hoan Bushman word for the mysterious force behind all of creation, something that can be personally experienced as an ecstatic emotion, heightened energy, somatic vibration, and song given by the Sky God. It is comparable to the Japanese word, seiki, and is similar to how Christian charismatics experience what they call holy ghost power. We call it the sacred vibration.

Pasturing
A term referring to departure from a small room and entry to the big room that is the vast sacred field of the Lord. Inspired in part by a line in Psalm 23, "He maketh me to lie down in green pastures," here everything feels fresh, newly born, holy, infused with creative life, ecstatically hot, naturally soulful, sweetly scented, and blessed by an anointment from God that is

discernable to those who are spiritually cooked. We often say that the spiritual crossroads is the choice between *posture* and *pasture.*

Posturing

Imitating ecstatic experience and expression while remaining in a small room with no spiritual heat. Postured praying, singing, shouting, dancing, trembling, dreaming, healing, ceremonial administration, and teaching, among other forms, take place when you are more concerned with proving your spiritual advancement and knowledge to yourself and others rather than surrendering to the divine. Postured action is inauthentic and incongruent and does not emit any soul-stirring sacred emotion—it simply lacks spiritual heat. It tends to spiritually backfire, resulting in self-inflation, room deflation, further refrigeration, and the absence of the inspiration and the performance of creative invention.

Posturing feels fake, lifeless and soulless and has a spiritual stink that is readily discernable to those who are spiritually cooked. We sometimes tease that the goal of Sacred Ecstatics is to move from posturing to pasturing—moving from an ego that likes to strut its stuff to the vast green pasture where you are led and fed by God. Posturing is a common trickster trap that is as old as humanity itself. The Bushmen, for example, have a word for a spiritual posturer, someone pretending to be cooked: *n=u'uhan.*

Prayer

Prayer is communicable expression and communion with God, the ultimate goal of which is whole and holy divine union. The form of prayer changes as the room gets bigger and hotter, moving from an emphasis on spoken words to rhythm, tones, and movement that become chant, song, dance, and all other ecstatic forms of expression. During the strongest, hottest praying there is no felt separation between the seeker, the Creator, and the whole of creation. What God hears in prayer, above all else, is how much one is in *need* of prayer. What God offers in prayer, beyond all else, is the joy that comes when the praying vessel is empty and wants nothing more than to be touched by and filled with God's sacred emotion, something that has been described as fire, molten lava, liquid heat, warm water, boiling steam, and holy smoke, among other similar forms. To experience the bliss of prayer, change your ecstatic condition by feeling the need for spiritual contrition that activates divine ignition. Receiving God's unconditional love is conditional upon your cup being empty and its emptiness becoming noticeably excitable as it is held up to receive the pour of prayer power.

Pulling sickness

In the hottest spiritual temperatures when an anointed healer is really cooking, the ecstatic body pump will activate and become strong enough to "pull" out sickness and tiredness. The Bushmen refer to this ecstatic action as removing "dirty nails." The experienced physical pulling is an automatism, a spontaneous action that feels like it is vacuuming and extracting whatever needs to be removed from others while doing the same to the healer's own body. Pulling has no need for conscious knowing about sickness—neither its name nor cause. Diagnosis takes place at cooler spiritual temperatures where effective pulling and removal of sickness is inhibited by presumed understanding. Less knowing and more pulling is the aim of ecstatic healing, the cleanup of whatever makes people sick, tired, and spiritually uninspired. The less you medically intuit, the better conduit you become for sacred pulling power.

Recipe for setting your soul on fire

Sacred Ecstatics provides a three-step action recipe for making yourself ready for the required spiritual conductance and divine sympathetic resonance that leads to the pinnacle spiritual experience of sacred ecstasy. It involves (1) building sacred ground and creating a big room; (2) spiritual cooking, where ecstatic expression and experience take place, followed by (3) instruction for how to return to the everyday in a way that sustains the warmth and fosters a desire to share the blessings that were received. The recipe is based on the steps that are followed by ecstatic lineages around the world and remains constant even when words, beliefs, names, songs, rhythms, dance forms, and other details change across traditions.

Reentering the everyday
The third and final step of the Sacred Ecstatics recipe includes a mystical prescription for action in order to sustain sacred expansion and spiritual heat. The descent from ecstatic flight to walking on everyday ground is as important as the ascent. The purpose of getting spiritually cooked is to ready you to help ecstatically warm the world by keeping your rope to God strongly felt.

Religion
The means of enacting a relationship with the divine, inspired by the desire for worship that further ties and binds a person's finite humanity with the whole universe's infinite divinity. A religion usually begins with a direct mystical encounter with the divine. As the resulting spiritual heat is shared with others, it binds the emergent community with whatever metaphors, prayers, songs, and movements were associated with the originating spiritual experience. With the arrival of political jockeying for leadership roles, the spiritual wisdom of the founding experience gets lost amidst the constant focus on social organizational needs. Here members emphasize social "community" more than divine communion. The spiritual heat required to experience the divine is now extinguished in favor of the frigid forms that maintain a rigid hierarchical institution. As a result, many people erroneously assume the word "religion" only refers to oppressive institutions. It's important to remember that while the formative years of a religion may spark spiritually hot liberation and a latter era may socially degenerate into cold oppression, the fire that launched its original birth may reignite at any moment to bring regeneration, another round of liberation, and more spirited ecstatic cooking.

Rhythm detox

Also known as the "budge smudge," the rhythm detox helps shake you free from stale and monotonous rhythms, readying you to subsequently board a more fascinating, changing rhythm. This is accomplished by physical shaking, especially that which imitates the natural shaking of an animal when in need of a physical reset.

Rope to God

The rope to God is the wholehearted connection you feel with God as well as the spiritual pipeline, the holy communication line, the divine fishing line that can hook and reel in a heart, and the mystical trail for visits to visionary locales that function as spiritual classrooms. The rope, which is a Ju/'hoan Bushman metaphor for relationship, is also a synonym for the melodic line of a song. You sing to awaken and uncoil the rope, and you sing to climb it. When the singing rope is strong enough, its tones and rhythms pull you to the highest destination — all the way to God. The rope is empowered by all the ecstatic expression of spiritual cooking. Each time you are cooked, the strands of the rope are cleaned and renewed while another strand is added. Value the rope above everything because it is the ecstatic lifeline connecting you to the divine.

Sacred Ecstatics

The art of (1) building and entering a room that is big enough for spiritual cooking, (2) conducting the actual spiritual cooking, (3) and making a resourceful return to the everyday where you share what you received. Regardless of the spiritual or religious traditions, names, or ideas you prefer, the recipe and engineering of Sacred Ecstatics help you access the sacred ecstasy, spiritual gifts, and holy guidance only found in the biggest room with the highest spiritual temperature. Sacred Ecstatics is a syncretic, always-changing form that prepares you to be spiritually cooked, receive and empower the sacred vibration, and grow a strong rope to God.

Sacred emotion

Ultimately, this emotion involves loving God and loving to receive and share God's love. In its more diluted forms, sacred emotion can refer to any degree of wonder and awe of divine mystery, a truly felt appreciation of God's creative presence in all things. In the most concentrated form, sacred emotion is felt as fire, a glorious burning in the heart that is also experienced as a vibration or electricity coursing throughout the body. Sacred emotion pours through your rope to God and is the most important of the four ingredients of spiritual cooking.

Sacred ground

A space vast enough to host the interaction of humanity and divinity. As opposed to a small self-centric room that is limited to personal intention, wishful thinking, and fulfillment of trivial desire, sacred ground lays the foundation for a big room where everything is surrendered to the higher power, the greater mind, and the emotive-and-locomotive heart of divinity.

Sacred song

A sacred song is the driver's license or conductor's permit of ecstatic spirituality. Without a sacred song—music that is inspired and given by the divine—one is neither spiritually cooked nor able to perform any anointed spiritual function. While all music is arguably sacred on some level, a sacred song is specifically and unambiguously born of divinity. It is the main vessel for transferring sacred emotion, the most important ingredient of ecstatic spirituality. Without a song, you can't get to the big room or make the temperature hot enough for healing or spiritual cooking to take place.

Sacred vibration

The sacred vibration involves both heightened sacred emotion and the physical trembling of the body, each inspired by sacred song. While it is arguably more accurate to use the hyphenated term, "sacred vibration-sacred emotion-sacred song," we use the single term, "sacred vibration," as an abbreviation of this whole complex. It is important to remember that a body vibration with no relationship to divinely inspired emotion is not a sacred vibration. The source of the sacred vibration is divine resonance—the beat and tone of the Creator's singing heart. God sings and human beings do their best to catch the songs, dances, emotion, and motion of creation. There are two main ways to receive the sacred vibration: either directly from the divine itself or by an intermediary, spiritually cooked human being (SCHB) who has either received it from the divine or from another SCHB. In either case, the sacred vibration is transmitted not only through touch but also through the acoustic vibrations of a song that has enough sacred emotion to simultaneously activate and pulse a mechanical vibration across the somatic border.

Second Creation
The Ju/'hoan Bushman term (*Manisi n!a'an-n!a'an*) for the mental world of knowing where trickster names a First Creation changing form, thereby giving the appearance of stilling, distilling, and freezing the world into discrete parts. Cognitive encapsulation brings small room containment that is distant from the formerly unconstrained changing of continuously reborn creation. Second Creation's production of endless cutouts and arbitrary reifications encourages pretending that you can conquer and control nature as well as explain away all mystery, including God. The more you are lost in a Second Creation carnival fun-house of self-reflecting mirrors, the more you are in need of a First Creation visitation that brings you back inside "the changing" where you feel inseparable from the whole of creation.

Seiki
An old Japanese word for the amplified life force, a notion akin to the Bushman word, n/om. Seiki jutsu is the art of working with this amplified life force. One of its greatest proponents, Ikuko Osumi Sensei, taught that seiki must be gathered and concentrated to be made strong enough to fill ourselves and

others with abundant vitality. Seiki is also regarded as the power source of healing, well-being, longevity, aesthetic inspiration, creative invention, and whole bodied connection to the cosmos.

Seiki movement

Spontaneous movement precipitated by the circulation of seiki within and around the body. The daily practice of seiki movement, called *seiki taisou*, makes one more receptive to seiki and builds up the seiki within. The seiki movement exercise is a time to milk seiki from the atmosphere and drink it through every pore of the body. It's an instant recharger of vitality and a powerful enhancer of daily performance and health.

Shaking medicine

The shaking of the body that comes from the sacred emotion of feeling a rope to God. If sacred emotion is not evoking the tremble, quake, or shake, then the spontaneous movement is nothing more than a body automatism more akin to a Charley horse or muscle spasm. Forced shaking may be useful in physical therapy, sports medicine, or exercise enhancement, but it lacks the additional transformational phenomena associated with sacred shaking medicine. Sacred Ecstatics teaches shaking that comes from above rather than from below. In other words, gather all the ecstatic ingredients, especially sacred emotion, and allow the blending to expand and heat the room, thereby igniting the highest spiritual shake. Allow God to shake you rather than assume you can shake yourself into divine mystery.

Shamanism

One of the earliest forms of ecstatic spirituality whose practition-ers were, above all else, spiritually cooked, a condition marked by spontaneous body shaking, wild shouting, enthusiastic singing, spirited dancing, changing rhythms, and ceremonial improvisation. The subsequent cooling of shamanism into hereditary entitlement and institutional training has meant that many anthropologists, foreign travelers, and observers witnessed degenerated forms of cold shamanism that had lost its ecstatic "shake and bake," resulting in reports that missed the originating experience. Contemporary so-called neo-shamanism similarly lacks the original core — the basic ecstatic ingredients and their blending that expands and heats the room to host the sacred vibration and the rope to God. Sacred Ecstatics aims to set shamanism on fire again, along with other religions, in order to recover its original soulful, sacred ecstasy.

Small room
A self-centric existential space constructed and maintained by thought and action that maintain the self as the primary reference point for all experience. "Small room" is another name for a spiritually cold container in which your sense of well-being rises and falls with the inflation and deflation of your ego. Here there is no sacred emotion, vibration, or felt relationship to holiness. Small rooms lack heart, soul, creative life force, humor, and the possibility of the utmost mystical impossibility. Such paucity breeds selfishness, impoverishing anger, and postured compassion and generosity. Even big room spiritual wisdom can be trapped and distorted in a small room, fostering cold piety, rigid dualisms, and overzealous moralism. The purpose of ecstatic spirituality is to provide an exit from small rooms and entrance to the big room where divinity resides. Here spirited cooking brings back mystical senses and uncommon wisdom sense no longer bound by a limiting trickster fence.

Soul
The quality of tone, rhythm, body movement, and emotion associated with performance inside a big room. Rather than regard this word as a noun that implies material-like presence or absence, Sacred Ecstatics depicts "soul" as a special quality and vital essence activated by the sacred vibration. (This definition of soul is similar to its historical use among African Americans in reference to music, dance, speech, and even food.) Soul is inseparable from the swamplike complexity whose contradictions and juxtapositions host the changing contraries

inherent in ecstatic transformation, rather than promote unsullied platitudes, non-literary attitudes, and sterilized spiritual altitudes.

"Soul loss," whether you conceptualize it as a misplaced spiritual essence or more generally as a loss of "mojo," is best treated by an infusion of soulfulness: fascinating rhythm, embellished tone, anointed body swagger, and sacred emotion. In contrast, the so-called soul retrieval protocol of new age shamanism emphasizes guided imagery that itself lacks "soul," thereby perpetuating the very dissociation and passionless presence it claims to mend. Spiritually hot shamanism uses soulful expression to cook all participants, circulating and infusing the soulfully ecstatic qualities that transport everyone back to the big room where all fragmented parts are made whole again.

Spirit
From the Latin word, *spiritus,* meaning breath, respiration, or wind associated with the animating or vital principle in all living forms — the breath of life or the life-giving breath of the Creator. Sacred Ecstatics uses this word to indicate the awakening, revitalizing, and ecstaticizing breath of God, something that is experienced as a mix of heightened sacred emotion and vibration in the body's expression. From a spiritual engineering standpoint, "working the spirit," a term that comes from Caribbean ecstatics, refers to the gathering and blending of ingredients to turn a mystical wheel of prayer, song, and dance.

Spiritual classrooms
Mystical travel takes you to locales in the spiritual universe where advanced instruction, gifting, and anointment take place. Teachers may be encountered in any form from angelic to vegetative, mineral, energy, light, or matter made of earthly or heavenly elements. The higher the classroom, the more the visit is a celebration of God's grace and love, emphasizing joy that is both heard and felt, with sight being a secondary sense. Spiritual lineages almost always have some kind of structure in place through which elders guide spiritual travelers and help them

discern whether a vision was a true visit to a spiritual classroom, an everyday psychological dream recycling autobiographical debris, or the display of consciously seeded wish projection.

Spiritual cold
The condition found in a small existential room with little to no room for holy influence, spiritual confluence, or sacred concordance. In their most impoverished form, cold spiritual temperatures are marked by the paucity of creative improvisation, spontaneous change, heightened emotion, fluidic body movement, complex polyrhythm, and embellished melodic tonality. Spiritual coldness fosters overly static beliefs, inflexible interpretations, and a feeling of distance from the divine. However, there also exists resourceful cognition amidst cold spiritual temperature, associated with the skilled use of language and thought that prepares the ground for later ecstatic expression. As one of the four directions of ecstatic living, "spiritual masonry" happens in the spiritual cold, though it warms the situation as it continues its expansive construction. Wise discernment and clear linguistic expression are needed to lay the right cornerstone for building sacred ground, starting in the cold and then moving to the warmer degrees.

Spiritual cooking
Spiritual cooking refers to the second step of the Sacred Ecstatics recipe in which ecstatic transformation is triggered by time spent in the spiritual fire of the big room. The installation of the sacred vibration, the buildup of your rope to God, and their mutual strengthening require extreme spiritual heat. The ecstatic temperature needed for spiritual cooking is ignited, sustained, and further elevated by rhythm and melody that effectively stir sacred emotion. As sacred emotion, movement, and music are induced and transduced from acoustic to mechanical vibration (and vice versa), the temperature soars and you are spiritually cooked, a term that is also used by the Ju/'hoan Bushmen to refer to what takes place in a n/om dance.

Spiritual engineering
The nuts-and-bolts, practical know-how behind preparing your body instrument to experience the sacred ecstasy that spiritual cooking brings, especially the installation of the sacred vibration, the strengthening of your rope to God, and the ongoing renewal, empowerment, and growth. A focus on spiritual engineering shifts the emphasis away from debating belief, understanding, or religious text to the phenomenology of ecstatic spiritual experience and the actions that prepare you to receive, hold, and share it.

Spiritual heat
A term used to indicate the emotional and somatic experience of the interactional blending of all the ecstatic ingredients as they form and turn the mystical prayer wheel. Spiritual heat brings a shift from stillness, lack of emotion, and calm speech to heightened sacred vibration, strong sacred emotion, the primacy of rhythm and song, and spontaneous movement. It fosters the outpouring of creative invention, spirited action, extreme joy, and untamed ecstatic fervor. Ecstatic spiritual lineages refer to their spirituality as "hot" and practically recognize that the spiritual temperature goes up as the room expands and allows more room for God to act without interference.

Spiritual temperature
This notion indicates the degree of ecstatic intensity associated with feeling closeness to divinity—the excitement of sacred emotion that energizes vocalized expression and spontaneous body movement, as well as the awakening of the sacred vibration. Spiritual temperature is the most reliable indication of your relationship with the divine and the sacred vastness of the existential room you presently occupy. Spiritual temperature, rather than professed belief, discerns the actual presence of "spirit" in any spiritual practice or ceremony.

Spirituality

How one relates to the breath of life that arises from the source and force of all creation. Religion is the room built by a lineage to host its spirituality. The name of the room or religion is less important than the degree of the room's sacred expansion and spiritual heat. All religions and their enacted spiritual practices take place at different spiritual temperatures, though some lineages have more spiritual cooking know-how than others. We reserve the term "ecstatic spirituality" to refer only to those lineages who regularly enter the spiritual heat.

Syncretic spirituality

A syncretic spirituality or religion is a blend of different spiritual traditions. The syncretic blend of Sacred Ecstatics consists of its main root lineages: the Kalahari Bushman way of handling n/om; the Japanese way of handling seiki; the St. Vincent Shakers' way of handling the holy spirit in what is already a syncretic mix of African and Christian religions; and the sanctified, holy ghost power ways of the traditional African American church whose roots are in the Deep South of the United States. As an ever-expanding and evolving syncretic orientation, Sacred Ecstatics also benefits from teachings that stem from other spiritual and secular traditions with whom we have studied firsthand or received in vision, including Islamic mysticism, Jewish mysticism, Zulu ancestralism, Native American relationalism, and Guarani forest communalism. In addition, we are inspired by how Australian Aboriginal elders sing their dreaming, how Brazilian folk healers dream a spiritual prescription, how Zen Buddhists empty the existential cup, and how Bushman n/om-kxaosi are taught while dreaming God's ostrich egg. Our work is enhanced by the art of Jamaican trumping, Balinese mystical drawing, Edgar Cayce unconscious reading, cybernetic circular thinking, and Charles Henry's sensory experimenting. Sometimes we are illumined by Nikola Tesla's former vision in a Budapest park, Vincent van Gogh's sacred hues for the blues, Frida Kahlo's magical butterflies and healing flights from pain, beat poets' cut out news, jazz rides on improvised tunes, European composers crossing the aural bridge, hymnists catching tonal grace, cooked preachers turning a prayer wheel, gospel singers garnishing a tone, tango and salsa dancers mounting a song, flamenco duende calling on n/om, impossible horns opening the gate, and Zora Neale Hurston thirstin' to uncover sparks found inside the mud, to name a few of what flew into the Sacred Ecstatics gumbo stew.

Tonal alignment
Here different localized body movements are aligned to the production of discrete musical tones that are either externally produced or internally sung. In this manner the body is sonically tuned by the alignment of its movement to tone. (The combination of tonal alignment and rhythm alignment comprises whole body tuning.) In its simplest form, a three-note tuning, the hips shake with a low bass note, the shoulders move with a mid-note, and the head has a higher frequency vibration corresponding to a high musical note. The more tones that are aligned with differentiated areas of body movement, the more music can be a physically, emotionally, and spiritually moving experience.

Transduction
The conveyance or transmittance of energy from one place to another (including from person to person, or from divinity to humanity) at the same time that the class or type of energy changes. In the context of Sacred Ecstatics, transduction occurs when acoustic vibration becomes mechanical vibration and vice versa. More importantly, the vibration of God's love and its inspired creative force can be transduced into the sound of song and the movement of dance, which takes place during intense spiritual cooking.

Trickster
A term derived from the Ju/'hoan Bushmen referring to the changing faces or aspects of God that you experience through cognition. Trickster is the agent of naming and presumed

understanding that freeze-frames the world into cognitive categories. It is essentially the basic operation of mind that casts a distinction, name, re-indication, and frame in order to construct the cognitive container of an experiential reality. The primary or originally selected distinction sets the cornerstone for what room can be built, providing the compass setting, temperature range, and breadth of stage for the whole of one's life. All subsequent action retraces or principally associates itself with the initial construct. This is the recursive reentry of a self-validating, homeostatic world that is resistant to out-of-the-box transformation.

Trickster is not the opposite of God, it is not evil, and it is not necessarily devilish. It is the knowing side of divinity — the mind of creation that creates and perceives difference, differentiating wholeness into parts that make possible a wider range of diverse phenomenal qualities for human experience. The slicing, dicing, sorting, and reshuffling of trickster mind make it tricky because it can arbitrarily change direction without notice. Trickster can help or hinder, be medicinal or iatrogenic, provide liberation or addictive imprisonment, reveal or conceal, open or close, and either expand or shrink the room. Trickster can help build sacred ground *or* it can reduce existential space into a small room that only has room for the invented illusion of a separate self.

Working the Spirit
Another term for spiritual cooking used in the African diaspora, especially among Afro-Caribbean lineages of ecstatic spirituality. Here the sanctified black church, Santeria, Vodou, King Revival, Pocomania, Shakers, Candomble, Umbanda, among others, all "work the spirit," that is, gather and blend the ecstatic ingredients that turn the mystical wheel and ignite a spiritual fire. Their spiritually engineered means are usually similar even though their preferred metaphors and beliefs often differ.

NOTES

[1] The Keeneys, *Sacred Ecstatics: The Recipe for Setting Your Soul on Fire* (Createspace Independent Publishing Platform, 2016).

[2] Bradford Keeney, *Shakers of St. Vincent* (Philadelphia, PA: Ringing Rocks Foundation and Leete's Island Press, 2002), 102–105.

[3] The Mother, *Notebook on Evolution,* September 21, 2017, 122, accessed October 22, 2017, http://www.kheper.net/topics/Aurobindo/Notebook_on_Evolution.pdf.

[4] William James, *The Varieties of Religious Experience* (Createspace Independent Publishing Platform, 2016), 139.

[5] Evelyn Underhill, *Mysticism: A Study in the Nature and Development of Spiritual Consciousness* (Mineola, NY: Dover Publications, 2002), 81.

[6] Meridee Duddelston and Bob Perkins, "Oscar Peterson, The Wonderful Wizard of the Piano!" WRTI.org, August 21, 2017, par. 2, accessed February 23, 2018, http://wrti.org/post/oscar-peterson-wonderful-wizard-piano.

[7] Charles Henry, "Essai de Generalisation de la Theorie du Rayonnement: Resonateurs Gravitiques et Resonateurs Biologiques," Paris, *Bulletin de Institut Psychologique,* no. 4 (1924).

[8] June Wieders, *Song of the Spine* (North Charleston, SC: BookSurge Publishing, 2004).

[9] Clifton Johnson, *God Struck Me Dead: Religious Conversion Experiences and Autobiographies of Ex-Slaves* (Philadelphia, PA: Pilgrim Press, 1969), 19.

[10] Rae Beth Gordon, *Why the French Love Jerry Lewis: From Cabaret to Early Cinema* (Stanford, CA: Stanford University Press, 2001), 9.

[11] Ibid., 10–11.

[12] Vincent van Gogh, "Letter from Vincent van Gogh to Theo van Gogh, Drenthe, 28 October 1883," accessed August 23, 2017, par. 33, http://www.webexhibits.org/vangogh/letter/13/336.htm.

[13] Edward Hall, *The Dance of Life: The Other Dimension of Time* (New York: Anchor, 1983), 224.

[14] Ibid., 184–185.

[15] Jane Goodridge, *Rhythm and Timing of Movement in Performance: Drama, Dance, and Ceremony* (London: Jessica Kingsley Publishers, 1999), 43.

[16] Roberto Assagioli, *Psychosynthesis: A Collection of Basic Writings* (New York: Viking, 1965), 214.

[17] Babatunde Olatunji, *The Beat of My Drum: An Autobiography* (Philadelphia, PA: Temple University Press, 2005), 29.

[18] Carl Jung, *Memories, Dreams, Reflections* (New York: Vintage Books, 1989).

[19] Ibid., 271.

[20] Ibid.

[21] Ibid., 273.

[22] Lin-Manuel Miranda interviewed by Terry Gross on NPR, "Lin-Manuel Miranda on Disney, Mixtapes and Why He Won't Try to Top 'Hamilton,'" January 3, 2017, accessed August 10, 2017, https://www.npr.org/templates/transcript/transcript.php?storyId=507470975.

[23] From the title of the book by Stephen Davis, *Miles/1973: "My Ego Only Needs a Good Rhythm Section"* (New York: Vigliano Books, 2014).

24 Eugenio Barba and Nicola Savarese, *A Dictionary of Theatre Anthropology: The Secret Art of Performer* (New York: Taylor & Francis, 2011), 75.

25 Nikola Tesla, "Mechanical Therapy," undated, par. 6, accessed December 6, 2017, http://www.tfcbooks.com/tesla/0000-00-00.htm.

26 As cited in W. Bernard Carson, *Tesla: Inventor of the Electrical Age* (Princeton, NJ: Princeton University Press, 2013), 186.

27 As cited in Deena Rosenberg, *Fascinating Rhythm: The Collaboration of George and Ira Gershwin* (Ann Arbor: University of Michigan Press, 1991), 92.

28 See Bradford Keeney, ed., *Ikuko Osumi, Sensei: Japanese Master of Seiki Jutsu* (Philadelphia, PA: Ringing Rocks Press & Leete's Island Books, 1999), and Bradford Keeney and Hillary Keeney, *Seiki Jutsu: The Practice of Non-Subtle Energy Medicine* (Rochester, VT: Healing Arts Press, 2014).

29 As quoted in W. Royal Stokes, *The Jazz Scene: An Informal History from New Orleans to 1990* (New York: Oxford University Press, 1991), 234.

30 Benjamin Jowett, trans., *The Republic of Plato* (Oxford: Clarendon Press, 1888), 88.

31 Hazrat Inayat Khan, *The Sufi Message of Hazrat Inayat Khan: The Art of Personality* (Egypt: Library of Alexandria, 2001), Kindle ed.

32 Alexander P.D. Mourelatos, ed., *The Pre-Socratics: A Collection of Critical Essays* (Princeton, NJ: Princeton University Press, 1974), 147.

33 Raymond Bernard, *Pythagoras: The Immortal Sage* (Whitefish, MT: Kessinger Publishing, 2003), 48.

34 Edward T. Hall, *The Dance of Life: The Other Dimension of Time* (New York: Random House, 1989), 3.

35 Donald Kinney, *The Poetry of Saint Thérèse of Lisieux* (Washington, DC: ICS Publications Institute of Carmelite Studies, 1995), eBook ed.

[36] Blaise Pascal, *Pensees and Other Writings*, trans. Honor Levi (New York: Oxford University Press, 1995), 59.

[37] Quote attributed to Beethoven by Bettina von Arnim, *Goethe's Correspondence with a Child* (London: Longman, Orme, Brown , Green, and Longmans, 1839), 207; Kahlil Gabran, *The Treasured Writings of Kahlil Gabran* (Edison, NJ: Castle Books, 2009), 484; quote by Walter Savage Landor from Kenneth W. Osbeck, *101 More Hymn Stories: The Inspiring True Stories Behind 101 Favorite Hymns* (Grand Rapids, MI: Kregel Publications, 1985), 145. This quote by Maria Von Trapp is widely attributed to her, but the original source is unknown.

[38] Nathan Haskell Dole, *Famous Composers: Volume 1* (New York: Thomas E. Crowell, 1902), 172.

[39] Edward Bulwer Lytton, *Zanoni* (Leipzig, Germany: Tauchnitz: 1842), 8.

[40] Anton Schindler, *The Life of Beethoven: Correspondence with his Friends*, ed. Ignace Moscheles (London: Henry Colburn, 1841), 276.

[41] Ibid., 282.

[42] As quoted in NPR Morning Edition, "Novelist Vonnegut Remembered for his Black Humor," April 12, 2007, par. 19, accessed December 6, 2017, https://www.npr.org/templates/story/story.php?storyId=955428.

[43] C.H. Spurgeon, "Better than Wine," June 2, 1872, verse 2, accessed October 7, 2017, http://www.biblebb.com/files/spurgeon/2459.htm.

[44] Ibid., verse 3.

[45] Ludwig van Beethoven, "Letter to Emilie, July 17, 1812," London, *Musical News* 3 (1892), 627.

[46] As quoted in David Hajdu, "Pete Seeger's Last War," *Mother Jones* (September/October 2004), par. 33, accessed October 7, 2017, http://www.motherjones.com/politics/2004/09/pete-seeger-last-war/#.

47 Bradford Keeney, ed., *Guarani Shamans of the Forest* (Philadelphia, PA: Ringing Rocks Foundation and Leete's Island Press, 2000), 66.

48 As quoted in Tracey R. Rich, "Prayers and Blessings," Judaism 101 (blog), par. 12, accessed September 21, 2017, http://www.jewfaq.org/prayer.htm.

49 As quoted in Many Cihlar, *Mystics at Prayer: A Collection of Inspirational Prayers from Around the World* (San Jose, CA: Grand Lodge of the English Language Jurisdiction, AMORC, 1997), 46.

50 Charles Spurgeon, *The Complete Words of C.H. Spurgeon, Volume 32, Sermons 2001-2061* (Harrington, DE: Delmarva Publications, 2013), eBook ed.

51 Charles Haddon Spurgeon, *The Metropolitan Tabernacle Pulpit: Sermons Preached and Revised by C.H. Spurgeon During the Year 1878, Volume XXIV* (London: Passmore & Alabaster, 1879), 214.

52 Lakota prayer attributed to Chief Yellow Lark. Original source unknown.

53 Sufi prayer by Hazrat Pir-o-Murshid Inayat Khan, Hidayat Inayat Khan, *Spiritual Liberty* (New Delhi: Readworthy Publications, 2011) 26.

54 In Glenn Hinson, *Fire in My Bones: Transcendence and the Holy Spirit in African American Gospel* (Philadelphia, PA: University of Pennsylvania Press, 200), 143.

55 The Keeneys, *Sacred Ecstatics*, 81.

56 Philip Schaff, ed., *Saint Augustin: Expositions of the Book of Psalms* (New York: Christian Literature Company, 1888), 107.

57 D.H.S. Nicholson and A.H.E. Lee, eds. *The Oxford Book of English Mystical Verse* (Oxford: Clarendon Press, 1917; repr., Bartleby.com, 2000), accessed December 21, 2017, www.bartleby.com/236/.

58 Saint Anselm, *Saint Anselm: Collection* (London: Aeterna Press, 2016), Kindle ed.

59 Robert Hall, ed., *Charles Spurgeon: The Power of Prayer in a Believer's Life* (Lynnwood, WA: Emerald Books, 1993), 85.

[60] Harvey Cox, *On Not Leaving It to the Snake* (New York: Macmillan, 1969).

[61] Bradford Keeney, ed., *Guarani Shamans of the Forest*, 66.

[62] From the hymn attributed to Sir Richard of Chichester, "Day by Day, Dear Lord, of Thee Three Things I Pray," accessed December 1, 2017, https://hymnary.org/text/day_by_day_dear_lord.

[63] Mirabai Starr, "Longing for the Beloved," *Parabola*, July 18, 2017, par. 2, accessed August 23, 2017, https://parabola.org/2017/07/18/longing-for-the-beloved-by-mirabai-starr/.

[64] C.H. Spurgeon, *Morning and Evening: Daily Readings* (Jersey City, NJ: Start Publishing, 2012), eBook ed.

[65] Charles Spurgeon, *The Complete Words of C.H. Spurgeon, Volume 41, Sermons 2394–2445*.

[66] Mohandas Karamchand Gandhi, *Autobiography: The Story of My Experiments with Truth* (Middletown, RI: B.N. Publishing, 2008), 63.

[67] This quote is widely attributed to D. L. Moody, original source unknown.

[68] Original source unknown.

[69] "God Is His Own Interpreter," *Apostolic Faith* 1, no. 5 (1907), 2.

[70] A.E. Stuernagel, "Being Filled with the Spirit: The Melodies of Heaven Overflow in the Soul," *The Latter Rain Evangel* 20, no. 10 (1928), 8.

[71] "Pentecostal Meetings," *Apostolic Faith* 1, no. 8 (May 1907), 3.

[72] Ibid., 2.

[73] Zora Neale Hurston, "Ritualistic Expression from the Lips of the Communicants of the Seventh Day Church of God, Beaufort, South Carolina" (Washington, DC: Library of Congress: Collections of the Manuscript Division, 1940), 22.

[74] As quoted in Wallace W. Zane, *Journeys to the Spiritual Lands: The Natural History of a West Indian Religion* (New York: Oxford University Press, 1999), 161.

75 Edric Connor quoted in Patricia Stephens, *The Spiritual Baptist Faith: African New World Religious Identity, History and Testimony* (London: Karnak, 1999), 18.

76 Archbishop Randoo quoted in Bradford Keeney, *Shaking Medicine: The Healing Power of Ecstatic Movement* (Rochester, VT: Destiny Books, 2007), 116.

77 Bradford Keeney, *Shakers of St. Vincent*, 65.

78 Ibid., 87.

79 Ibid., 74–75.

80 Bradford Keeney, *Shaking Medicine*, 118.

81 Ibid., 119.

82 Evangelista Torricelli, *Opera Geometrica* (Florence, 1644), trans. Paolo Mancosu, *Philosophy of Mathematics and Mathematical Practice in the Seventeenth Century* (Oxford: Oxford University Press, 1996), accessed November 1, 2017, par. 3, http://imaginaryinstruments.org/torricellis-trumpet-or-gabriels-horn/.

83 Bradford Keeney, ed., *Shakers of St. Vincent*, 93.

84 Ibid., 73.

85 Ted Gioia, *Healing Songs* (Durham, NC: Duke University Press, 2006), 56.

86 As quoted in Oliver Sacks, *Awakenings* (New York: Vintage Press, 1999), 281.

87 As quoted in Margaret Schevill, *The Pollen Path: A Collection of Navajo Myths Retold* (Palo Alto, CA: Stanford University Press, 1956), 166.

88 Ibid., 164.

89 Ibid., 165.

90 Bradford Keeney and Hillary Keeney, eds., *Way of the Bushman as Told by the Tribal Elders: Spiritual Teachings and Practices of the Kalahari Ju/'hoansi* (Rochester, VT: Bear & Company, 2015), 46.

91 The Keeneys, *Sacred Ecstatics*, chapter 7.

92 See Alan Dundes, ed., *Sacred Narrative: Readings in the Theory of Myth* (Berkeley: University of California Press, 1984), 81.

93 From Marilyn Nelson, *Ostrich and Lark* (illus. Kuru Art project) (Botswana and South Africa: Boyd Mills Press, 2012), 19.
94 Joseph Hart, *Hymns' on Various Subjects* (London: Hamilton, Adams, 1850), 148–149.
95 From Joseph Hart's autobiography, which can be found online. See Kevin Twit, "The Preface to Joseph Hart's 'Hart's Hymns' from 1759 Is a Classic in Spiritual Autobiography," Indelible Grace Hymn Book, October 7, 2013, par. 17–18, accessed February 19, 2015, http://hymnbook.igracemusic.com/resources/joseph-harts-preface
96 The Keeneys, "The Ropes are Back," *Climbing the Rope to God: Mystical Testimony and Teaching* (Createspace, 2017), 181–183.
97 José A. Argüelles, *Charles Henry and the Formation of a Psychophysical Aesthetic* (Chicago, IL: University of Chicago Press, 1972), 24–25.
98 Ibid., 155–156.
99 Ibid., 156.
100 Morris Allen Grubs, ed., *Conversations with Wendell Berry* (Jackson: University Press of Mississippi, 2007), 194.
101 Wendell Berry, "The Burden of the Gospels," *The Way of Ignorance* (Washington, DC: Shoemaker and Hoard, 2005), 137.
102 Wendell Berry, *Standing By Words: Essays* (Berkeley, CA: Counterpoint Press, 2005), 97.
103 Wendell Berry, *A Continuous Harmony: Essays Cultural and Agricultural* (Berkeley, CA: Counterpoint, 2012), 41.
104 Wendell Berry, *Hannah Coulter* (Berkeley, CA: Counterpoint, 2004), 113.
105 Wendell Berry, *Jayber Crow* (Berkeley, CA: Counterpoint, 2000), 51.
106 Morris Allen Grubs, *Conversations with Wendell Berry*, 23.
107Wendell Berry, *This Day: Collected and New Sabbath Poems* (Berkeley, CA: Counterpoint, 2013), 38.
108 Klaus Laczika, et al., "'Il flauto magico' Still Works: Mozart's Secret of Ventilation," *Multidisciplinary Respiratory Medicine* 8, no.

23 (2011), accessed November 2, 2017, https://mrmjournal.biomedcentral.com/articles/10.1186/2049-6958-8-23.

[109] Ibid., 7.

[110] Zora Neale Hurston, *The Sanctified Church: The Folklore Writings of Zora Neale Hurston* (New York: Marlowe & Company, 1997).

[111] Jacquel Trescott, "The Fabulous Zora Neale Hurston," *Washington Post*, May 21, 1978, par. 4, accessed December 8, 2017, https://www.washingtonpost.com/archive/lifestyle/1978/05/21/the-fabulous-zora-neale-hurston/83226feb-3114-4b3a-8c18-f3acb11378b5/?utm_term=.b0a42778d34d.

[112] Ibid., par. 5.

[113] Deborah G. Plant, ed., *The Inside Light: New Critical Essays on Zora Neale Hurston* (Santa Barbara, CA: ABC-CLIO, 2010), 241.

[114] Deborah G. Plant, "The Folk Preacher and Folk Sermon in Zora Neale Hurston's Dust Tracks on a Road," *Folklore Forum* 21, no. 6 (1988), 1–19.

[115] Ibid., 12.

[116] Larry Neale, "A Profile: Zora Neale Hurston," *Southern Exposure* 1 (1974), 160–168, as cited in Deborah G. Plant, "The Folk Preacher.

[117] M. Cooper Harriss, "The Preacher in the Text: Zora Neale Hurston and the Homiletics of Literature," *Religion and Culture Web Forum* (February 2008), 17.

[118] Zora Neale Hurston, "Ritualistic Expression, 2.

[119] M. Cooper Harriss, "The Preacher in the Text, 24.

[120] Zora Neale Hurston, *Their Eyes Were Watching God* (Chicago: University of Illinois Press, 1937), 16.

[121] NPR's Jazz Profiles, "Erroll Garner: 'The Joy of a Genius,'" September 19, 2007, accessed November 22, 2017, http://www.npr.org/2007/09/19/14501602/erroll-garner-the-joy-of-a-genius.

[122] Quoted by the Erroll Garner Jazz Project, February 26, 2017, accessed December 22, 2017, https://www.facebook.com/

officialerrollgarner/photos/a.426277457533836.1073741828.300539
896774260/727119560782956/?type=3&theater.

[123] Quoted by the Erroll Garner Jazz Project, November 5, 2017,
accessed November 10, 2017, https://www.facebook.com/
pg/officialerrollgarner/posts/?ref=page_internal.

[124] Marshall Winslow Stearns, *The Story of Jazz* (New York: Oxford
University Press, rev. ed., 1970), 5-6.

[125] "Garner, Erroll," Contemporary Musicians.
Encyclopedia.com, December 21, 2017, accessed December 22, 2017,
http://www.encyclopedia.com/education/news-wires-white-
papers-and-books/garner-erroll.

[126] Quoted in NPR, "Erroll Garner."

[127] Woody Allen quoted in Tom Reney, "No One Can Hear You
Read," October 23, 2013, accessed December 23, 2017,
http://digital.nepr.net/music/2013/10/23/erroll-garner-no-one-
can-hear-you-read/.

[128] Woody Allen, Steve Allen, George Avakian, and Billy Taylor all
quoted in "Erroll Garner" (blog), January 7, 2009, par. 3–5.,
accessed December 23, 2017,
http://errolgarner.blogspot.com/2009/01/httperrollgarner.html.

[129] Roderick Nordell, "The Jazz Musician Who Played the Y,"
Christian Science Monitor, August 13, 1992, par. 23, accessed
December 22, 2017, https://www.csmonitor.com/1992/0813/
13161.html.

[130] Joachim-Ernst Berendt and Günther Huesmann, *The Jazz Book:
From Ragtime to the 21st Century* (Chicago, IL: Lawrence Hill
Books, 2009), 378.

[131] Cited in Will Friedwald, "Garner's Serendipitous Hit," *Wall
Street Journal*, September 17, 2009.

[132] This story is reported in Faith Stewart-Gordon, *The Russian Tea
Room: A Love Story* (New York: Scribner, 1999), 136–137.

[133] David Summers and Ruth O'Rourke-Jones, eds., *Music: The
Definitive Visual History* (London: Dorling Kindersley, 2013), 232.

[134] Zora Neale Hurston, *Their Eyes Were Watching*, 109.

135 Saint Teresa of Avila, interpreted by Daniel Ladinsky in *Love Poems from God* (New York: Penguin Group, 2002), 276.

136 Marv Hiles and Nancy Hiles, "Friends of Silence" (blog), June 2010, accessed February 23, 2018, http://www.friendsofsilence.net/quote/2010/06/rise-and-fall-songline.

137 Plato, *Plato in Twelve Volumes, Vol. 1*, trans. Harold North Fowler (Cambridge, MA: Harvard University Press, 1966), sections 60d–61b, accessed December 17, 2017, http://www.perseus.tufts.edu/hopper/text?doc=Perseus%3Atext%3A1999.01.0170%3Atext%3DPhaedo%3Apage%3D61.

138 Quoted in John Arierhi Ottuh and Reuben Edafenene Ojighoro, "The Concept of Elohim and Theos in an Urhobo Cosmological Context: A Biblical Perspective," *International Journal of Philosophy and Theology* 3, no. 1 (2015), 148.

139 From *Glossary of Kabbalah and Chassidut* (website), accessed November 22, 2017, http://www.inner.org/glossary/gloss_c.htm.

140 haRold Smith, "Fullness of Joy," *He That Has an Ear* (blog), par. 3, accessed December 22, 2017, http://hethathasanear.com/Joy.html.

141 E.A. Hoffman, "What a Fellowship, What a Joy Divine" (1887), accessed December 23, 2017, https://hymnary.org/text/what_a_fellowship_what_a_joy_divine.

142 Cited in Philip Zaleski and Carol Zaleski, *Prayer: A History* (New York: Mariner Books, 2006), 75.

143 Mohandas K. Gandhi, *Young India*, May 20, 1926, 187.

144 Mohandas K. Gandhi, *Harijan*, April 27, 1947, 122.

145 Mohit Chakrabarti, *Gandhian Mysticism* (New Delhi, India: Atlantic Publishers and Distributors, 1989), 3.

146 Gandhi, *Autobiography*, x.

147 Mohandas K. Gandhi, cited in John Moniz, *Liberated Society* (Rome: Editrice Pontifica Universita Gregoriana, 1996), 62.

Made in the USA
Coppell, TX
18 June 2022

78979459R00193